A History of Roman Coinage in Britain

by Sam Moorhead

Illustrated by finds recorded with the Portable Antiquities Scheme

Dedication

*For Atticus, who arrived when this
book was being completed*

Editor
Greg Payne

Design & Origination
Christine Jennett

Published by
Greenlight Publishing
The Publishing House, 119 Newland
Street, Witham, Essex CM8 1WF
Tel: 01376 521900

info@greenlightpublishing.co.uk
www.greenlightpublishing.co.uk

Printed in Great Britain

ISBN 978-1-897738-54-2

© Sam Moorhead

Contents

Introduction

This book emanates from a series of 22 articles written for *Treasure Hunting* magazine between 2008 and 2011 about Roman coins found in Britain and recorded with the Portable Antiquities Scheme. Together, these pieces provide a chronological overview of Roman coinage from the Republican period to the early 5th century, with an emphasis on Roman coinage used in Britain. The text provides an introduction to the history of each period and then outlines the coinage (denominations, mints, contemporary copies etc.), using Portable Antiquities Scheme (PAS) and British Museum (BM) coins as illustrations. Throughout, indications are made of the numbers and distribution of particular Roman coin finds in Britain. Where relevant, important coin hoards are also included, but this book is primarily concerned with stray or single finds recorded with the PAS. For this book, some statistics in particular chapters have been updated, but readers are asked to consider that this work was written over a four year period so there will be some minor inconsistencies[1].

---

[1]Variation in totals can occur when the Welsh data (which includes hoards) is included.

Acknowledgements

I would like to thank Greg Payne and Dan Golbourn at Greenlight Publishing for publishing the articles and this book. I am very grateful to Philippa Walton, Dan Pett and Richard Kelleher for providing statistics and maps in the text, and Richard Abdy, Roger Bland and Philippa Walton for making comments on the text. I would also like to thank Jason Lundock for helping with production of the images, and Richard Abdy and David Stuttard for permission to use some of their site pictures. I am deeply indebted to all the Finds Liaison Officers and volunteers who work with the Portable Antiquities Scheme for this book would not be possible without their recording of coins. Furthermore, I am deeply grateful to all those detectorists who have recorded their material with the Portable Antiquities Scheme – without their co-operation, support and generosity, the Portable Antiquities Scheme would not be the success that it is today. At the end of the original articles, published in *Treasure Hunting*, I did thank many detector clubs who let me speak at their meetings; I have removed these references because they seem rather odd in a book, but I would like to re-iterate my thanks here. Finally, I would like to thank Richard Beleson whose generosity has enabled Philippa Walton and me to have more capacity to record and study Roman coins from Britain.

Chapter I
Recording Roman Coins

The Treasure Act and the Portable Antiquities Scheme

The new "Treasure Act" was passed in 1996. This meant that two or more gold and silver coins, or 10 or more base-metal (copper, bronze or brass) coins found together, and over 300 years in age, constituted "Treasure" under the new Act. This means that nearly all Roman coin hoards can now be recorded as part of the Treasure process; furthermore, museums are able to acquire any hoards that they deem of local or national importance, for example the Frome Hoard of 52,503 radiates which has been acquired by the Museum of Somerset in Taunton. Up until 1997, around 2,150 Roman coins hoards had been recorded to varying degrees of accuracy. Since the implementation of the Treasure Act in 1997, up until the end of 2012, over 560 Roman hoards have been declared Treasure. This is an increase of 20% in only 15 years. Furthermore, the Act has resulted in much more precise recording of hoards.

The Treasure Act also made provision for the founding of the Portable Antiquities Scheme, which encourages the voluntary recording, on the Portable Antiquities Scheme Database (www.finds.org.uk) of all objects which do not constitute Treasure. At the end of 2012, there were 837,655 objects on the PAS Database, ranging from Palaeolithic hand axes to post medieval finger rings. It is the largest dataset of its kind in the world and a glowing testament to all finders and those who work with the PAS.

The Importance Of Recording All Roman Coins

The PAS has made it possible to record the thousands of stray finds of Roman coins made by detectorists across the country. In the early years of the scheme, 1997-2006, 43,789 Roman coins were recorded on the PAS Database. After a drive to record *all* Roman coins, including poorly preserved 3rd century radiates and 4th century nummi (often called "grots" by detectorists), the number had risen to 145,752 by the end of 2012. When coin finds from Wales are added, the total of Roman coins on the database is 198,427. As you will read below, the analysis of Roman new coin finds recorded with the PAS is beginning to highlight important new questions for historians and archaeologists, so it is an excellent example of how detectorists who record with the PAS are making a genuine impact on the study of Roman Britain. I urge all detectorists to continue recording *all* of their Roman coins with the PAS (however worn they might be). It is also heartening to see an increasing number of detectorists beginning to "self-record" on the Database. I do recommend, however, that they seek as much training as possible from their FLO; Philippa Walton and I are always happy to check your records for you if you email us the PAS record number.

Among the many thousands of Roman coins recorded on the PAS Database there are rare pieces of individual numismatic significance, ranging from gold *aurei* and *solidi* to fine silver *denarii, miliarenses* and *siliquae* to sometimes unique base metal radiates and *nummi*. A number of these coins are included in this book. For me, at the moment, it is the coins of Carausius and Allectus which are particularly interesting (see Chapter XXII) as I am re-writing the *Roman Imperial Coinage* volume for these rulers: the PAS Database has a number of previously unknown types which will be included in the new volume. Some PAS records have already been included in the new edition of *Roman Imperial Coinage II* on the coinage of Vespasian, Titus and Domitian (AD 69-96) published in 2007.

However, equally important is the archaeological information afforded by large assemblages of coins from one site. Some detectorists have provided over 1000 coins from one defined area of search (mostly grots); many have provided more than 20 coins from one site, which is

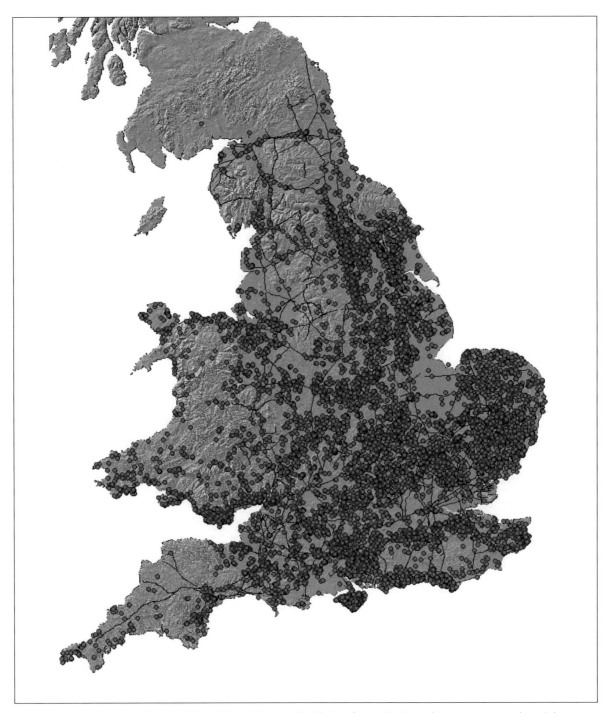

Map 1. Map of all Roman coins found in Britain and recorded with PAS. [Note that in outlying regions one dot might represent only one coin; in areas of prolific Roman coin loss a dot can represent hundreds, or even over a thousand coins.] (Map created by Philippa Walton)

generally enough to carry out statistical analysis. Many findspots where scattered coins have been found have been subsequently researched and have shown the site to have been that of a Roman settlement, whether the site is a villa, smaller rural settlement, or even a religious site. Philippa Walton and I have looked at all coin assemblages across the country (Table 1). In theory, any parish with 20 or more coins could contain a new Roman site; this means that up to around 900 parishes might contain a Roman site and it is known that many of these sites have not been previously recorded in county Sites and Monuments or Historic and Environment Records. In Lincolnshire, it is estimated by the FLO, Adam Daubney, that there are 100 new Roman sites; on

Number of Coins Found in a Parish	Number of Parishes
Fewer than 20	3,161
20-50	426
50-100	249
100-500	205
500-1000	20
Over 1000	5

Table 1. Number of Roman coins from Parishes across England.

the Isle of Wight, Philippa Walton's PhD research into PAS finds has identified around 30 new sites; in Devon and Cornwall, although Roman coins are scarce, they are being found in areas where Roman activity has not been previously recorded by archaeologists. Finally, several decades ago it was said that there was not a great use of Roman coins in East Anglia; the enormous number of finds in Norfolk and Suffolk refutes this statement entirely.

The PAS Roman coin data is also showing that there are marked differences in coin use across Britain. For example, Philippa Walton has shown that coin use north of the Roman road, the Fosse Way (that runs from Exeter to Lincoln) tends to be on a much smaller scale that coin use to the south of the road (Walton 2012), and that silver *denarii* are proportionally more common in the north while brass *sestertii* are more common in the south. Furthermore, the number of Roman coins in particular regions varies greatly in different periods. To analyse finds of Roman coins, we often use Reece Periods (see Table 2), pioneered by Richard Reece (who has written several books on coinage in Roman Britain – see Further Reading) in the early 1970s. Reece Period 1 covers all coins struck before the reign of Claudius (pre-AD 41) and subsequent periods cover different rulers and dynasties until Period 21 deals with the late Roman coins of the Theodosian dynasty (AD

1	pre-AD 41	Pre-Claudian & Iron Age
2	AD 41-54	Claudian
3	54-68	Neronian & Civil Wars
4	69-96	Flavian
5	96-117	Trajanic
6	117-138	Hadrianic
7	138-161	Antonine I
8	161-180	Antonine II
9	180-193	Antonine III
10	193-222	Severus to Elagabalus (Severan I)
11	222-238	Later Severan (Severan II)
12	238-260	Gordian III to Valerian
13	260-275	Gallienus (sole reign) to Aurelian
14	275-296	Tacitus to Allectus
15	296-317	The Tetrarchy
16	317-330	Constantinian I
17	330-348	Constantinian II
18	348-364	Constantinian III
19	364-378	Valentinianic
20	378-388	Theodosian I
21	388-402	Theodosian II
22	402-445	5th Century I (added by Sam Moorhead)
23	445-498	5th Century II (added by Sam Moorhead)

Table 2. Reece Periods, as used on the PAS Database.

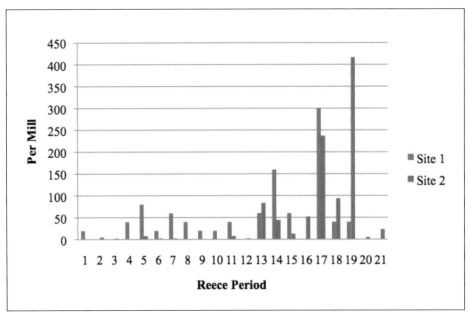

Fig.1. Proportions of coins (per mill) by Reece Period from two sites in Wiltshire. (See Table 2 for Reece Period dates; proportions are shown out of a thousand – per mill – rather than as a percentage. This is standard practice as it makes the numbers more manageable.)

388-402). I have added two more periods to cover the 5th century because an occasional later Roman coin is found in Britain (See Chapter XXVI). On the Database, where possible, we record a Reece Period for each coin, which enables us to generate statistics at the click of a switch for a particular site, region or county. It should be emphasised that most "grots" can be assigned to a Reece Period, making their recording extremely important – this is why we need to record *all* Roman coins found.

By using Reece periods, we can generate a coin-loss profile for a particular site, a county, a broad region or even the whole country. Fig.1. shows two different sites in Wiltshire that have very different profiles. Site 1 is much stronger in the early Roman period, Site 2 in the later period. In fact, these two sites are examples of two different types of sites from different parts of Wiltshire, showing that the nature of settlement and activity in the Roman period was not uniform across the county. This immediately asks questions about why these sites have different profiles, questions that need to be answered by archaeologists and historians. Eminent scholars, such as the Professor of Roman Archaeology at Cambridge University, and a research team at Reading University, are beginning to use such data to reappraise the nature of Roman settlement in Britain. A number of detectorists who are engaged in local research of their sites are also generating graphs like these; such work adds a completely new dimension to the discovery and recording of coin finds.

Sometimes, it is informative to compare different counties. Fig.2. shows the profiles for Surrey, Hampshire and the Isle of Wight. We might expect, given their close proximity to each other, that they would have similar profiles. This is not the case. The Isle of Wight peaks in the earlier periods, especially 7, 8 and 9 (AD 138-82), is weaker in the 3rd century and rises again at the end of the 4th century. Hampshire is not so strong in the early periods, but really peaks in the late 3rd and 4th century. Surrey is strongest in the early periods, but falls away significantly in the 4th century. There is not the space to discuss possible reasons for these differences, but data such as this does provoke many questions for archaeologists and historians to answer.

On a national level, Richard Reece generated an average of all sites from Roman Britain in 1995; Philippa Walton generated an average for all PAS sites in 2008 which is slightly different (Fig.3.). The PAS average shows a higher proportion of 4th century coins which can be partly explained by the fact that 4th century coins tend to me most common on rural sites, the kinds of sites most likely to be searched by detectorists. Much of Reece's data came from military and urban sites, which tend to have more 1st to 3rd century coins. However, the similarity of the graphs does confirm that the PAS data is valid for research, refuting claims by those critical of the PAS in the early years that the data would be useless.

Philippa Walton's new book, *Rethinking*

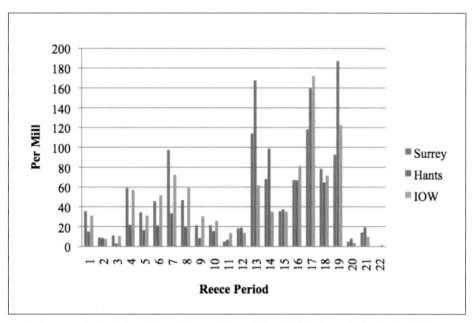

Fig.2. Roman coin finds from Surrey, Hampshire and Isle of Wight (recorded with the PAS). (See Table 2 for Reece Period dates; proportions are shown out of a thousand – per mill – rather than as a percentage.)

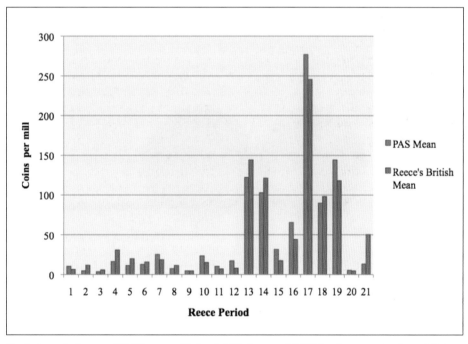

Fig.3. Reece's Average (1995) versus Walton's PAS Average (2008) for Roman coins from Britain. (See Table 2 for Reece Period dates; proportions are shown out of a thousand – per mill – rather than as percentages).

Roman Britain – Coinage and Archaeology (Moneta, 2012), is based on her research of the PAS Roman coin data up until 2008. It contains numerous case-studies about how PAS data is changing our understanding of Roman coinage in Britain from the pre-Roman to late-Roman periods. Some of her research is included in this book, but much of her work post-dates the writing of the articles in *Treasure Hunting*. Other thoughts are included in my book (written with David Stuttard), *The Romans who Shaped Britain* (Thames and Hudson, 2012). What is clear, the PAS Roman coin data is helping to re-write the history of Roman Britain, so please do continue to record your finds with us.

Chapter II
Roman Currency Systems

Fig.1. Gold Roman Republican *aureus* of the moneyer Q. Voconius Vitulus, struck in Rome c.40 BC or later, showing the head of Octavian, named as the son of the Divine Julius Caesar (IVLI. F. DIVI). RRC 526/1. © British Museum (20mm)

Fig.2. Silver Roman Republican *denarius* of Rome, "Crescent" issue, c.207 BC. The obverse shows the helmeted head of Roma, the reverse the Dioscuri (heavenly twins: Castor and Pollux). This coin is exceptionally well preserved suggesting that it may have arrived in Britain well before the Claudian invasion of AD 43. RRC 57/2. Found in Berkshire, BERK-65D307. © Portable Antiquities Scheme (18.5mm)

Fig.3. Silver Roman Republican *quinarius* of Mark Antony, struck in Gaul, 43-42 BC. This rare coin shows a worn Victory on the obverse and a lion standing right on the reverse. RRC 489/6. Found in Hampshire, HAMP-EE4687. © Portable Antiquities Scheme (14mm)

Fig.4. Copper Roman Republican *as* struck by followers of Pompey the Great (died 48 BC), in Spain or Sicily, after 45 BC. The obverse shows the head of Janus with features of Pompey the Great. The reverse shows a prow. RRC 479/1. © British Museum (29mm)

The Republican Coinage c.212-27 BC

The earliest Republican coinages before 212 BC were quite complex (see Chapter VII) but after this period there was a more systemised coinage based upon the silver *denarius* – Republican *denarii* are commonly found in Britain (Fig.2.). There were a few issues of gold *aurei*, but they are rare and none have been recorded with the PAS (Fig.1.). There were also occasional issues of silver fractions (e.g. the *quinarius* and the *victoriatus*), but these are rarely found in Britain (Fig.3.). The lower value coins were copper pieces ranging from the *as,* which was the most common base metal denomination, to the *uncia* and *semiuncia*. These copper coins were nearly all struck before Caesar's expeditions to Britain (55 and 54 BC) and are therefore very rarely found in Britain (Fig.4.).

The Augustan System c.27 BC-AD 260

The reformed coinage of the first Roman emperor, Augustus (27 BC-AD 14), was to provide the structure for the coinage down to the middle of 3rd century (see Chapters VIII-XVIII).

The gold *aureus* (c.7-8g) was at the head of the system (Fig.5.), being tariffed at 25 silver *denarii* (c.3-4g; Fig.6.); the *denarius* was broken down further into a variety of base metal coins, being equal to four brass *sestertii* (15-25g; Fig.7.), eight brass *dupondii* (up to 12.5g; Fig.8.), 16 copper *asses* (up to 11g; Fig.9.), 32 brass *semisses* (c.5g; Fig.10.) and 64 copper *quadrantes* (c.3g; Fig.11.) (see table on right). In Britain, the *semis* and the *quadrans* are very rare because they were probably never officially issued in the province; however, the PAS is recording a significant number of

8

Fig.5. Gold *aureus* of Trajan (AD 98-117), P M TR P COS VI P P S P Q R PARTHIA CAPTA, two Parthian captives seated either side of trophy, struck at Rome, AD 114-7. RIC II, 324. Found in Hertfordshire BH-80B838. © Portable Antiquities Scheme (18.5mm)

Fig.6. Silver *denarius* of Severus Alexander (AD 222-35), P M TR P II COS P P, Pax standing left, struck at Rome, AD 223. RIC IV, pt 2, 27. Found in Norfolk, NMS-AE0825. © Portable Antiquities Scheme (17mm)

Fig.7. Copper-alloy *sestertius* of Domitian as Caesar (AD 69-81), TR P COS VII DES VIII PP SC, Minerva with javelin and shield, struck at Rome, AD 80-1. RIC II (2nd ed), cf. 294. Found in Sussex, SUR-2C1A52. © Portable Antiquities Scheme (30.5mm)

Fig.8. Copper-alloy *dupondius* of Antoninus Pius (AD 138-61), SALVS AVG COS IIII SC, Salus feeding snake at altar, struck at Rome, AD 151-2. RIC III, 894. Found in County Durham, FAPJW-6091B3. © Portable Antiquities Scheme (26mm)

Fig.9. A copper-alloy *as* of Philip I (AD 244-9), AEQVITAS AVGG S C, Aequitas with scales and cornucopiae, struck at Rome. RIC IV, pt. 3, cf. 166a. Found in Hertfordshire, BH 8144F1. © Portable Antiquities Scheme (23.5mm)

Fig.10. Copper-alloy *semis* of Nero (AD 54-68), PONTIF MAX TR POT P P S C, Roma seated left, struck at Lyon, c.AD 66. RIC I, 550 var. Found in Hampshire, HAMP-F9B448. © Portable Antiquities Scheme (22mm)

Fig.11. Copper-alloy *quadrans* of Trajan (AD 98-117), S C, she wolf, struck at Rome. RIC II, 691. Found in Leicestershire, LEIC-6910A3. © Portable Antiquities Scheme (17mm)

Denomination	Gold Quinarius	Silver Denarius	Silver Quinarius	Brass Sestertius	Brass Dupondius	Copper As	Copper Semis	Copper Quadrans
Gold Aureus	2	25	50	100	200	400	800	1600
Gold Quinarius		12.5	25	50	100	200	400	800
Silver Denarius			2	4	8	16	32	64
Silver Quinarius				2	4	8	16	32
Brass Sestertius					2	4	8	16
Brass Dupondius						2	4	8
Copper As							2	4
Brass Semis								2

Table 1. The coin denominations used in the coinage of Augustus.

Fig.12. Copper-alloy *radiate* (which would have originally been silver-washed) of Probus (AD 276-82), PAX AVGVSTI, Pax standing left, struck at Ticinum. The mintmark T - // VXXI includes the XXI mark introduced after the reforms of Aurelian. RIC V, 516. Found in Somerset, SOM-832622. © Portable Antiquities Scheme (24mm).

Fig.13. Gold *solidus* of Honorius (AD 393-423), VICTORIA AVGGG, emperor trampling captive, struck at Milan, AD 395-402. RIC X, 1206c. Found in Hampshire, HAMP-F927E7. © Portable Antiquities Scheme (21.5mm).

Fig.14. Gold *tremissis* of Pulcheria (daughter of Arcadius and Augusta from AD 414 to 453), cross in wreath, struck at Constantinople, c.AD 430-40. RIC X, 280. © British Museum (13mm).

Fig.15. Silver *miliarensis* of Constantius II as Augustus (AD 337-361), FELICITAS ROMANORVM. Two emperors in archway, struck at Sirmium, AD 351-355; RIC VIII, 13. Found in Bedfordshire, BH-45E723. © Portable Antiquities Scheme (23mm).

quadrantes which probably reflect movement of troops into Britain from places on the Continent where *quadrantes* were available. Frances McIntosh and Sam Moorhead have written an article about these new finds in an article in the *British Numismatic Journal* (81, 2011, pp. 223-30).

The "Radiates"c.238-296
(See Chapters XVIII-XXII)

In the 3rd century the silver content of coins dropped from around 50% at the start of the century to as low as 1% in the early 270s. In 215, Caracalla issued a new silver coin (Chapter XVI, 29) which was probably tariffed at two *denarii* although it only weighed one and a half *denarii*. This coin bore a bust of the emperor wearing a radiate crown (used earlier to denote the *dupondius* or double *as*). This coin which we now call the "radiate" (sometimes called the *antoninianus* after Caracalla, but with no good reason) did not initially catch on, but from 238 it became increasingly dominant and swiftly pushed out the *denarius*. However, the "radiate" was rapidly debased in the 240s and 250s so that the larger base metal denominations, now largely *sestertii* and *asses*, became relatively more valuable than their face value and thus uneconomic to produce.

By the 260s, only the debased radiates were commonly found in circulation. Gold coins continued to be struck, but in very small numbers. Radiates continued to be struck in vast quantities until Diocletian's reforms of AD 294-6. There were numerous issues under the Central Empire rulers Gallienus and Claudius (AD 260-70) before Aurelian (AD 270-5) reformed the coinage by increasing the silver content to 5%: coins marked with XXI show that the metal content was one part silver to 20 parts copper, therefore 5% silver (Fig.12.; Chapter XXI). In parallel, the breakaway Gallic Empire (AD 260-74) struck enormous

numbers of radiates, probably striking at least a million pieces a day under Victorinus and Tetricus I-II (AD 269-74) (Chapter XX). With the demise of the Gallic Empire, there was a massive rise in the number of radiate copies, called "barbarous radiates", produced in Britain and Gaul around AD 275-85 (Chapter XXI). The last major issue of radiates in Britain was during the reigns of Carausius and Allectus (AD 286-96) (Chapter XXII).

Solidi, Siliquae and Nummi of the 4th century
(See Chapters XXIII-XXVIII).

In AD 294-6, the emperor Diocletian (AD 284-305) introduced a new coinage reform which resulted in the stabilisation of the gold coinage (the *aureus*), the introduction of a good quality silver coin (the *argenteus*, struck at 96 to the pound, see Chapter XXIII, 3) and of a large silver-washed *nummus* with a silver content of 2·5-5%. The "radiate"

Fig.17. Silver half-*siliqua*, anonymous issue (probably c.AD 392-4), struck at Trier. The coin depicts a helmeted bust of Roma and X in wreath. Frome *siliqua* hoard (2010). © Museum of Somerset, Taunton (13.5mm).

Fig.18. Copper-alloy *nummus* (AE1) of Magnentius (AD 350-353), SALVS D D N N AVG ET CAES, large chi-rho flanked by small alpha and omega, struck at Amiens, AD 353. RIC VIII, 41. Found in Somerset, SOM-14B8B6. © Portable Antiquities Scheme (24mm)

Fig.16. Silver *siliqua* of Julian (AD 355-363), VOT X MVLT XX in wreath, struck at Arles, AD 361-363. RIC VIII 309. Found in Buckinghamshire, BH-E3F1A0. © Portable Antiquities Scheme (18mm)

Fig.19. A copper-alloy *nummus* (AE2) of Constans (AD 333-50), FEL TEMP REPARATIO, soldier leading small figure from hut, struck at Trier, AD 348-50. RIC VIII, 223. Found in Nottinghamshire, FAPJW-1D4005. © Portable Antiquities Scheme (21mm)

Fig.21. A copper-alloy *nummus* (AE4) of Theodosius I (AD 379-95), VICTORIA AVGGG, Victory advancing left, struck at Siscia, AD 388-92. LRBC, cf. 1576/80. Found in Nottinghamshire, NCL-B67B67. © Portable Antiquities Scheme (13mm)

Fig.20. Copper-alloy Roman *nummus* (AE3) of Crispus (AD 317-26), BEATA TRANQVILLITAS, altar inscribed VOT/IS/XX, struck at London, AD 321-2. RIC VII, 230. Found in Warwickshire, WAW-5E0202. © Portable Antiquities Scheme (20mm)

coinage ceased, although a few smaller denominations bore a radiate crown for a while and are called "post-reform radiates" (Chapter XXIII, 6).

The emperor Constantine (AD 306-37) introduced a new gold coin, the *solidus* (c. 4.5g; Fig.13.), which was to remain the standard Roman gold coin well into the Byzantine period; the emperor Magnus Maximus (AD 383-8) introduced the third of a *solidus*, called the *tremissis* (Chapter XXVIII, 18; Fig.14.) – this coin was to become very popular in post-Roman barbarian coinages. Furthermore, Constantine also introduced the silver *siliqua* (3.38 to 2.25g; Fig.16.) which was to become very common between c.AD 357 and 402, many of the examples in Britain being clipped; there was also the scarcer heavy silver coin called the *miliarensis* (5.4-4.5g; Fig.15.). There were also occasional issues of half-*siliquae* which are very rare (c.1g; Fig.17.).

As the 4th century progressed, the *nummus* varied greatly in silver content, size and weight.

At times, there were different denominations of bronze coins, but we cannot be sure what they were called and we tend to call all 4th century bronze coins *nummi*. Some books use the terms AE1 (25mm plus), AE2 (20-25mm), AE3 (16-20mm) and AE4 (up to 16mm) to differentiate the sizes of the coins (Figs.18-20.). From AD 364, bronze *nummi* did not contain any silver; in Britain such *nummi* of the House of Valentinian and House of Theodosius are very common.

Gold *solidi* ceased to arrive in Britain in significant numbers after c.AD 408; silver *siliquae* ceased to arrive in large numbers after the closure of the Milan mint in AD 402; bronze *nummi* only arrived in small numbers after c.AD 395. After Britain ceased to be part of the Roman Empire under Constantine III (AD 407-11), very few Roman coins arrived in Britain, although it is possible to argue for the use of coins in some form of monetary economy in parts of Britain until around AD 430.

Chapter III

Emperors and Empresses Represented on Coins Found in Roman Britain

Between Augustus (27 BC-AD 14) and the last Roman emperors in the Western Roman Empire, Romulus Augustulus (AD 475-6) and Julius Nepos (AD 474-80), there were over 230 rulers (emperors, junior emperors, usurpers and empresses) represented on Roman coins. Table 4, below, lists most of the rulers from Augustus to the early 5th century; very few coins for 5th century rulers after Honorius, are found in this country. After a while it became the convention for senior emperors to be titled Augustus and for junior emperors to take the title Caesar. For example, Marcus Aurelius was Caesar under Antoninus Pius (AD 139-61) (Chapter XIV, Fig.3.), and then became senior emperor, or Augustus, in his own right (AD 161-80) (Chapter IV, Fig.5.). Many emperors struck coins for their empresses who took the title Augusta, for example Faustina I under Antoninus Pius (Chapter IV, Fig.9.).

The following listing (Table 1) provides totals for rulers from the Republican period to the 5th century. Not only are coins listed which can be assigned to a particular ruler, but also coins which can only be identified more imprecisely: there are tens of thousands of coins that can only be assigned to a general period, such as "uncertain radiate ruler, AD 260-75" or "House of Constantine". This list does give an indication of the relative rarity of coins in Britain; do remember that some emperors common in Britain are rarer in other parts of the Empire (i.e. Carausius) and that others which are rare in Britain and more common elsewhere (i.e. Maxentius). The totals below exclude the Welsh data which includes hoards. However, a few very rare coins (marked with an asterisk) are included from the Welsh data. A number of very minor rulers, for whom the PAS does not have coins recorded, are not included on the list. I provide chapter references so you can look up a particular emperor quickly.

12

Table 1. Number of coins by Ruler on the PAS Database.

Ruler		Chapter	Ruler		Chapter
Roman Republican (211-32 BC)	819	VII	Antonine uncertain	161	
Mark Antony (32-31 BC)	158	VII	Uncertain 1st-2nd Century	627	
			Uncertain 2nd Century	262	
Octavian/Augustus (31 BC-AD 14)	170	VIII			
Tiberius (14-37)	153	IX	Didius Julianus (193)	4	XVI
Caligula (including Agrippa) (37-41)	29	IX	Manlia Scantilla (under D. Julianus)	2	XVI
Agrippina the Elder	1	IX	Didia Clara (under D. Julianus)	0	XVI
Claudius (41-54)	404	IX	Pertinax (AD 193)	12	XVI
Antonia (died 37; under Claudius)	15	IX	Pescennius Niger (193-40)	0	XVI
Agrippina the Younger (died AD 59)	0	X	Clodius Albinus (193-7)	40	XVI
Nero (54-68)	289	X	Septimius Severus (193-211)	947	XVI
Julio-Claudian uncertain	15		Caracalla (196-217)	460	XVI
Civil Wars (68-9)	15	X	Plautilla (died 211)	35	XVI
Galba (68-9)	31	X	Geta (198-212)	179	XVI
Otho (69)	22	X	Julia Domna (AD 193-217)	351	XVI
Vitellius (69)	65	X	Macrinus (217-80)	14	XVII
Vespasian (69-79)	1040	XI	Diadumenian (217-8)	5	XVII
Domitilla (under Vespasian)	1*		Elagabalus (218-22)	260	XVII
Titus (69-81)	126	XI	Julia Paula (under Elagabalus)	14	XVII
Domitian (69-96)	662	XI	Aquilia Severa (under Elagabalus)	3	XVII
Domitia (under Domitian)	1*		Annia Faustina (under Elagabalus)	0	XVII
Flavian uncertain	53		Julia Soaemias (under Elagabalus)	41	XVII
Nerva (96-8)	160	XII	Julia Maesa (under Elagabalus)	80	XVII
Trajan (98-117)	1452	XII	Severus Alexander (221-35)	535	XVII
Plotina (under Trajan)	1	XII	Julia Mamaea (222-35)	197	XVII
Marciana (died 114)	2	XII	Orbiana (under Severus Alexander)	9	XVII
Matidia (under Trajan)	1	XII	Severan uncertain	27	
Hadrian (117-38)	1588	XIII			
Sabina (under Hadrian)	89	XIII	Maximinus I (235-8)	84	XVII
Aelius Caesar (138)	19	XIII	Maximus (235-8)	8	XVII
Antoninus Pius (138-61)	1567	XIV	Gordian I (238)	1*	XVII
Faustina I (died 141)	507	XIV	Gordian II (238)	0	XVII
Marcus Aurelius (139-80)	1195	XIV, XV	Balbinus (238)	5	XVII
Faustina II (145-75)	601	XIV, XV	Pupienus (238)	3	XVII
Lucius Verus (161-9)	122	XV	Uncertain 1st-3rd centuries	1539	
Lucilla (164-9, under Lucius Verus)	221 †	XV			
Commodus (180-92)	624	XV	Gordian III (238-44)	244	XVIII
Crispina (c.180-3)	72	XV	Tranquillina (under Gordian III)	0	XVIII

13

Ruler		Chapter
Philip I (244-9)	79	XVIII
Philip II (244-9)	31	XVIII
Otacilia Severa (AD 244-9)	43	XVIII
Pacatian (c.248)	0	XVIII
Jotapian (c.248)	0	XVIII
Trajan Decius (249-51)	27	XVIII
Herennia Etruscilla (249-51)	8	XVIII
Herennius Etruscus (249-51)	7	XVIII
Hostilian (249-51)	4	XVIII
Trebonianus Gallus (251-3)	26	XVIII
Volusian (251-3)	22	XVIII
Aemilian (253)	6	XVIII
Cornelia Supera (under Aemilian)	0	XVIII
Uranius Antoninus (253-4)	0	XVIII
Valerian I (253-60)	123	XIX
Mariniana (under Valerian)	5	XIX
Valerian II (c.256-8)	39	XIX
Saloninus (258-60)	11	XIX
Regalianus (c.260)	0	XIX
Dryantilla (under Regalianus)	0	XIX
Radiate uncertain 238-60	14	
Gallienus (253-68)	1939	XIX
Salonina (253-68)	223	XIX
Macrianus (260-1)	1*	XIX
Quietus (260-1)	0	XIX
Claudius II Gothicus (268-70)	2601	XIX
Divus Claudius (270-85)	551+ † †	XIX
Quintillus (270)	106	XIX
GALLIC EMPIRE (AD 260-74)		
Postumus (260-9)	775	XX
Laelian (269)	8	XX
Marius (269)	15	XX
Victorinus (269-71)	1801	XX
Domitianus (271)	0	XX
Tetricus I (271-4)	2416	XX
Tetricus II (273-4)	1054	XX

Ruler		Chapter
Aurelian (270-5)	126	XXI
Aurelian and Vabalathus (270-2)	1	XXI
Severina (275)	10	XXI
Tacitus (275-6)	99	XXI
Florian (276)	7	XXI
Probus (276-82)	226	XXI
Carus (282-3)	14	XXI
Numerian (282-4)	3	XXI
Carinus (282-5)	18	XXI
Magnia Urbica (under Carinus)	1*	XXI
Nigrinian (struck under Carinus)	1*	XXI
Julian of Pannonia (284-5)	0	XXI
Barbarous Radiates (c. 275-85)	4167	XXI
Radiates uncertain	4564	
Carausius (c.286-93)	2025	XXII
Allectus (c.293-6)	1087	XXII
Diocletian (284-305)	297	XXIII
Maximian (286-310)	282	XXIII
Constantius I (293-306)	227	XXIII
Galerius (293-311)	100	XXIII
Galeria Valeria (under Galerius)	2	XXIII
Domitius Domitianus (296-7)	1*	XXIII
Severus II (305-7)	13	XXIII
Tetrarchic ruler uncertain	40	
Constantine I (306-37)	6736	XXIII-XXV
Maxentius (306-12)	21	XXIII
Romulus (under Maxentius)	0	
Alexander (311)	0	
Maximinus II Daia (309-13)	110	XXIII
Licinius I (308-24)	371	XXIII, XXIV
Licinius II (317-24)	47	XXIV
Martinian (324)	0	XXIV
Crispus (317-26)	1014	XXIV
Fausta (died 326)	93	XXIV
Helena (House of Constantine)	877	XXIV, XXV

Ruler	Chapter	Ruler	Chapter
Delmatius (335-7)..23..............XXV		Theodosius I (379-95)..........................223..........XXVIII	
Theodora (House of Constantine)........715..............XXV		Aelia Flacilla (under Theodosius I)...........0..........XXVIII	
Constantine II (317-40)......................2742....XXIV, XXV		Arcadius (383-408)..............................350..........XXVIII	
Constans (333-50) ....2817....XXV, XXVI		Eudoxia (under Arcadius)........................0..........XXVIII	
Vetranio (350) ....0..............XXVI		Magnus Maximus (383-8)...................108..........XXVIII	
Nepotian (350) ....0..............XXVI		Flavius Victor (387-8)............................32..........XXVIII	
Magnentius (350-3)............................1808..............XXVI		Magnus Maximus or Flavius Victor 16	
Decentius (351-3) ....144..............XXVI		Eugenius (392-4) ....41..........XXVIII	
Magnentius or Decentius......................33		Honorius (393-423) ....160..........XXVIII	
Constantius Gallus (351-4) ....68..............XXVI		House of Theodosius uncertain 1030	
Constantius II (323-361) ....4275... XXIV-XXVI			
Constantius II or Constans....................69		Theodosius II (402-450) ....5..........XXVIII	
Julian (355-63) ....336..............XXVI		Constantine III (407-11)...........................0	
Jovian (363-4)..27..............XXVI		Maximus (409-11) 1	
House of Constantine 20,972		Jovinus (411-13)......................................1..........XXVIII	
		Valentinian III (425-50) ....0 † † † XXVIII	
Valentinian I (364-75)..........................1326..........XXVII			
Valens (364-78) ....2611..........XXVII		Uncertain 4th Century 4641	
Procopius (365-6) ....1..........XXVII		Uncertain c.260-402.......................4,042	
Gratian (367-83)................................2002..........XXVII		Late 4th- Early 5th Century.................196	
House of Valentinian uncertain..........6664		Uncertain 18,002	
Valentinian II (375-92).........................158..........XXVIII		Total 128,593	

*   These coins come from Welsh hoards.

†   I do wonder if Marcus Aurelius continued to strike coins for Lucilla after the death of Lucius Verus as her coins are much more numerous than those of Verus.

† †   Note that many Divus Claudius coins are recorded as barbarous radiates.

† † † A number of later rulers are represented in finds such as the Patching Hoard. (See Bland and Loriot 2010, p.361, in Further Reading appendix.)

Chapter IV
Obverse Inscriptions (Legends) and Types

Fig.1. Copper-alloy *as* of Nero (AD 54-68), struck in Lyon, AD 65.
Obverse: NERO CLAVD[ius] CAESAR AVG[ustus] GER[manicus] P[ontifex] M[aximus] TR[ibunicia] P[otestas] IMP[erator] P[ater] P[atriae]; laureate head right, globe at neck.
Reverse: S[enatus] C[onsulto]; Victory flying left, holding globe inscribed S[enatus] P[opulus]Q[ue] R[omanus].
RIC I, 477. Found in London on the foreshore of the River Thames, LON-0C0210. © Portable Antiquities Scheme (24mm)

Fig.2. Silver *denarius* of Commodus (AD 180-92), struck at Rome, AD 189.
Obverse: M[arcus] COMM[odus] ANT[oninus] P[ius] FEL[ix] AVG[ustus] BRIT[annicus] P[ater] P[atriae]; Laureate head right.
Reverse: MIN[erva] VICT[rix] P[ontifex] M[aximus] TR[ibunicia] P[otestas] XIIII CO[n]S[ul] V [Consul] DES[ignatus] VI; Minerva standing left holding Victory and spear; to left, shield; to right, trophy.
RIC III, 189. Found in East Yorkshire, YORYM-9E35C7. © Portable Antiquities Scheme (17.5mm)

This chapter is intended to assist you to read and identify the obverse legend and type of your Roman coins. I provide most of the common titles and bust types that you are likely to come across.

Common Titles on Roman Coins

As with modern British coins, the ruler's inscription ("obverse legend") normally contained a variety of titles which were often abbreviated. When you look at a Roman coin you will often find the emperor's name in the middle of the inscription with titles on either side. Sometimes, the emperor's title is continued in the reverse legend (Figs. 1-13).

The following titles are commonly found on Roman coins, before and after the emperor's or empress's name; they are often abbreviated. Note that in Latin inscriptions the letter U was represented by a V.

IMP – IMPERATOR

Commander-in-chief of the army or victorious general. Sometimes a number follows IMP (i.e.

IMP III) showing how many victorious campaigns have occurred in an emperor's reign. This helps with the dating of coins.

AVG – AUGUSTUS

Title taken by senior emperors.

AUGUSTA for empresses.

C, CAE, CAES – CAESAR

Title taken by senior and junior emperors, but used alone by Junior Emperors.

COS – CONSUL

Consul. COS is often followed by a number denoting how many times the emperor has been declared Consul (i.e. COS III). This also helps with the dating of coins.

COS DES – CONSUL DESIGNATUS

Consul Designate. Consuls were elected or nominated the summer before taking office, so received this title until they took office.

Fig.3. Copper-alloy *as* of Domitian (AD 81-96), struck in Rome, AD 86.
Obverse: IMP[erator] CAES[ar] DOMIT[ianus] AVG[ustus] GERM[anicus] CO[n]S[ul] XII CENS[or] PER[petuus] P[ater] P[atriae].
Reverse: FORTVNAE AVGVSTI, S C; Fortuna standing left holding rudder and cornucopiae.
RIC II (2nd ed), 488. Found in Lincolnshire, Lin-E74A15. © Portable Antiquities Scheme (28mm)

Fig.4. Copper-alloy *sestertius* of Trajan (AD 98-117), struck in Rome, AD 114-7.
Obverse: IMP[erator] CAES[ar] NERVAE TRAIANO AVG[ustus] GER[manicus] DAC[acicus] PARTHICO P[ontifex] M[aximus] TR[ibunicia] P[otestas] CO[n]S[ul] VI P[ater] P[atriae]; Laureate and draped bust right.
Reverse: ARMENIA ET MESOPOTAMIA IN POTESTATEM P[opuli] R[omani] REDACTAE, S C; Trajan standing, holding spear and parazonium, reclining figures of Armenia, Euphrates and Tigris at his feet. RIC II, 642. Found in Northamptonshire, NARC-CE14A4. © Portable Antiquities Scheme (33mm)

Fig.5. Silver *denarius* of Marcus Aurelius as Augustus (AD 161-180), struck at Rome, AD 164.
Obverse: ANTONINVS AVG(ustus) ARMENIACVS.
Reverse: P[ontifex] M[aximus] TR[ibunicia] P[otestas] XVIII IMP[erator] II CO[n]S[ul] III; Mars standing right, holding spear and leaning on shield.
RIC III, 92. Found in Hertfordshire, BH-09CE61. © Portable Antiquities Scheme (17mm)

TR P (or POT) – TRIBUNICIA POTESTAS

Power of the Tribune. This office was founded in the Republican period, but was adopted by the emperors. It is often followed by a number as the office was re-affirmed regularly, often annually (i.e. TR P XVII = holder of the Tribunician Power for the seventeenth time). This enables us to date some coins quite precisely.

P M or PONT MAX – PONTIFEX MAXIMUS

Chief Priest (a title still used by the Pope).

P P – PATER PATRIAE

Father of his Country. A title adopted by Augustus and conferred on several later emperors.

CENS (PERP) – CENSOR (PERPETUUS)

Censor or Censor forever. Oversaw the Census and morals.

GERM – GERMANICUS Conqueror of Germania.

PARTH – PARTHICUS Conqueror of Parthia.

Fig.6. Silver *siliqua* of Valens (AD 364-78), struck at Lyon, AD 364-7.
Obverse: D[ominus] N[oster] VALENS P[ius] F[elix] AVG[ustu]S Pearl-diademed, draped and cuirassed right.
Reverse: REISTITVTOR REI P[ublicae]; Emperor with labarum and victory on globe; mintmark: PLVG.
RIC IX, 6e. Found in Somerset, SOM-05DD97. © Portable Antiquities Scheme (16.5mm)

DAC – DACICUS Conqueror of Dacia.

ARM – ARMENIACUS Conqueror of Armenia.

BRIT – BRITANNICUS Conqueror of Britannia.

SARM – SARMATIACUS Conqueror of the Sarmatians.

P F – PIUS FELIX
(Pious to the Gods; and blessed by the Gods.)

D N – DOMINUS NOSTER
(Our Lord) – commonly used on late Roman coins in the Christian period. Some historians call this period the "Dominate".

IVN – JUNIOR
For coins of Licinius II and Constantine II.

NOB – NOBILISSIMUS
(Most noble) – commonly used for junior emperors on late Roman coins.

PP or PERP – PERPETUUS
(Forever). This title was used on late Roman coins.

DIVUS/DIVO
Titles used on commemorative coins to indicate

that the dead emperor had been deified – i.e. DIVO CLAVDIO coins for Claudius II (AD 268-70) (XIII, 31-2)

DIVA
Title used on commemorative coins to indicate that a dead empress had been deified – i.e. DIVA FAUSTINA for Faustina I (died AD 141) and II (died AD 176) (Fig.9.)

MAX – MAXIMUS
(Greatest or supreme) – Septimius Severus was Parthicus Maximus; Gallienus was Germanicus Maximus; Constantine I was Maximus Augustus (Fig.10.)

M – MARCUS (or MAUSAEUS? for Carausius)

CL – CLAUDIUS
A family name of various emperors.

FL – FLAVIUS
A family name of various emperors.

Fig.7. Copper-alloy Roman *nummus* of Constantine II as Caesar (AD 317-37), struck at Trier, AD 332-3.
Obverse: CONSTANTINVS IVN[ior] NOB[ilissimus] C[aesar]; Laureate and cuirassed bust right.
Reverse: GLORIA EXERCITVS; two soldiers and two standards; mintmark TR•P.
RIC VII, 539. Found in West Sussex, SUSS-12A357.
© Portable Antiquities Scheme (18mm)

Fig.9. Silver *denarius* of Diva Faustina (died AD 141), struck at Rome under Antoninus Pius, AD 141-61).
Obverse: DIVA FAVSTINA; draped bust right.
Reverse: AVGVSTA; Venus standing left holding apple and resting left hand on shield.
RIC III, no. 366. Found in North Yorkshire, DUR-CB4720.
© Portable Antiquities Scheme (18mm)

Fig.8. Silver *siliqua* of Julian (AD 360-3), struck at Lyon, AD 361-3.
Obverse: FL[avius] CL[audius] IVLIANVS P[er]P[etuus] AVG[ustus]; Pearl-diademed, draped and cuirassed right.
Reverse: VOT / X / MVLT / XX in wreath; mintmark: PVLG.
RIC VIII, no. 233. Found in Bedfordshire, NMS-73A266.
© Portable Antiquities Scheme (17mm)

Fig.10. Copper-alloy *nummus* of Constantine I (AD 306-37), struck at Arles, AD 332-3.
Obverse: CONSTANTINVS MAX[imus] AVG[ustus]; Rosette diademed, draped and cuirassed right.
Reverse: GLORIA EXERCITVS; Two soldiers and two standards; mintmark: branch//PCONST.
RIC VII, p. 273, no. 364. Found in Lincolnshire, LIN-554774. © Portable Antiquities Scheme (16mm)

IVL – IVLIVS
A family name of various emperors.

M AVR – MARCUS AURELIUS
A name used by several 3rd century emperors, such as Elagabalus, Severus Alexander and Probus.

Two common abbreviations:

S P Q R – SENATUS POPULUS QUE ROMANUS
The Senate and People of Rome. (See Fig.1.; chapter IX Figs.15&16; chapter X Figs.19&23.)

S C – SENATUS CONSULTO
By authority of the Senate. S C was occasionally used on Republican *denarii*, probably to denote an emergency issue. It was used on the reverse of base metal coins from the reign of Augustus until the second half of the 3rd century AD. (See chapter VII Figs.8-10., and subsequent chapters up to XVIII.)

Common Obverse Types on Roman Coins
Below, I list the most common obverse types that occur on Roman coins. There are a large number of minor varieties, especially in the later 3rd century and the early 4th century. These are listed in volumes of the *Roman Imperial Coinage* and the *Coin Hoards of Roman Britain* series.

BARE-HEADED

Fig.12. Silver *denarius* of Marcus Aurelius as Augustus (AD 161-80), PROV DEOR TR P XVI COS III, Providentia standing with globe and cornucopiae, struck in Rome, AD 161-2. RIC III, 48. Found in County Durham, BM-088398. © Portable Antiquities Scheme (17mm)

BARE-HEADED AND CUIRASSED BUST

Fig.13. Copper-alloy *nummus* of Decentius (351-353), VICTORIAE DD NN AVG ET CAE, struck at Lyons, AD 351-353. RIC VIII, 137. Found in Berkshire, PUBLIC-78EB06. © Portable Antiquities Scheme (22mm)

BARE-HEAD, DRAPED AND CUIRASSED BUST

Fig.14. Copper-alloy Roman *nummus* of Magnentius (AD 350-353), VICTORIAE DD NN AVG ET CAES, two Victories holding wreath inscribed VOT/V/MVLT/X, struck at Lyons, AD 351-3. RIC VIII, 121. Found in Berkshire, BERK-D7F916. © Portable Antiquities Scheme (22mm)

LAUREATE HEAD

Fig.15. Copper-alloy *sestertius* of Lucius Verus (AD 161-9), FORT RED TR P VIII IMP V COS III S C, Fortuna seated left, struck at Rome in AD 168. RIC III, cf. 1476. Found in Sussex (SUSS-113C77). © Portable Antiquities Scheme (29.3mm)

Fig.11. Silver-washed copper-alloy *nummus* of Constantine I (AD 306-37), struck at Ostia, AD 312-3. Obverse: IMP[erator] C[aesar] CONSTANTINVS P[ius] F[elix] AVG[ugustus]; cuirassed bust right. Reverse: S[enatus] P[opulus]Q[ue] R[omanus] OPTIMO PRINCIPI ("best of princes"); Legionary eagle flanked by two vexilla (standards). RIC VI, 94. Found in North Lincolnshire, NLM-1D4686. © Portable Antiquities Scheme (22.5mm)

**LAUREATE AND
DRAPED BUST**

Fig.16. Silver *denarius* of Trajan (AD 98-117), S P Q R OPTIMO PRINCIPI, Trajan's Column, struck at Rome, AD 112-4. RIC II, 292. Found in Sussex, SUSS-5D0A00. © Portable Antiquities Scheme (19mm)

**LAUREATE AND
CUIRASSED BUST**

Fig.17. Copper-alloy *nummus* of Maximian (AD 286-310), GENIO POP ROM, Genius standing left, struck at London, AD 307. RIC VI, 85. Found in Dorset, DOR-A2AD53. © Portable Antiquities Scheme (27mm)

**LAUREATE, DRAPED
AND CUIRASSED BUST**

Fig.18. Silver *denarius* of Caracalla as Augustus (AD 198-217), PONTIF TRP III, Caracalla holding globe and spear, struck at Rome, AD 199-200. RIC IV, pt 1, 305. Found in North Yorkshire, DUR-A84742. © Portable Antiquities Scheme (19.5mm)

**RADIATE
HEAD**

Fig.19. Copper-alloy radiate of Gallienus (sole reign, AD 260-8), VIRTVS AVG, Mars standing, struck at Rome. Cunetio 921. Found in Hampshire, HAMP-4B1284. © Portable Antiquities Scheme (19mm)

**RADIATE AND
CUIRASSED BUST**

Fig.20. Copper-alloy radiate of the emperor Probus (AD 276-282), VIRTVS AVG, Emperor with spear and globe, struck at Rome. RIC V, pt 2, 801 (wrongly attributed to Siscia). Found in Dorset, SOM-5A8312. © Portable Antiquities Scheme (22mm).

**RADIATE, DRAPED AND
CUIRASSED BUST**

Fig.21. Silver radiate of Postumus (AD 260-9), MONETA AVG, Moneta with scales and cornucopiae, struck at the "Principal Mint" in Gaul. Cunetio 2404. Found in Hampshire, HAMP-4C4E81. © Portable Antiquities Scheme (20mm).

**DIADEMED AND DRAPED
(FOR EMPRESS)**

Fig.22. Silver *denarius* of Julia Mamaea (AD 222-35), struck at Rome, VESTA, Vesta holding patera and sceptre. RIC IV, pt 2, 362. Found in Lincolnshire, ESS-EEBD65. © Portable Antiquities Scheme (18.5mm)

**DRAPED BUST ON CRESCENT
(FOR EMPRESS)**

Fig.23. Copper-alloy radiate of Salonina, sole reign (AD 253-68), IVNONI CONS AVG, Capreolus left, struck at Rome. Cunetio 1418. Found in Wiltshire, WILT-65CFD2. © Portable Antiquities Scheme (19mm)

**HELMETED AND
CUIRASSED**

Fig.24. Copper-alloy Roman *nummus* of Crispus (AD 317-26), BEATA TRANQVILLITAS, altar inscribed VOT/IS/XX, struck at London, AD 321-2. RIC VII, 230. Found in Warwickshire, WAW-5E0202. © Portable Antiquities Scheme (20mm)

**HELMETED AND CUIRASSED BUST,
HOLDING SPEAR AND SHIELD**

Fig.25. Copper-alloy *nummus* of Constantine I (AD 306-37),VICTORIAE LAETAE PRINC PERP; Two Victories holding shield inscribed VOT/PR over altar, struck at London, AD 319-20. RIC VII, 159. Found on the Isle of Wight, IOW-E86503. © Portable Antiquities Scheme (18mm)

**RADIATE AND HELMETED
CUIRASSED BUST**

Fig.26. Copper-alloy radiate of Carausius (AD 286-93), ADVENTV[S AVG?], Emperor left on horseback, struck at an unattributed mint. Unpublished. Found in Hampshire, DUR-EE2DD3. © Portable Antiquities Scheme (23mm)

**PEARL-DIADEMED, DRAPED
AND CUIRASSED BUST**

Fig.27. Gold *solidus* of Arcadius (AD 383-408), VICTORIA AVGGG; Emperor standing right holding standard and Victory on globe, spurning captive, struck in Ravenna, AD 402-406. RIC X, 1286. Found on the Isle of Wight, IOW-DA6D56. © Portable Antiquities Scheme (20.5mm)

ROSETTE-DIADEMED, DRAPED AND CUIRASSED BUST

Fig.28. Copper-alloy *nummus* of Constantine I (AD 306-37), GLORIA EXERCITVS, two soldiers and two standards, struck at Lyon, AD 330-1. RIC VII, Lyon 236. Found in Wiltshire, SOM-084907. © Portable Antiquities Scheme (18mm)

ROSETTE AND LAUREATE DIADEMED, DRAPED AND CUIRASSED BUST

Fig.29. Gold *solidus* of Constantius II (AD 337-61), VICTORIA DD NN AVGG, Victory advancing left with trophy and palm-branch, struck at Trier AD 342-3. RIC VIII, 122. © British Museum (21mm)

RADIATE BUST IN CONSULAR ROBES, HOLDING EAGLE-TIPPED SCEPTRE ("SCIPIO")

Fig.30. Silver-washed radiate of Probus (AD 276-82), ERCVLI PACIF, Hercules standing, struck at Ticinum. RIC V, pt 2, 375. Frome Hoard. © British Museum (24mm)

FACING DIADEMED AND HELMETED BUST, HOLDING SPEAR AND SHIELD

Fig.31. Gold *solidus* of Honorius (AD 393-423), CONCORDIA AVGG, Constantinopolis seated holding Victory on globe and sceptre, foot on ship's prow. Struck at Constantinople, AD 397-402. RIC X, 8. Found in Gloucestershire, GLO-0BB2D8. © Portable Antiquities Scheme (19mm)

LAUREATE BUST IN CONSULAR ROBES (SOMETIMES CALLED A *TRABEA* OR IMPERIAL MANTLE), HOLDING EAGLE-TIPPED SCEPTRE

Fig.32. Copper-alloy *nummus* of Constantine I (AD 306-37), BEATA TRANQVILLITAS, globe on altar, struck at Trier, AD 321. RIC VII, 321. Found in Hampshire, SUR-293900. © Portable Antiquities Scheme (20mm)

LAUREATE AND DRAPED BUST HOLDING VICTORY ON GLOBE AND *MAPPA*

Fig.33. Copper-alloy radiate of Constantine II as Caesar (AD 317-37), BEATA TRANQVILLITAS, globe on altar, struck in Trier, AD 321. He holds the *mappa* (a cloth thrown down by the emperor to start chariot races) in his left hand. RIC VII, 312. Found in Somerset, SOM-288406. © Portable Antiquities Scheme (20.5mm)

Chapter V
Reverse Types on Roman Coins

Fig.1. Silver-washed copper-alloy radiate of Carausius (AD 286-93), struck at "C" Mint. The obverse shows Carausius in military attire, holding a spear and shield. The reverse shows the emperor distributing largesse, with a statue of Liberalitas standing in front of him. RIC V, pt 2, 277var. Frome Hoard. © British Museum (25mm)

The reverses of Roman coins cover an enormous range of topics and themes relating to the Roman world. In this chapter, I discuss the variety of reverse types by theme. Most of the reverse types are represented on coins illustrated in this book, but one or two extra coins are included here to make the lists more complete.

The Emperor & His Family

From the reign of Augustus (27 BC-AD 14), the emperor often appears on the reverse of coins in a variety of guises and activities. He can be in military dress, often holding a standard. He also spears, spurns or drags enemies (Chapter XXVIII, Fig.32.). Some issues show him celebrating a victory or another major event such as the return of the Parthian standards in the reign of Augustus (Chapter VIII, Fig.14.). On some coins, the emperor even holds a statuette of Victory, or appears alongside Victory (Chapter XXVI, Fig.12.).

Occasionally the emperor appears on a galley which can, at a basic level, represent the emperor's progress around the Empire (for example Hadrian) or a naval event (for example possibly Constans' trip to Britain), but on a more conceptual

level can reflect the "ship of state" (Chapter XXVI, Fig.2.). The emperor is often shown as the ruler or restorer of the world (RESTITVTOR ORBIS/REIPVB), holding spear and globe, or raising a female personification (Chapter XXVIII, Fig.7.). A few coins show the emperor elevating or confirming minor or client-kings on the fringes of the Roman Empire. In the case of Carausius, he tries to muscle in on the world of the rulers of the central Roman Empire (Chapter XXII, Fig.30.). When there were emperors ruling jointly, their coins often show them working in concord (CONCORDIA) (Chapter XVII, Fig.36.).

The emperor is sometimes represented wearing traditional Roman dress, the toga, with attributes of power such as the globe and sceptre (Chapter VIII, Fig.7.). When new emperors first visited Rome, their arrival (ADVENTVS) in the city was celebrated on coins, normally with the emperor on horseback; in the case of Carausius, he was celebrating his arrival in London (Chapter XXII, Fig.5.). One of the most important events for the emperor was the handing out of largesse to the population, coins often celebrating his generosity [LIBERALITAS] (Fig.1.).

Another important role carried out by the emperor, who was often the Pontifex Maximus (chief priest), was sacrificing to the gods (Chapter XI, Fig.22.).The emperor could even be depicted with gods, most often with Jupiter, king of the gods (Chapter XXI, Fig.14.).

Members of the wider imperial family appeared on the reverses of his coins, Augustus honouring his grandsons Lucius and Caius (Chapter VIII, Fig.18.), Vespasian depicting his sons Titus and Domitian (Chapter XI, Fig.3.) and Caracalla clasping hands with Plautilla (Chapter XVI, Fig.21.). On a late Roman coin, Constantine appears with his sons Crispus, Constantine II and Constantius II.

Young emperors often took the title Princeps (PRINCIPI IVVENTVTIS – "The Prince of Youth") (Chapter XVII, Fig.3.) and were shown in military dress. In the reign of Augustus, a series of coins depicted a Capricorn, representing the star sign during which the emperor was conceived. There are some very unusual depictions; it is thought clumsy that Nero appears as Apollo playing the lyre on a coin that apparently celebrates Nero's victory at the Olympic Games (Chapter X, Fig.7.).

Emperors rarely retired, but when they did the event could be celebrated as in the case of Diocletian and Maximian (Chapter XXIII, Fig.15.).

Posthumous Types

Deceased emperors and empresses were often commemorated on coins where they were accorded divine status (DIVVS, DIVO and DIVA; see "Titles" section above). The tradition started in the imperial period with Augustus who was titled *Divus Augustus Pater* (Our Divine Father Augustus) (Chapter VIII, Fig.20.). Deceased rulers were normally depicted bare-headed or veiled on the obverse. The reverses often depicted an eagle, the spirit of the dead emperor or a peacock, the spirit of the dead empress (Chapter XIV, Fig.22. & Chapter XIX, Fig.12.).

Sometimes the deceased is shown riding on the flying bird to heaven. Other common types include funeral pyres and altars and even eagles and an altar (Chapter XXIII, Fig.23.). The last posthumous coins were struck for Constantine the Great who was the last emperor to have a consecration issue (Chapter XXV, Fig.11.). From then onwards, Christian emperors were not declared gods on their death and posthumous issues ceased.

Military Types

Without the support of the army, the emperor could not hold power. Hence, many coin types honoured the army. Some coins declared a good relationship (Concordia) between the emperor and army (CONCORDIA MILITVM/EXERCITVM) often with clasped hands or standards (Chapter XXII, Fig.13.). Other coins praised the "glorious army" (GLORIA EXERCITVS) while others praised the "faithfulness of the army" (FIDES MILITVM /EXERCITVS) or the "spirit or genius of the army" (GENIVS EXERCI) (Chapter X, Fig.27.).

Some emperors honoured particular legions, notably Gallienus and Carausius (Chapter XXII, Fig.20.), while Hadrian honoured the armies of particular provinces. The appearance of the galley alludes to the Roman navy. Some coins depicted weapons while a large number show military standards. One coin, depicting an eagle on a globe is thought to have been struck by Vespasian especially for issue to the army (Chapter XI, Fig.10.).

Many emperors struck coins celebrating military victories, using a variety of types: triumphal arches; triumphant emperor; defeated enemies; Victory/Victories; trophy and weapons, and Victories and trophy (Chapter X, Fig.4.).

One common 4th century type shows a Roman soldier spearing a fallen horseman with the inscription FEL[icium] TEMP[us] REPARATIO ("Happy days are here again") (Chapter XXVII, Fig.31.).

Another enigmatic type from the same period shows a soldier leading a small figure from a hut – is this a soldier leading off a captured barbarian, or does it show the Roman army assisting the lowly farmer in the Roman Empire? Even the empress was sometimes honoured as the Mother of the Camp (i.e. army) (Chapter XXVII, Fig.5.).

Geographical Types: Cities, Provinces & Rivers
Rome & Constantinople

From her depiction on Roman Republican *denarii* to her appearance on late Roman coins, Roma, the personification of Rome, was a common type on coins. She was normally depicted as a warrior, like Minerva, often seated on a shield or cuirass holding weapons or Victory (Chapter X, Fig.22.).

Sometimes, the city of Rome (VRBS ROMA) was honoured, often with a depiction of the wolf with Romulus and Remus (Chapter XXV, Fig.5.). Romulus and Remus could appear by themselves. On many coins, reference was made to the Senate and People of Rome (SPQR) and on one late Roman issue, the people of Rome were honoured (Chapter IX, Fig.15.). In the later Roman period, Constantinople was honoured in a similar way (Chapter XXV, Fig.7.).

Fig.2. Copper-alloy *as* of Antoninus Pius (AD 138-61), struck in Rome, AD 140-44, showing the River Tiber reclining placing her hand on the prow of a ship. BMC IV, 1389. © British Museum (26mm)

Fig.3. Copper-alloy *sestertius* of Caracalla (AD 198-217), struck at Rome, AD 213. The obverse includes the title BRIT[annicus], taken by Caracalla after the imperial expedition in Britain led by Septimius Severus in AD 208-11. The reverse shows the Circus Maximus in Rome with several chariots racing inside. BMC IV, 251. © British Museum (34mm)

Other Peoples, Provinces, Cities & Rivers

In the Republican period, a number of coins represented people from the fringes of the Roman world, for example a Gaulish warrior on a piece of 118 BC (Chapter VII, Fig.16.). The three-legged symbol (*triskelis*) of Rome's first overseas province, Sicily, appears on some coins (Chapter X, Fig.18.). Augustus celebrated the capture of Egypt from Cleopatra after the Battle of Actium in 31 BC (Chapter VIII, Fig.5.). Trajan honoured the new province of Arabia, created out of the old Kingdom of Nabataea in AD 106 (Chapter XII, Fig.20.).

Hadrian struck a famous series of coins, which honoured most of the provinces, including Germania and Britannia, and another series of pieces on which he declared himself the restorer of particular provinces (Chapter XIII, Fig.7.). Antoninus Pius struck a copious issue of coins depicting Britannia (Chapter XIV, Fig.14.). One coin of Commodus shows the emperor as Hercules alongside the personification of Africa, while a late Roman coin depicts the personification of the great African city of Carthage (Chapter XXIII, Fig.13.). Some coins even celebrated great rivers, such as the Tiber (Fig.2.).

Carausius showed himself being greeted by Britannia, with the inscription "Welcome, O long awaited one" (EXPECTATE VENI) (Chapter XXII, Fig.8.), while a coin of Constantius I shows the emperor raising Britannia after the defeat of Allectus in AD 296 (Chapter XXIII, Fig.22.).

Architectural Types

Buildings occur frequently on coins. Temples are commonly depicted on coins, including the Temples of Mars Ultor, Vesta, Janus, and Divus Antoninus and Diva Faustina, all in Rome (Chapter XIV, Figs.9-10.). The Colosseum, started by Vespasian, appears on the coins of his son Titus (Chapter XI, Fig.14.). Trajan's coins have a

Fig.4. Gold *aureus* of Valerian I (AD 253-60) struck at Rome. The reverse shows Apollo the Protector, holding a branch and lyre. RIC V, pt 1, 32. © British Museum (17mm)

range of structures, including the famous bridge over the Danube, monuments in Rome, his new Basilica Ulpia and Trajan's Column (Chapter XII, Fig.17.). The Circus Maximus in Rome, where chariot races and other major parades were held, was depicted on a later coin of Caracalla (Fig.3.).

Even the construction of new ports and roads could be commemorated (Chapter XII, Fig.10.). Architectural types tend to be rarer in the later Roman period, although Maxentius (AD 306-12) struck numerous temple types at Rome and the camp gate becomes a common type in the 4th century (Chapter XIV, Fig.23.). The dwellings of humble people are alluded to on a late Roman coin showing a soldier leading a small figure from a hut.

Gods & Other Religious Types

Deities are very common on Roman coins, ranging from Olympian gods and goddesses to the deities of eastern "mystery cults". Below, I list the gods who appear on coins in this book; the list is not exhaustive, but includes the deities you are most likely to come across.

Many Olympian and other Graeco-Roman

Fig.5. Silver *denarius* of Septimius Severus (AD 193-211), struck at Rome, AD 197. The reverse shows Bacchus with his *thyrsus* and panther, and called by his Italian name: LIBER PATER. RIC IV, pt 1, 99. Found in Hampshire, SUR-29F313. © Portable Antiquities Scheme (15mm)

Fig.7. Silver *denarius* of Clodius Albinus (AD 193-7), struck at Rome, AD 193. The reverse shows Aesculapius standing with a snake wreathed around his staff. RIC IV, pt 1, 2. Found in Lincolnshire, LIN-EA0992. © Portable Antiquities Scheme (19mm)

Fig.6. Base silver radiate of Valerian I (AD 253-60) struck in Gaul. The reverse shows Vulcan holding his hammer and pincers by an anvil on the ground. Cunetio 706. © British Museum (20mm)

Fig.8. Silver *denarius* of Claudius (AD 41-54), struck at Rome, AD 46-7. The reverse proclaims Augustan Peace and shows Pax-Nemesis advancing right holding a caduceus and pointing at a snake; she also holds a fold of drapery at her neck. Found in Leicestershire, LEIC-20DE25. © Portable Antiquities Scheme (19.5mm)

gods and goddesses appear on coins, as in the examples given below.

Jupiter – King of the Gods.

He is commonly shown holding a sceptre and thunderbolt and often has an eagle in attendance (Chapter XIV, Fig.32.). On the coins of Gallienus, he is represented by his sacred animal, the goat and on one coin the young Jupiter is shown riding a goat (Chapter XIX, Figs.8 & 18.).

Juno – Queen of the Gods.

She is often shown holding a sceptre and with a peacock in attendance (Chapter XV, Fig.17.). One piece shows her mythical beast, the capreolus (a cross between a goat and a deer) (Chapter IV, Fig.23.).

Minerva – Goddess of War and Wisdom.

She is normally shown dressed as a warrior, sometimes with an owl in attendance (Chapter XIV, Fig.16.).

Mars – God of War.

He is normally shown as a warrior, although he can appear in an heroic naked pose as well (Chapter XV, Fig.2.).

Neptune – God of the Sea.

He is often shown with a trident and a dolphin (Chapter IX, Fig.10.).

Apollo – God of the Sun, the Arts, Music and Prophecy.

He is normally depicted with a lyre although he is also often associated with his sacred animal, the griffin (Fig.4.).

Diana – Goddess of the Moon, Hunting and Protector of the Young.

She is rarely shown on Roman coins although she is honoured with her sacred animal, the deer, stag or gazelle on common coins of Gallienus (Chapter XIX, Fig.19.).

Mercury – The Messenger God who was god of travellers, merchants and thieves.

He is well known for his caduceus (wand with entwined serpents) and petasus (winged hat) (Chapter XI, Fig.27.).

Venus – Goddess of Love, Reproduction and Beauty.

She is often depicted naked or semi-naked and sometimes holds an apple (Chapter XVII, Fig.8.).

Ceres – Goddess of Agriculture, most commonly associated with grain.

She is often shown holding corn ears and a torch (Chapter XIX, Fig.7.).

Bacchus (Liber Pater) – the Greek Dionysus who was often called Liber on Roman coins and was the God of Wine and Drama.

He is often shown holding his staff entwined with ivy (the *thyrsus*) and is accompanied by his panther (Fig.5.).

Vulcan – The God of Volcanoes and Smiths.

He is rarely depicted on Roman coins, but on a piece of Valerian he holds his hammer and pincers with an anvil on the ground (Fig.6.).

Aesculapius – God of Healing.

He is normally shown holding a staff with a snake wrapped around it. (Fig.7.).

Castor and Pollux – also known as the Dioscuri (Heavenly Twins).

They are commonly depicted on Republican *denarii*, the Dioscuri reputedly fought on horseback beside the Romans in their defeat of the last Etruscan king of Rome and the Latin League at the battle of Lake Regillus in the 490s BC (Chapter VII, Fig.5.).

Nemesis – Goddess of Retribution, sometimes associated with Pax.

She is often winged, holds a caduceus and has a snake in attendance. (Fig.8.).

Hercules – Greek demi-god, famous for his Twelve Labours. He is often depicted as a powerful man with his attributes of a club, bow and lion-skin (Chapter IV, Fig.30.).

Janus – Two-Faced God of Beginnings and Ends (Chapter VII, Fig.7.).

When there was no war in the Empire, the doors of his temple in Rome were closed (Chapter X, Fig.5.).

Vesta – Traditional Roman Goddess of the Hearth and Family.

Her Temple, in the Roman Forum, was tended by the Vestal Virgins. She is often shown veiled, holding a sceptre, patera and the Palladium (statuette of Athena from Troy) (Chapter XIII, Fig.11.).

Sol – Sol or Sol Invictus (the "Invincible Sun") became increasingly popular in the Roman Imperial Period.

He is depicted with a radiate crown and often holds a whip or globe; sometimes he appears in his chariot (Chapter XXIII, Fig.38.).

Eastern Cults

Cybele – the Magna Mater – Great Mother Goddess, from Anatolia, Turkey.

She is often depicted with a drum and lions (Chapter XV, Fig.14.).

Elagabal – The "Sun God of the Ridge/Mountains".

He had a sacred stone at Emesa in Syria. The emperor Elagabalus (AD 218-22) brought the stone to Rome and set up his cult in the city (Chapter XVII, Fig.7.).

Serapis – This Egyptian god combined the powers of various Greek deities: Aesculapius, Jupiter, Osiris and Pluto; his consort, Isis, was also worshipped across the Roman world and appears on coins struck by Julian, AD 360-3 (Chapter XVI, Fig.29.).

Christ – Christian imagery began to appear on coins from the reign of Constantine I, AD 306-37.

The Chi-Rho symbol was most commonly used in the 4th century (Chapter XXVI, Fig.23.), but the cross became more common in the 5th century. One coin even spells out the text Constantine saw in a vision before the Battle of the Milvian Bridge in AD 312; HOC SIGNO VICTOR ERIS ("In this sign you will conquer") (Chapter XXIII, Fig.26.).

Pagan Backlash – The Emperor Julian (AD 360-3) tried to turn back the tide against Christianity and issued coins with a bull (the most important sacrificial animal in Roman religion) and two stars (possibly referring to Castor and Pollux) (Chapter XXVI, Fig.37.).

Miscellaneous Religious Types

Altar of Roma and Augustus – built at Lyon, Gaul, in the reign of Augustus (Chapter VIII, Fig.19.).

Sacrificial Implements Increasingly, sacrificial implements were used on coins of young junior emperors (Caesars) as one of their first positions was a priesthood (Chapter XIX, Fig.10). On one specific issue, the emperor Vitellius celebrated a priesthood that he held (Chapter X, Fig.31.).

Personifications

A wide range of personifications appear on coins. Below, I list all the common personifications, although not all are covered in the book.

Fig.9. Copper-alloy radiate of Gallienus, sole reign (AD 260-8), struck at Rome. The reverse shows Abundantia emptying a cornucopiae. Cunetio 1159. Found in Sussex, SUSS-A98AE6. © Portable Antiquities Scheme (20mm)

Fig.11. Silver *denarius* of Marcus Aurelius as Caesar (AD 139-61), struck at Rome, c.AD 145-7. The reverse shows Honos standing left holding branch and cornucopiae. RIC III, 429a. Found in Leicestershire, SWYOR-604195. © Portable Antiquities Scheme (18mm)

Fig.10. Silver *denarius* of Hadrian (AD 117-38), struck at Rome, AD 117-22. The reverse shows Clementia (note CLEM in exergue) sacrificing at an altar with sceptre and patera. RIC II, 116. Found in Somerset, SOM-696C24. © Portable Antiquities Scheme

Fig.12. Silver *denarius* of Hadrian (AD 117-38), struck at Rome, AD 132-4. The reverse shows Indulgentia seated holding a sceptre. RIC II, 212. © British Museum (17mm)

Abundantia – Abundance.

She is often shown emptying a cornucopiae (horn of plenty) (Fig.9.).

Aequitas – Equity.

She holds scales and cornucopiae (Chapter II, Fig.9.).

Aeternitas – Eternity; Stability; Continuity.

She often holds globe, torch, sceptre or the heads of the sun and moon (Chapter XXI, Fig.11.).

Annona – Corn harvest and supply.

She often holds corn ears and cornucopiae and can appear with a modius (corn measure) and the prow of a ship. The modius often appears as a type by itself (Chapter XI, Figs.8 & 25.).

Bonus Eventus – Good outcome, event or luck (Chapter X, Fig.20).

Clementia – Mercy; Clemency.

She is often shown with a patera or branch and sceptre, and sometimes at an altar. (Fig. 10.).

Comes – Companion or Protector, normally of an emperor.

The *comes* could be one of several gods or personifications, for example Jupiter, Hercules or Victory (Chapter XX, Fig.22.).

Concordia – Concord or Harmony.

She normally holds a patera and cornucopiae – some Concordia types show clasped hands (Chapter XIII, Fig. 15.).

Fecunditas – Fecundity; Fertility.

She is commonly shown on coins of empresses and she is often associated with children (Chapter XIX, Fig.23.).

Felicitas – Prosperity; Happiness.

She normally holds a long-handled caduceus in combination with various other attributes (Chapter XXI, Fig.12.).

Fides – Faithfulness; Confidence.

She is most commonly associated with the army: Fides Militum who holds two military standards (Chapter XI, Fig.9.).

Fig.13. Silver radiate of Gordian III (AD 238-44), struck at Rome, AD 240. The reverse shows Liberalitas holding her coin scoop and cornucopiae. RIC IV, pt 3, 36. Found in Hampshire, SUR-E7F263. © Portable Antiquities Scheme (22mm)

Fig.14. Silver *denarius* of Geta as Caesar (AD 198-209), struck in Rome, AD 200-2. The reverse shows Nobilitas holding the Palladium and sceptre. RIC IV, pt 1, 13a. Found in Wiltshire, WILT-864E11. © Portable Antiquities Scheme (18mm)

Fortuna – Fortune; Good Luck.

She normally holds a rudder on globe and cornucopiae, sometimes with a wheel (Chapter XI, Fig.24.).

Fortuna Redux – Fortune the Home-bringer.

She is associated with travel (Chapter XVIII, Fig.2.).

Genius – "Genius" or spirit.

He is normally shown sacrificing at an altar with patera and cornucopiae (Chapter X, Fig.16.).

Genius Populi Romani – Spirit of the Roman People.

This was a very common type of the Tetrarchy (AD 294-305) (Chapter XXIII, Fig.5.).

Hilaritas – Cheerfulness; Rejoicing.

He holds a palm branch and cornucopiae (Chapter XVI, Fig.6.).

Honos – Honour.

He holds a branch or sceptre and cornucopiae. (Fig.11.).

Indulgentia – Indulgence.

She can hold a variety of attributes, including corn ears, sceptre, flower, baton and cornucopiae. (Fig.12.).

Justitia – Justice.

She can hold a patera, branch, sceptre or scales (Chapter VI, Fig.5.).

Laetitia – Joy; Happiness.

She holds a wreath and sceptre or rudder/baton (Chapter XX, Fig.24.).

Libertas – Liberty; Freedom.

She normally holds the *pileus* (cap of liberty) and a sceptre (Chapter XIV, Fig.18.).

Liberalitas – Generosity; Liberality.

She normally holds a scoop for distributing coins at festivals, and a cornucopiae (Fig.13.). Sometimes, she appears next to the emperor while he is distributing largesse. (Fig.1.).

Moneta – Money or Mint.

She holds scales and cornucopiae (Chapter XXIII, Fig.11.).

Nobilitas – Nobility.

She can hold the Palladium (statuette of Athena from Troy), globe and sceptre. She was often associated with junior emperors (Fig.14).

Pax – Peace.

She normally holds an olive branch and sceptre (Chapter XXII, Fig.12.).

Pietas – Piety; Dutifulness, normally towards the gods or state.

She is often shown veiled and sacrificing with a patera, and holding a sceptre or box of incense (Chapter XX, Fig.18.).

Providentia – Foresight; Providence.

She often holds a baton over globe and cornucopiae or sceptre (Chapter XX, Fig.22.).

Pudicitia – Modesty and Chastity.

She is normally associated with empresses and usually appears seated and veiled (Chapter XV, Fig.16.).

Fig.15. Base-silver radiate of Postumus (AD 260-9), struck at the Principal Mint in Gaul. The reverse shows Uberitas standing left holding a purse or grapes and cornucopiae. Cunetio 2439. Found in Wiltshire, WILT-19D401. © Portable Antiquities Scheme (19.5mm)

Fig.16. Copper-alloy medallion of Antoninus Pius (AD 138-61), struck at Rome (AD 140-44). The reverse shows the Capitoline Triad: Minerva, Jupiter and Juno. Gnecchi 66. Three other examples of this medallion are known, in Milan, Paris and Vienna. Found in Sussex, SUSS-5C54B2. © Portable Antiquities Scheme (39mm)

Salus – Health; Safety.

She is normally shown feeding a snake rising from an altar (Chapter XVII, Fig.28.).

Securitas – Security.

She is often shown reclining or nonchalantly leaning against a column (Chapter XXVI, Fig.13.).

Spes – Hope.

She holds a flower and lifts the hem of her skirt (Chapter XX, Fig.26.).

Uberitas – Fertility; Fecundity.

She holds a purse or bunch of grapes and cornucopiae. (Fig.15.).

Victoria – Victory.

She is normally winged and holds a wreath and palm. Sometimes she appears in a chariot, or two Victories appear together (Chapter XXV, Fig.25.).

Virtus – Courage; Bravery.

This inscription normally accompanies a figure of Mars, the god of war. Virtus herself is a female personification looking like Roma, but barely features on coins (XVIII, Fig.30.).

Vota & Anniversary Coins
Vota Coins

Roman emperors celebrated jubilees with coins proclaiming oaths of office. They would express thanks (vota) for a number of years ruled and for more in the future (multis) to the next jubilee. So, a coin with VOT V MVLT X would mean "thanks for five years of rule, looking forward to ten". The Romans counted their years inclusively

so their fourth year is our fifth (Chapter XXVII, Fig.11.) It can be dangerous dating coins precisely using vota types because emperors often celebrated their jubilees early! One common issue of the House of Constantine, praised the "blessings of peace" (BEATA TRANQUILLITAS) on the 20th jubilee of Constantine (VOTIS XX) (Chapter XXIV, Fig.15.).

Anniversary Coins

In AD 148, Antoninus Pius celebrated the 900th anniversary of the foundation of Rome. It is thought that a large series of medallions were struck at the time to prepare for this event – one example was found in Sussex a few years ago (Fig.16.).

In AD 248, Philip I celebrated the 1000th anniversary of the traditional date of Rome's foundation (753 BC) with lavish anniversary "secular games", some coins bearing the inscription SAECULARES AVGG. One piece of Philip bore the wolf and twins while another for his empress, Otacilia Severa, depicted a hippopotamus, a potent symbol of fecundity in the ancient world (Chapter XVIII, Figs.11 & 16.). On the 1100th anniversary in AD 348, Constantius II and Constans struck numerous coins showing the legendary bird, the phoenix, which rose from the ashes, alluding to a prophecy that Rome would be destroyed after 1100 years (Chapter XXVI, Fig.9.)

Miscellaneous Types

Especially in the Roman Republican period, mythological scenes and characters were depicted, Aeneas carrying his father, Anchises, being a famous example (Chapter VII, Fig.14.). One

Fig.17. Copper-alloy *nummus* of Constantine I (AD 306-337) struck at Arles, AD 313-5. The obverse shows the emperor laureate, wearing consular robes (*trabea*) and holding an eagle-tipped sceptre. The reverse, with the inscription VTILITAS PVBLICA, shows the emperor (?) holding Victory and globe receiving Moneta who stands on the prow of a ship holding scales and cornucopia. This very rare coin also commemorates the movement of the mint from Ostia to Arles in AD 313. RIC VII, 51. Found in Staffordshire,WMID-CBFFB7. © Portable Antiquities Scheme (22mm)

Republican coin shows citizens voting at one of the assemblies (*comitia*) at Rome, whilst another marks a political assassination with Brutus striking a coin celebrating the murder of Julius Caesar on the Ides of March, 44 BC (Chapter VII, Fig.15.). Occasionally emperors cancelled debts or lightened the tax load – Nerva commemorated taking the burden of paying for the imperial postal service (*cursus publicus*) in Italy (Chapter XII, Fig.5.).

Finally, some low value late Roman coins bore the inscription VTILITAS PUBLICA ("for the common good"), denoting that they were indeed struck for the benefit of the people, in this case to enable small transactions (Fig.17.).

Chapter VI
Roman Mints

In the Republican period, Rome was the most important mint. Coins were also struck elsewhere in Italy and at times in some of Rome's early provinces such as Sicily and Spain. The most common Republican coins to be found in Britain, the *denarii* of Mark Antony (struck 32-31 BC) were produced at a mint which travelled with Antony, probably operating in Greece and western Turkey.

After the coinage reforms of Augustus (27 BC-AD 14) until around AD 253, Rome continued to be the major mint in the Empire. In the 1st centuries BC and AD, Lugdunum in Gaul (Lyons in France) struck large numbers of coins from the reigns of Augustus through to Vespasian (Fig.2.). Furthermore, a number of eastern mints, notably Antioch in ancient Syria (now in modern Turkey) (Fig.5.) and Caesarea in Cappadocia (Fig.11.), struck for many emperors. Imperial coins were sometimes struck elsewhere during civil wars (for example Galba minted in Spain and Clodius Macer in Africa) (Chapter X, Fig.18.).

With the increasing threat to Rome's frontiers in the middle of the 3rd century AD, coins needed to be minted closer to the armies, which were defending the Empire. In the second half of the 3rd century, Rome was joined by a large number of mints across the Empire, primarily in the production of "radiates": Trier and Cologne in Germany; Lyons in France; Ticinum (Pavia) in Italy; Siscia (Sisak) in Croatia; Viminacium (Kostalac) in Serbia; Serdica (Sofiya) in Bulgaria; Heraclea and Cyzicus in Turkey; Antioch (Turkey); Tripolis in Lebanon.

With the reforms of Diocletian and Constantine I (AD 294-early 4th century), the system of mints across the Empire was formalised: Trier, Lyons and Arles in Gaul; Rome and Aquileia in Italy; Siscia in Croatia; Thessalonica in Greece; Heraclea, Constantinople, Nicomedia and Cyzicus around the Sea of Marmara in Turkey, Antioch in south-east Turkey, and Alexandria in Egypt. Other mints which were operational for parts of the 4th and early 5th centuries were: London; Ambianum (Amiens) in Gaul; Barcelona (Barcino) in Spain; Ticinum, Milan, Ravenna and Ostia in Italy; Sirmium (Sremska Mitrovica) in Serbia; Serdica in Bulgaria; Carthage in North Africa.

Mint	Count	Mint	Count
Alexandria	47	Ravenna	15
Amiens	193	Rome	11,701
Antioch	108	Rouen	6
Aquileia	474	Serdica	6
Arles	c. 4,300	Sirmium	19
"C" Mint (Britain)	417	Siscia	712
Carthage	11	Spain	45
Constantinople	c. 50[1]	Tarraco	5
Cyzicus	65	Thessalonica	110
Gallic Mints (Gallic Empire)	1,949	Ticinum	143
Heraclea	48	Trier	10,616
London	2,987	Tripolis	5
Lyon	4,012	Viminacium	1
Milan	10		
Nicomedia	37	Total	38,441
Ostia	15		

Table 1. Numbers of coins from major Roman mints on the PAS Database. [1]A number of coins for Arles (Constantina) have been catalogued for Constantinople. These are in the process of being edited back to their correct mint.

Mintmarks

In the Republican period, many silver *denarii* struck at Rome are marked ROMA (Fig.1.). Coins from other mints often require more research to determine their origin, but the standard catalogue of Republican coins (Crawford, *Roman Republican Coinage* and the British Museum collection on-line – see Further Reading) records all the various mints.

In the Augustan period (27 BC-c.AD 253) gold and silver coins do not tend to have mint-marks and it is often find-spots and style which enable attribution. However, base metal coins from Rome (*sestertii, dupondii, asses, semisses* and *quadrantes*) are nearly always marked with S C (*Senatus Consulto*). At Lyons, it is possible to distinguish the base metal coins of this mint from those of Rome because Lyons' coins have a globe at the end of the point of the neck of the emperor's portrait (Fig.2.).

After c.AD 253, mintmarks began to appear more commonly as mints proliferated. The mint-marks for "radiate" coins often do not give an obvious clue to the mint, but a study of hoards and style has enabled attribution. However, by the 4th century, the system of mintmarks is much more logical.

Fig.1. Silver Roman Republican *denarius* of Cnaeus Lucretius Trio, showing Roma and the Dioscuri, struck at Rome (ROMA), 136BC. RRC 237/1a. Found in Leicestershire, LEIC-9D14B2. © Portable Antiquities Scheme (19mm)

Fig.2. A copper-alloy Roman *as* of Nero (AD 54-68), S C Victory advancing holding shield, Mint of Lyon (globe at base of neck), c.AD 66. RIC I, 544. Found in Norfolk, SF-0C7B00. © Portable Antiquities Scheme (28mm)

Map 1. Roman mints. (© Richard Kelleher)

33

Various Mintmarks Found On Later Roman Coins

Core Mintmarks

Some radiates and most 4th century coins bear mintmarks, which include letters specific to the mint of the coin. For example, coins of Trier normally bear the letters TR, Lyons, LVG or LG, Siscia, SIS, and so on. These marks are noted in the summary of mints below.

XXI – sometimes KA in the East

On radiates after the reforms of Aurelian (AD 270-5) until the reforms of Diocletian (AD 294-6), XXI often occurred as part of a mintmark; in the East, KA (21 in Greek) could be used. It is now known that XXI stands for 20 parts copper to one part silver (i.e. 5% silver). Coins marked XXII have been shown to have 10% silver, proving this interpretation.

SM – *Sacra Moneta* (Sacred Mint/Money)

A number of mintmarks start with SM, or sometimes just M. For example SMALA on coins of Alexandria (Fig.3.); ML or MC on coins of London under Carausius and Allectus (Chapter XXII, Figs.23 & 45).

P – *Pecunia* (Money)

Some mintmarks start with P (not to be confused with P for Prima in first workshop, see below). For example PLON or PLN for coins of London (Chapter XXIII, Figs.34-38).

OB & PS

Early in the reign of Valentinian (AD 364-78), the gold and silver coinages were reformed, ensuring that pure metal was used. From now onwards, gold coins often had OB (*obryzum aurum* = pure gold added to the mintmark (i.e. CONOB = pure gold, struck in Constantinople); silver coins were marked with PS (*pusulatum* = pure silver) so MDPS means "pure silver, struck at Milan" (Fig.22.).

COM

In the late Roman period, much gold coinage was struck at the court (*comitatus*) of the emperor. Because the emperor was often on the move, this meant that *comitatensian* coins were struck at a variety of cities, for example Rome, Milan, Ravenna, Arles and Lyons. See Fig.25. for a coin from the Comitatensian mint at Ravenna.

Officina (Workshop) Numbers & Letters

Most mints had more than one workshop – London only had one; Trier had two for most of its life; at some stages, mints such as Rome, could have as many as 12 workshops; eastern mints often had 11, with Antioch having 15 between 347 and 355. These workshops were each assigned a number, a Roman letter or even a Greek letter, normally in a logical sequence which could comprise symbols from all three groups. Western mints tended to use numerals and Roman letters, whereas eastern mints used Greek letters; however, in the 3rd century, Rome used a combination of all three in the reigns of Gallienus and Claudius II (AD 260-7). See Table 2 for a summary listing of the common *officina* marks.

Other Letters

There are often other letters and/or symbols in the fields on the reverse of the coins – on Constantine's coinage there are T F, S F, F B, etc. (see Chapters XXIII-XXIV). Although people have attempted to interpret the meaning of these letters, we cannot be sure what they mean. However, they are always recorded as part of the mintmark and they often represent different issues and help to create a chronology of a particular mint's coinage, as noted in volumes of *Roman Imperial Coinage*.

Symbols

Many mints used symbols to differentiate issues. Dots (Fig.7.), crescents (Fig.4.), dots in crescents, stars (Chapter XXVI, Fig.22.), palm branches (Chapter XXV, Fig.30.), wreaths (Chapter XXVI, Fig.21.) leaves, chi-rho symbols (Chapter 26, Fig.23.), and letters on standards (Chapter XXV, Fig.17.) are found on many 4th century coins. These were often used to mark a new issue of coins from a mint and are recorded in detail in *Roman Imperial Coinage*. For a useful index, see Carson, Hill and Kent, *Late Roman Bronze Coinage*, pp. 36-39.

Summary Of Mints

Below is a quite comprehensive, but necessarily condensed, listing of mints which struck Roman Imperial coins. In some cases we only know the regions where coins were struck (i.e. Spain) and cannot be certain about the exact location of the mint.

Note: for examples of late 3rd and 4th century mintmarks, I only provide mintmarks for the first *officina* (workshop) at the mint, normally the letter P (for Prima) or A (for Alpha). Of course this letter can change depending on how many workshops were operating at the mint. For example, I list SMALA for Alexandria, noting that there are four workshops. Therefore, the mintmark could be SMALA, SMALB, SMALΓ or SMALΔ.

Africa

Some coins were struck at unspecified mints in Africa in the late Roman Republican period. In AD 68, Clodius Macer struck coins in Africa during the Civil War (Chapter X, Fig.18.). See

Workshop No.	Roman numeral[2]	Latin letter	Greek letter
1	I / OF I[3]	P (Prima)	A (Alpha)
2	II / OF II	S (Secunda)	B (Beta)
3	III / OF III	T (Tertia)	Γ (Gamma)
4	IIII	Q (Quarta)	Δ (Delta)
5	V		E (Epsilon)
6	VI		S (Sigma)
7	(VII)		Z (Zeta)
8	(VIII)		H (Eta)
9	(VIIII / IX)	N (Nona)	Θ (Theta)
10	X		I (Iota)
11	XI		IA (Iota Alpha) or AI
12	XII		BI (Beta Iota)
13			ΓI (Gamma Iota)
14			ΔI (Delta Iota)
15			EI (Epsilon Iota)

Table 2. Table of *Officina* (workshop) numbers and letters.
[2] Roman numerals VII-IX are generally not used as officinae letters; none exist after XII.
[3] OF(ficina) I-III used on bronze coinage of the House of Valentinian (AD 364-75) at Lyons and Arles (see Chapter XXVII, Figs.25, 28 & 29.).

Alexandria and Carthage (below) for the only official Roman Imperial mints in Africa.

Alexandria (Egypt)

Until the reforms of Diocletian (AD 294-6), increasingly debased *tetradrachms* were struck at the imperial mint in Alexandria. These coins were only intended for use in Egypt which had a closed economy; however, many left the province and some have been found in Britain. After Diocletian's reforms, Alexandria continued to strike coins into the Byzantine period, ceasing in the 7th century AD.

Core mintmark: ALE and AL
Number of workshops: four (Greek letters)
Examples of full mintmark: ALEA; SMALA
Coins of Alexandria quite rare in Britain.

Ambianum (Amiens in France)

Amiens was reputedly the birthplace of the usurper Magnentius (AD 350-3) who opened a mint in the city. It was soon closed after his death by Constantius II (AD 337-61).

Core mintmark: AMB
Number of workshops: one
Example of full mintmark: AMB•
Coins of Ambianum are quite common in Britain.

Fig.3. Copper alloy *nummus* of the House of Constantine, VRBS ROMA wolf and twins type, struck at Alexandria (SMALB), AD 333-5. RIC VII, 63. Found in Lincolnshire, NCL-09E6E4. © Portable Antiquities Scheme (19mm)

Fig.4. Roman copper-alloy *nummus* of Magnentius (350-353), VICTORIAE DD NN AVG ET CAES two Victories type, struck at Amiens (AMB•), AD 351-353. RIC VIII, 23. Found in Somerset, SOM-34F767. © Portable Antiquities Scheme (23mm)

Antioch (Antakya in modern Turkey)

Antioch was a major mint for much of the Imperial period, continued to strike into the Byzantine period until the 7th century AD. Severan (AD 193-211) coins previously attributed to Laodicea (Syria) were probably struck at Antioch.

Core mintmark: ANT and AN
Number of workshops: up to 15 (Greek letters)
Examples of mintmarks: ANA; SMAN; SMANA; SMANTA
Coins of Antioch quite rare in Britain.

Fig.5. Gold *aureus* of Vespasian (AD 69-79), IVSTITIA AVG, struck at Antioch, AD 72-3. BMC II, p. 75, no. *. Found in North Lincolnshire, FASAM-2CD627. © Portable Antiquities Scheme (19mm). It is highly likely that this coin was struck from gold taken by the Romans from the Temple treasury in Jerusalem (see Judaea, below).

Fig.6. A Roman silver *siliqua* of Valentinian I (AD 364-75), RESTITVTOR REIP emperor and standard type, struck at Antioch (ANT), AD 364-367. RIC IX, 7a. Found in Kent, KENT-867C56. © Portable Antiquities Scheme (17mm)

Aquileia (west of Trieste, Italy)

Aquileia opened under Diocletian (c.AD 294) and was closed after a final issue of coins in AD 425.

Core mintmark: AQ; AQVIL
Number of workshops: up to three (Latin and Greek letters)
Examples of mintmarks: AQP; SMAQ; SMAQP; SMAQA; AQPS
Coins of Aquileia are relatively common in Britain.

Fig.7. Copper-alloy *nummus* of Constantius II (AD 337-61), FEL TEMP REPARATIO, Emperor on galley reverse, struck at Aquileia (AQT•), AD 348-50. RIC VIII, 97. Found in Leicestershire, LEIC-B10692. © Portable Antiquities Scheme (24mm)

Arelate (Arles, France), also named Constantina in the 4th Century

Arles was founded in AD 313 when the mint of Ostia (port of Rome) was moved there. It remained in use until around the time of the fall of the Western Roman Empire in AD 476. The city was renamed Constantina in honour of Constantine II, although between AD 340 and 353 it reverted to Arelate, before the name Constantina was reinstituted in 353 for the rest of the century. Most coins with CON in the mintmark found in Britain come from Arles, *not* from Constantinople (see below).

Core mintmark: A; AR; ARL; LPAR; CON; CONST; KON; KONSTAN
Number of workshops: up to four (Latin letters)
Examples of mintmarks: PA; PAR; ARLA; PARL; PCON; PCONST; KONOB
Coins of Arles are common in Britain.

Fig.8. A copper-alloy *nummus* of Constantius II (AD 337-61), dating to AD 350-1 (Reece Period 18), FEL TEMP REPARATIO, soldier and fallen horseman type, struck at Arles (- • // PAR), AD 350-1. RIC VIII, 141. Found in North Yorkshire, SWYOR-A5D944. © Portable Antiquities Scheme (24mm)

Barcino (Barcelona, Spain)

Barcino only minted coins for the usurper Maximus (AD 409-10).

Mintmarks: SMB; SMBA

Coins of Maximus are extremely rare anywhere in the Roman Empire; there are none on the PAS Database.

Fig.9. Silver *siliqua* of Maximus (AD 410-11), VICTORA AAVGGG, Roma seated left, struck at Barcelona, AD 410-11. RIC X, c.f. 1601. © British Museum (15mm)

"C Mint" (Uncertain location in Britain)

In the reigns of Carausius (AD 286-93) and Allectus (AD 293-6), there was a major mint that marked its coins with a C or CL. Numerous theories have suggested possible locations of the mint: Camulodunum (Colchester), Clausentum (Bitterne), Colonia (for York), Corinium (Cirencester) and Glevum (Gloucester) are some. It could possibly stand for Classis (fleet). It does appear that the mint was most likely also based in London, although I believe it may have travelled with the emperor when he was away from London.

Core mintmark: C; CL

Examples of mintmarks: C; G; CL; CXXI; MC; MCXXI; SC; SMC; SPC; MSCC; QC

"C Mint" coins are common in Britain.

Fig.10. A silver-washed radiate of Carausius (AD 286-293), PROVID AVGGG. Providentia with globe and cornucopiae type, struck at "C Mint" (S P//MC). Found in Essex, ESS-EEBD65. © Portable Antiquities Scheme (23mm)

Caesarea in Cappadocia (Turkey)

Caesarea was a major Roman provincial mint and in the reign of Septimius Severus (AD 193-211) was used to strike imperial *denarii*. These coins were previously attributed to Emesa in Syria. The coins often share types with coins from Rome, but many have distinctive inscriptions and types and are generally of a distinct "eastern" style.

Fig.11. Silver *denarius* of Septimius Severus (AD 193-211) FELICIT TEMPOR, corn ear between crossed cornucopiae, probably struck at Caesarea, Cappadocia. RIC IV, pt 1, p. 141, c.f. 373 (which is attributed to Emesa). Found in Kent, KENT-4402B2. © Portable Antiquities Scheme (17mm)

Carthago (Carthage, Tunisia)

Although destroyed by the Romans in 146 BC, Carthage grew again into a major city, being at the heart of the grain supply to Rome. It was briefly operational AD 296-311, but was to become an important mint in the Byzantine period, until the 7th century.

Core mintmark: K; KART (as part of reverse legend)

Workshops: up to four (Latin and Greek letters)

Examples of mintmarks: PK; PKP; FK; KART with Off letter in exergue (A-Δ)

Coins of Carthage are quite rare in Britain.

Fig.12. A copper-alloy *nummus* of Galerius as Caesar (AD 293-305), SALVS AVGG ET CAESS AVCTA KART, Carthage standing, struck in Carthage (KART = Carthage; Δ in exergue = workshop 4), c.AD 298-9. RIC VI, 28b. Found in Herefordshire, WMAS-E627C7. © Portable Antiquities Scheme (28mm)

Cologne

During the Gallic Empire (AD 260-74), Cologne (*Colonia Claudia Agrippinensium*) operated for some of the time. We know this was the case under Postumus as the illustrated coin notes the mint's name on the reverse. It is probable that the Gallic mint of Victorinus and the Tetrici that we call Gaul Mint II was situated at Cologne.

Fig.13. Base-silver radiate of Postumus (AD 260-9), COL CL AGRIP COS IIII, struck at Cologne, AD 268. The reverse legend is an abbreviation of the city's name: *Colonia Claudia Agrippinensium*. RIC V, pt 2, 286. © British Museum (20mm)

Constantinople (Istanbul, Turkey)

Constantinople's mint was opened in AD 326 and remained in use throughout the Byzantine period (down to AD 1453). Note that most of the coins with CON in their mintmark found in Britain come from Arles (Constantina), *not* Constantinople (see Arelate, above).

Core mintmark: CN; CON; CONS
Workshops: up to 11 (Greek letters)
Examples of mintmarks: CN; CON; CONA; CONS; CONSA; CONSPA
Coins of Constantinople are quite rare in Britain.

Fig.14. Gold *solidus* of Honorius (AD 393-423), CONCORDIA AVGGΘ Constantinopolis enthroned type, minted at Constantinople (CONOB = of pure gold from Constantinople), AD 408-20. RIC X, 201. Found in Bedfordshire, BH-FCFC92. © Portable Antiquities Scheme (21mm)

Cyzicus (Aydincik, Turkey)

Cyzicus struck Roman Provincial coins for much of the Roman period until it began to strike "radiates" under Claudius II (AD 268-70). It was certainly a mint under Aurelian (AD 270-5). It continued into the Byzantine period, being closed in the 7th century.

Core mintmark: CVZ and KVZ; CY/VZIC; KY/VZICEN; K
Number of workshops: up to 10 (Greek letters)
Examples of mintmarks: SMKA; CVZICENA; CVZICA; CVZA
Coins of Cyzicus quite rare in Britain.

Fig.15. Copper-alloy *nummus*, Licinius I (309-24), IOVI CONSERVATORI, Jupiter standing type, minted in Cyzicus (SMKΔ), AD 321-4. RIC VII, 15. Found in Leicestershire, LEIC-F8D9F4. © Portable Antiquities Scheme (20mm)

Eastern Mints

There is much debate about which Eastern mints were used to strike Roman Imperial coinage. We know that coins were struck at Antioch (see above), but other mints were situated elsewhere, such as at Caesarea in Cappadocia (Turkey, see above), Tripolis (Lebanon, see below) and in Judaea (see below). Severan (AD 193-211) coins previously attributed to Emesa (Syria) are now reckoned to be the products of Caesarea in Cappadocia. It is also highly likely that Severan (AD 193-211) coins attributed to Laodicea (Syria) were actually struck at Antioch.

Emerita (Mérida, Spain)

The colony of Emerita was founded in 26-25 BC by P. Carisius, governor of Lusitania, under instructions from the emperor Augustus (27 BC-AD

14). Carisius struck imperial coins at the city until 23 BC.

Fig.16. Silver *denarius* of Augustus (27 BC-AD 14), P CARISIVS LEG PRO PR, helmet between dagger and battle-axe, struck at Emerita, between c.25-23 BC (RIC 7a). Found in Hampshire, HAMP-49EB77. © Portable Antiquities Scheme (20mm)

Ephesus (Selçuk, Turkey)

Emperors such as Augustus (27 BC-AD 14) and Hadrian (AD 117-38) struck large silver *cistophoroi* on an eastern weight standard (12g) at Ephesus. These coins were struck for use in the east and did not travel to Britain. However, in the reign of Vespasian (AD 69-79), imperial *aurei* and *denarii* were also struck at the city.

Fig.17. Silver *denarius* of Vespasian (AD 69-79), PACI AVGVSTAE, Victory advancing right, struck at Ephesus in AD 71. RIC II (2nd ed.), 1431. © British Museum (18mm)

Gaul – Principal and Mint I and II

Coins were struck in Gaul during the Civil Wars (AD 68-9), possibly at Lyon, Vienne and Narbo. During the Gallic Empire (AD 260-74), coins were struck at two or more mints. It is suggested that the Principal Mint of Postumus (AD 260-9) and Gaul Mint I of Victorinus and the Tetrici (AD 269-74) was situated at Trier (see below). Archaeological evidence for a mint at Trier has been discovered. It is now thought that Gaul Mint II for Victorinus and the Tetrici was at Cologne (see above). It has also been suggested that Laelian (AD 269), might have struck coins at Mainz. However, there is still an on-going debate about the locations of these mints.

Heraclea (Marmara Ereglisi, Turkey)

Heraclea began to strike coins under Diocletian, around AD 291, and continued to be a mint until the reign of Leo (AD 457-74).

Core mintmark: H; HT; HERAC; HERACL
Workshops: up to six (Greek letters)
Examples of mintmarks: HA; HTA; HERACA; HERACLA; SMH; SMHA
Coins of Heraclea are quite rare in Britain.

Fig.18. Copper-alloy *nummus* of Galerius as Caesar (AD 293-305), GENIO POPVLI ROMANI, Mint of Heraclea (HTB), AD 296-7. RIC VI, 18b. Found in Surrey, SUR-CC9245. © Portable Antiquities Scheme (27mm)

Italy

In the Roman Republican period, coins were struck at, generally unspecified, mints in Italy and Sicily, other than Rome. For Roman Imperial mints in Italy, see Rome, Ticinum, Milan, Aquileia, Ostia and Ravenna.

Judaea

A number of gold *aurei* of Vespasian, Titus and his sons (AD 69-79) have been attributed to a mint in Judaea that operated at the time of the First Jewish Revolt (AD 66-73). It is possible that this mint was situated at Caesarea Maritima on the coast of modern Israel where Herod the Great (40-6 BC) built a massive port. So much gold was taken from the Jewish Temple treasury that the value of gold fell against silver in the East, from 25 to 12 *denarii*.

Fig.19. Gold *aureus* of Titus as Caesar under Vespasian (AD 69-79), CONCORDIA AVG, struck in Judaea, AD 70. RIC II (2nd ed.), 1534. © British Museum (18mm)

Londinium (London, Great Britain)

London was a mint under Carausius and Allectus, through to the middle of Constantine I's reign (c.AD 286-325) and then again briefly under Magnus Maximus (AD 383-8), when the city was called Augusta.

Core Mintmarks: unmarked (in early years of Diocletian); L; LN; LON; AVG

Workshops: Only one

Examples of mintmarks: L; ML; MLXXI; MSL; MLL; MLN; PLN; PLON; AVG; AVGOB; AVGPS

Coins of London are common in Britain from the period AD 286-325; but very rare for the period 383-8.

Fig.20. A copper-alloy radiate of Carausius (AD 286-93) struck in the name of Maximian Herculeus (AD 286-305), PAX AVGGG, London (S P//MLXXI), c.AD 290-2. RIC V, pt 2, 34. Found in Hampshire, HAMP-D380B6. © Portable Antiquities Scheme (24mm)

Lugdunum (Lyon, France)

Lugdunum was an important mint from the reign of Augustus (27 BC-AD 14) and continued to strike coins intermittently until AD 294 when it became a major mint under Diocletian. It closed in the early 5th century.

Core mintmark: Under Nero and Vespasian, globe at neck; LG; LVG; LVGD

Workshops: two (in 4th century)

Examples of mintmarks: PLG; RPLG; FPLG; LPLG; CPLG; MPLG; PLVG; LVGP; LVGPA-D; LVGVP; LVGAP; LVGSP; LVGPR

Coins of Lyons are very common in Britain
For a 1st century coin from Lyon, see Fig.2.

Fig.21. Copper-alloy Roman *nummus* of Crispus (AD 317-26), PROVIDENTIAE CAESS camp-gate type, struck at Lyon (PLG), AD 324-325. RIC VII 228. Found in Wiltshire, WILT-5731A4. © Portable Antiquities Scheme (18mm)

Mediolanum (Milan)

Milan opened in the reign of Valerian I (AD 253-60) and continued in use as a Roman mint until the end of the 5th century.

Core Mintmark: MD; MED

Examples of mintmarks: MD; MED; MDOB; MDPS

The only common coins from Milan found in Britain are the silver *siliquae* of Arcadius and Honorius, struck c.397-402 (RIC X, 1227-8; see Chapter XXVIII, Figs.27-9).

Fig.22. Silver *siliqua* of Arcadius (AD 383-408), VOT/X/MVLT/XV in wreath, struck at Milan (MDPS), AD 388-93. RIC IX, 27a Found in East Yorkshire, NCL-9A6D66. © Portable Antiquities Scheme (18mm)

Nicomedia (Izmit, Turkey)

Nicomedia was founded as mint under Diocletian, around AD 294, and continued to operate well into the Byzantine period.

Core mintmark: N; NIC; NIC; NICO; NIK

Workshops: up to 10

Examples of Mintmarks: NA; MN; SMN; SMNA; NIC; NICO; NIKA

Coins of Nicomedia are quite rare in Britain.

Fig.23. Copper-alloy *nummus* of Constantine II as Caesar (AD 317-37), GLORIA EXERCITVS, two soldiers and two standards, struck at Nicomedia (SMNA), AD 330-5. RIC VII, p. 633, no. 189. Found in Leicestershire, LEIC-02C5F1. © Portable Antiquities Scheme (18mm)

Ostia (Port of Rome, Italy)

The mint of Ostia was opened by the emperor Maxentius (AD 308-12) and remained operational until AD 313 when it was transferred to Arles (see above).

Core mintmark: OST
Workshops: four (Latin and Greek letters)
Examples of mintmark: POST; MOSTA; MOSTP
Coins of Ostia are rarely found in Britain.

Fig.24. Copper-alloy *nummus* of Maximinus I (AD 308-313), SOLI INVICTO COMITI, Sol standing left, struck at Ostia (MOST[T]), AD 312-3. RIC VI, 86a. Found in Wiltshire, WILT-F10705. © Portable Antiquities Scheme (21mm)

Ravenna (Italy)

Ravenna became the effective capital of Roman Italy after Honorius retreated from Milan to this important port on the Adriatic Sea in AD 402. It remained an important mint until the end of the 5th century.

Core mintmark: RV
Examples of mintmark: RV (in field over COMOB in exergue); RVPS
The few coins of Ravenna found in Britain tend to be gold *solidi*.

Fig.25. Gold *solidus* of Arcadius (AD 383-408), VICTORI AAVGGG; Emperor holding standard and Victory on globe and spurning captive, struck at Ravenna (R V//COMOB = struck in pure gold at the Comitatensian mint in Ravenna), AD 402-406. RIC X, 1286. Found on the Isle of Wight, IOW-DA6D56. © Portable Antiquities Scheme (20.5mm)

Roma (Rome, Italy)

Rome was a mint throughout our period and continued to strike coins intermittently in the Byzantine period.

Core mintmark: R; RM; ROM; ROMA; S C on reverse of early base metal coins
Workshops: up to 12 (Roman numerals, Latin and Greek letters)
Examples of mintmark: ROMA; R; RP; RPRIMA; SMRP; RM; RBP; RFP; VRB ROM; SMROM; SMVRM
Coins of Rome are very common in Britain from the Republican to radiate periods, but are scarcer in the 4th century.
See Fig.1. for a Republican coin of Rome.

Fig.26. Copper-alloy *nummus* of Constantine I (306-37), D N CONSTANTINI MAX AVG, VOT XXX, struck at Rome (RP), AD 329. RIC VII, 320. Found in Northants, FASAM-E62997. © Portable Antiquities Scheme (18mm)

Rouen (Rotomagus) (?)

It is generally accepted by scholars that Carausius (AD 286-93) set up his first mint at Rouen, around AD 286-7, where he minted gold *aurei* and small, poor quality, radiates.

Core mintmark: R
Examples of mintmark: OPR; OPA
Coins of Rouen are rare in Britain.

Fig.27. Copper-alloy radiate of Carausius (AD 286-93) with Salus or Tutela on the reverse, struck at Rouen, c.AD 286-7. Found in Wiltshire, WILT-1522F2. © Portable Antiquities Scheme (16mm)

Serdica (Sofia, Bulgaria)

Serdica operated from the reign of Aurelian (AD 270-5) to Probus (AD 276-82) before reopening under the Tetrarchs briefly in the early 4th century (AD 303-8 and 313-4).

Core mintmark: SD; SERD
Workshops: five
Examples of mintmark: SMSD; SMSDA
Coins of Serdica are rare in Britain.

Fig.28. Silver-washed copper-alloy radiate of Aurelian (AD 270-5), SOLI INVICTO Sol and two captives type, struck at Serdica in AD 274. This is a good example of a radiate coin which does not have a clearly identifiable mintmark. Over the years scholars have attributed many radiate coins to mints by finding clues on some coins and using the evidence of hoards and style. RIC V, pt 2, cf. 308. Found in Leicestershire, LEIC-F4D9B7. © Portable Antiquities Scheme (23mm)

Sirmium (Sremska Mitrovica, Serbia)

Sirmium operated as a mint intermittently during the 4th century (AD 320-6; 351-64; 379; 393-5). It is possible, but unlikely, that it struck coins in the early 5th century.

Core mintmark: SIRM; SIR
Workshops: up to two
Examples of mintmark: SIRM; ASIRM; SM (in field with COMOB in exergue); SMSPV; SIROB
Coins of Sirmium are rare in Britain.

Fig.29. Silver *siliqua* of Constantius II (AD 337-61), VOTIS/XXX/MVLTIS/XXXX in wreath, struck at Sirmium (SIRM), AD 355-61. RIC VIII, 68. Found in Lincolnshire, WMID-E59C87. © Portable Antiquities Scheme (18mm)

Siscia (Sisak in Croatia)

The mint at Siscia was founded around AD 259 under Valerian and Gallienus and continued in use until around AD 392; it possibly struck some coins for Honorius in the early 5th century.

Core mintmark: SIS; SISC
Workshops: five (Greek letters)
Examples of mintmarks: SIS; ASIS; ASISR; SISC; ASISC; DASISC; ASISCA; ASISCE; ASISCR; ASISCP
Coins of Siscia are quite common in Britain.

Fig.30. Copper-alloy *nummus* of Constantine II (AD 317-37), GLORIA EXERCITVS, two soldiers and one standard, struck at Siscia, AD 337. RIC VII, 262. Found in Wiltshire, WILT-8BEAC7. © Portable Antiquities Scheme (16mm)

Spain (Roman *Hispania*)

Surprisingly, the Iberian peninsula never really had any major Roman mints. Some coins were struck there in the Roman Republican period and Augustus had coins struck at Emerita (Spain, see above) and two unspecified mints in Spain. Coins were struck at more than one mint in Spain during the Civil Wars (AD 68-9) and in the reign of Vespasian (AD 69-79). One of these mints was probably at Tarraco (see below).

Tarraco (Tarragona, Spain)

During the Civil Wars (AD 68-9), Galba (AD 68-9) and Vitellius (AD 69) struck coins in Spain at a mint thought to be at Tarraco. It is also reckoned that the same mint continued to strike coins under Vespasian (AD 69-79) (Chapter X, Fig.32.).

Fig.31. Silver *denarius* of Vitellius (AD 69), CONSENSVS EXERCITVVM, Mars with spear, legionary eagle and standard, probably struck at Tarraco in Spain. RIC I, 24. Found in Cambridgeshire, CAM-5B48E3. © Portable Antiquities Scheme (18mm)

In older books coins of Ticinum were incorrectly attributed to Tarraco.

Thessalonica (Greece)

Thessalonica opened as a mint under Diocletian, c.AD 298/9, and continued to be an important Byzantine mint for centuries to come.

Core mintmark: TS; TES; THS; THES
Workshops: up to five (Greek letters)
Examples of mintmark: TS; TSA; SMTS; SMTSA; TES; SMTES; TESA; SMTESA; THS; THES; COM and COMOB on gold
Coins of Thessalonica are scarce in Britain.

Fig.32. Copper-alloy *nummus* of Constantius II as Caesar (AD 324-37), PROVIDENTIAE CAESS, camp-gate with two turrets, struck at Thessalonica (SMTSB), AD 326-8. RIC VII, 158. Found in Leicestershire, LEIC-4F1CA3. © Portable Antiquities Scheme (19mm)

Ticinum (Pavia, Italy)

Ticinum operated from the reign of Aurelian (AD 270-5) until it closed under Constantine I in AD 327.

Core mintmark: T
Workshops: three (Latin letters)
Examples of mintmarks: T; MT; PT; SMT
Coins of Ticinum are quite numerous in Britain.

Fig.33. Copper alloy *nummus* of Constantine I (AD 306-37), D N CONSTANTINI MAX AVG, wreath enclosing VOT/XX, struck at Ticinum (TT), AD 320-1. RIC VII, 140. Found in Somerset, SOM-E8DF77. © Portable Antiquities Scheme (19mm)

Travelling Mints

In the Roman Republican period, a number of leading figures had mints that travelled with their armies. The most famous example is Mark Antony who issued an enormous number of "legionary *denarii*" from travelling mint(s) which were probably operating in Greece and western Turkey in 32-31 BC (see Chapter VII, Fig.11.).

Treveri (Trier, Germany)

Trier first opened as a mint under Postumus (AD 260-9) and continued to be a mint of the Gallic Empire until AD 274. It was reopened under Diocletian around AD 291 and was to be the most prolific mint in the north-western empire for most of the 4th century. It finally closed around AD 430.

Core mintmark: TR
Workshops: two
Examples of mintmark: TR; ATR; PTR; PTRE; TRP; TRPS; TROB; SMTR; SMTRP
Coins of Trier are extremely common in Britain.

Fig.34. Silver *siliqua* of Valentinian I (AD 364-375), VRBS ROMA, Roma seated left on throne holding sceptre and victory, struck at Trier (TRPS•), AD 367-375. RIC IX, 27d. Found in Somerset, SOM-AE6A03. © Portable Antiquities Scheme (18mm)

Tripolis (al-Fayha'a, Lebanon)

Tripolis was operational from the reign of Aurelian (AD 270-5) to around AD 290 during the reign of Diocletian (AD 284-305). In the later years of its operation, the letters TR appeared in the field of the reverse of coins.

Fig.35. Copper-alloy radiate of Diocletian (AD 284-305), IOVI CONSERVATORI AVG, Victory and Jupiter, struck at Tripolis (TR) in AD 284. RIC V, pt 2, 328. © British Museum (20mm)

Viminacium (Kostalac, Serbia)

Roman provincial coins had already been struck at Viminacium from the reign of Gordian III (AD 238-44), but in the joint reign of Valerian I and Gallienus (AD 253-60) Roman Imperial pieces were issued at the mint. They are identified by style, rather than by a particular mint-mark. Coins of Viminacium are rarely found in Britain and generally come from hoards.

Fig.36. Silver radiate of Gallienus (joint reign, AD 253-60), SALVS AVGG, Salus feeding snake at altar, struck at Viminacium, AD 257-8. RIC V, pt. 1, 397. Found in Monmouthshire, PUBLIC-C95EB6. © Portable Antiquities Scheme (20mm)

Chapter VII
Coinage of The Roman Republic
(c.300-27 BC)

Fig.1. Cast bronze currency bar (*aes signatum*), Rome, c.280-242 BC. Bull on both sides. RRC 5. © British Museum (1790 grams; 17cm across)

Fig.2. Silver *didrachm* minted at Rome, c.269-266 BC. Head of Hercules; wolf suckling Romulus and Remus. RRC 20/1. © British Museum (19mm)

Fig.3. Cast bronze coin (*aes grave*), Rome, c.269-266 BC. Head of Minerva on both sides. RRC 21/2. © British Museum (121 grams; 5cm)

This is the first chapter on the history of Roman coins. I intend to cover the entire period of Roman coinage from the Republic to the 5th century AD when the Western Roman Empire finally fell to the barbarians. I will trace the development of Roman coinage in general, but will place a special emphasis on the nature of Roman currency circulating in Britain, as represented by coins found by detectorists which are recorded on the Portable Antiquities Scheme database (www.finds.org.uk).

The First Roman Coinage (c.300 BC)

Given that the first ever coins were struck around 600 BC in western Turkey, the Romans started to use coinage relatively late, sometime around 300 BC. The first currency, issued down to c.212 BC, consisted of four major elements:-

1. Large cast pieces called today *aes signatum*, up to 1800 grams (c.63 ounces) in weight (Fig.1.). They were inspired by bars used by the Etruscans to the north. Roman bars have been found in hoards around Rome which does suggest that they were used as currency. The Roman author Livy even tells us that Roman senators used wagons to carry their wealth around.

2. Struck silver coins with the inscription ROMANO and then ROMA which circulated mostly south of Rome in the region of Campania (Fig.2.).

3. Struck bronze coins, also inscribed ROMANO, circulated more in central Italy.

4. Large cast coins (*aes grave*) made to different

Fig.4. Copper Carthaginian coin, c.300-264 BC, struck in Sardinia. Found in Lincolnshire (LINC0E9D7). © Portable Antiquities Scheme (18mm)

fractions of the Roman pound (Fig.3.).

These different forms of currency were struck at a variety of mints across Italy ranging from the Etruscan city of Volterra in the north to the former Greek cities of Naples and Metapontum further south. These coins are not found in Britain; the earliest coins to arrive in Britain were Iron Age coins from the Continent and coins from the Mediterranean world, possibly as early as the 3rd century BC (Fig.4.).

Fig.5. Silver *denarius*, anonymous issue of Rome, from 211 BC. Helmeted head of Roma and X (denoting 10 asses) and the Dioscuri (Castor and Pollux). RRC 44.5. © British Museum (20mm)

Fig.6. Silver *quinarius* of C. Egnatuleius, struck at Rome in 97 BC. Apollo, and Victory with trophy and carnyx (war trumpet). Note the mark of value, Q, on the reverse. Found in Cheshire (LVPL-D19795). © Portable Antiquities Scheme (15mm)

Fig.8. Silver *denarius* of C. Cossutius Maridianus, who titles himself as a moneyer on the reverse: AAAFF. Struck at Rome in 44 BC, the obverse showing the veiled head of Julius Caesar. RRC 480.19. © British Museum (18mm)

Fig.9. Silver *denarius* of C. Calpurnius Piso Frugi, struck at Rome in 67 BC. His name is abbreviated to C PISO L F FRVG. There are two control marks, an unclear one to the left of the head, and a Δ (delta) below the horseman. This is one of over 400 control mark varieties. Found in Lancashire (LANCUM-7032F7). © Portable Antiquities Scheme (20mm)

Fig.7. Copper *as* of C. Fabius, minted in Rome in 102 BC. Head of Janus and ship's prow, with moneyer's name above prow. Because these coins were used for tossing in gambling, the Roman expression "Heads or Ships" stuck. RRC 322.2. © British Museum (30mm)

The Denarius Coinage (c.212-27 BC)

The first coinage collapsed during the Second Punic War against Hannibal (218-201 BC). This required a completely new coinage, starting in around 212 BC, that was to be struck at several mints in Italy, Sicily, Sardinia and Spain. The backbone of the coinage was the silver *denarius*, struck at 84 to the Roman pound (c.3.90g) (Fig.5.). Occasionally, there were silver *quinarii* and *sestertii* (half and quarter *denarii*) struck normally in times of emergency or for Roman colonies in Gaul (Fig.6.). Initially, there were six bronze denominations, ranging from the *as* (Fig.7.) to the *uncial* (ounce; one-twelfth of an ounce). Originally the *denarius* was tariffed at 10 *asses*, represented by a large "X" by the head of Roma on the obverse of many *denarii*. In the first half of the 2nd century BC the *as* was struck in such large numbers that the *denarius* was re-tariffed at 16 *asses*. This remained the exchange rate until the *denarius* and *as* ceased as denominations in the 3rd century AD.

Mint Officials in the Roman Republican Period

It is thought that each year, after 212 BC, there were three magistrates appointed annually to be moneyers responsible for the striking of coinage. They were called the *Tresviri Auro Argento Aere Flando Feriundo* –"The Board of Three for the casting and striking of gold, silver and bronze". A few coins actually record a reference to this title, normally abbreviated to AAAFF (Fig.8.). However, on nearly all coins one of the names of the three moneyers was recorded, either in full or abbreviated (Fig.9.).

These moneyers came from the most influential families of Rome and the office of moneyer was regarded as one of the most desirable junior magistracies; several went on to hold the senior office of consul. Because of the naming of magistrates on coins, we are able to date most issues to a particular year which helps researchers enormously. Furthermore, many engravers marked each die with a different number, letter or symbol which helps us to determine the size of a particular issue (Figs.9 & 12.).

Rome increasingly became the major centre for striking coins, the mint being situated by the Temple of Juno Moneta on the Capitoline Hill (Fig.10.). In the last decades of the Republic the various generals and triumvirs, such as Pompey, Caesar and Mark Antony, struck coins across the empire and even in travelling mints (Figs.11 &

Fig.10. Silver *denarius* of T. Carisius, struck at Rome in 46 BC. The obverse shows Moneta and the reverse an anvil and punch die, with hammer and tongs, for making coins. Found in Hampshire (HAMP-E92417). © Portable Antiquities Scheme (18.45mm)

Fig.11. Silver *denarius* of Mark Antony, struck at a travelling mint, 32-13 BC. This coin shows a legionary eagle between two standards, and a galley. These very common coins honoured different legions, in this case Legio X. Found in Somerset (SOM-71C234). © Portable Antiquities Scheme (17mm)

Fig.13. Silver *denarius* of Safra, struck at Rome in 150 BC. This coin also shows Roma, but with Victory in a biga (two-horse chariot) on the reverse. Found in Denbighshire (LVPL-914DD1). © Portable Antiquities Scheme (18mm)

Fig.12. Silver *denarius* serratus of Tiberius Claudius Nero, struck at Rome in 79 BC. The coin is marked with a control mark CXXXX[?] (140+); the largest recorded number is CLXV (155). Found in Surrey (SUR-2F0954). © Portable Antiquities Scheme (18.5mm)

Fig.14. Silver *denarius* of Julius Caesar, struck in Rome, 47-46 BC. Caesar claimed descent from Venus, who is on the obverse of this coin, which meant he was related to the Trojan hero Aeneas who is seen carrying his father from Troy on the reverse. Found in Leicestershire (LEIC-97F7A2). © Portable Antiquities Scheme (17mm)

15.). Some Republican *denarii* had serrated edges (Fig.12.); if this was to prevent forgery it was not entirely successful as serrated copies are known!

Designs on Roman Republican Denarii

The earliest *denarii* had a standard design with the head of Roma on the obverse and the heavenly twins, Castor and Pollux, on the reverse (Fig.5.). In the 2nd century Victory in a chariot (two or four horse) also became a common reverse type (Fig.13.). Increasingly, the designs became more varied. Some moneyers made references to their ancestors (Fig.14.) or created designs which punned with their names. A few coins actually marked events, such as the Ides of March *denarii* of Brutus which celebrated the assassination of Caesar (Fig.15.).

A number of coins also celebrated victories in war, for example over the Gauls (Fig.16.), while one even shows Roman citizens voting in an assembly (Fig.17.).

In the last few decades of the Republic, the coinage reflects the jockeying for power amongst powerful men like Caesar, Pompey and Mark Antony and some coins honoured more than one person; for example, Octavian and Mark Antony (Figs.18 & 15.).

Fig.15. Silver *denarius* of Brutus, struck at a travelling mint, 43-42 BC. This coin shows two daggers and the cap of liberty, and celebrates the assassination of Caesar on the Ides of March 44 BC. RRC 508/3. © British Museum (17mm)

Fig.16. Silver *denarius* of L Pomponius, struck at the Roman colony of Narbo in Gaul, 118 BC. This coin shows a Gaulish warrior with shield and carnyx (war trumpet) in a chariot and celebrates a Roman victory over the Gauls. Found in Greater Manchester (LVPL-6896E7). © Portable Antiquities Scheme (19mm)

Fig.17. Silver *denarius* of P. Licinius Nerva, struck at Rome, 113-112 BC. The reverse shows citizens voting at an assembly in Rome. Found in Hampshire (HAMP-EA4B73). © Portable Antiquities Scheme (16.5mm)

Fig.19. Silver *denarius* hoard found at Shapwick in 1998. You can see one or two worn Mark Antony *denarii* in the picture. © Portable Antiquities Scheme

Fig.20. Silver *denarius* of C. Maianius struck at Rome, 153 BC. This is one of the earliest coins on the PAS database. Found in Lincolnshire (LIN-739914). © Portable Antiquities Scheme (17mm)

Fig.18. Silver *denarius* depicting both Mark Antony and Octavian, struck at a travelling mint in 41 BC. Found in Staffordshire (WMID-154F76). © Portable Antiquities Scheme (19mm)

Roman Republican Denarii Found in Britain

Until the advent of the Portable Antiquities Scheme, the vast majority of Republican *denarii* were found in coin hoards which were buried after the Claudian invasion in AD 43. We know from hoards that Republican coins were still in circulation in great numbers in the 1st century AD, hence the worn nature of most of the recorded coins. However, the debasement of the *denarius* under Nero (AD 54-68) and then under Trajan (98-117) led to the withdrawal of most Republican coins from circulation as they had a higher silver content. There was one exception, the *denarii* of Mark Antony with military standards and galley designs (Fig.11.). Ancient writers tell us that they had an inferior silver content and as a result they survived in circulation until the

Fig.21. Silver *denarius* of the Triumvir Lepidus, struck in Italy, in 42 BC. It shows Lepidus and Octavian and is from quite a small issue. Found in Suffolk (SF-7DD9F2). © Portable Antiquities Scheme (17mm)

Fig.22. Copper *as of* Cnaeus Lentulus, struck in Rome in 88 BC. This appears to be the only Republican copper coin with a secure provenance in Britain. Found in Essex (ESS-05C304). © Portable Antiquities Scheme (20.5mm)

Map 1. Map showing the find spots of Roman Republican *denarii* recorded on the PAS database. (© Dan Pett)

3rd century AD when very worn examples are still found in hoards: the Shapwick hoard of 9,238 *denarii*, buried around AD 224, contained 260 worn Mark Antony coins (Fig.19.). These pieces are also the most common Republican coin found by detectorists.

Over 800 Republican *denarii* have been recorded on the PAS database (see Map). They have been found all over England, even in Cornwall, showing how they were circulating in everyday use across the Province. The earliest recorded coins pre-date 150 BC (Fig.20.), but most of the coins date between 150 and 27 BC. Many, as would be expected, come from very large issues which had over 100 obverse and reverse dies (Figs.9 & 12.), but there are a few scarcer pieces (Fig.21.).

One commonly asked question is whether Republican coins arrived in Britain before the Roman invasion of AD 43. Only two appear to have been found in secure archaeological contexts that date them to the pre-Roman period. However, it is quite likely that they did come to Britain

from the Roman world in considerable numbers, alongside products such as wine amphorae, silverware and glass, before AD 43. Furthermore, contrary to popular belief, the Britons were not mining silver before the Roman Conquest. However, the Britons did produce a large quantity of silver coins, notably issues of the tribes such as the Iceni and kings like Cunobelinus and Verica. This silver had to come from somewhere and Roman *denarii* are surely the major source. Philippa Walton has used PAS data to suggest that some Republican *denarii* did arrive before AD 43.

In Britain, despite the presence of thousands of Republican *denarii*, only one copper *as* has been found (Fig.22.). This is mainly because these coins were in use before Britain became part of the Roman Empire. Furthermore, only gold and silver coins tend to cross the boundaries between different currency systems as they have an intrinsic value. How this *as* arrived in Britain remains a mystery, but it is possible that it came with a batch of imperial copper coins in or soon after the invasion of AD 43.

Chapter VIII
Coinage of Augustus, First Emperor of Rome
(27 BC-AD 13)

Fig.1. The Temple of Mars Ultor in the Forum of Augustus, built to celebrate the victory over Caesar's assassins, Cassius and Brutus, at the Battle of Philippi in 42 BC. © Sam Moorhead

Early Life 63-31 BC

C. Octavius (Octavian) was born in 63 BC, the great nephew of Julius Caesar. In his will, Caesar nominated Octavian as his heir. This meant that after Caesar's assassination in 44 BC, Octavian became a major force in Roman politics. Octavian stated that a comet which appeared in 44 BC was in fact Caesar's soul going to heaven, resulting in the placing of comets on coins (Fig.2.). Caesar was then declared a god in 42 BC, enabling Octavian to title himself "son of a god" (*divi filius*) on his coins.

Octavian formed the Second Triumvirate with Mark Antony and Lepidus in 42 BC. In the same year, Brutus and Cassius were defeated at the Battle of Philippi – Octavian promised the god Mars a temple if he won the battle, and the temple of Mars the Avenger (*Mars Ultor*) was finally dedicated in 20 BC (Figs.1 & 3.). Relationships with Mark Antony deteriorated until the final showdown at the Battle of Actium where Octavian and Agrippa defeated Mark Antony and Cleopatra in 31 BC (Figs.4 & 5.). One of the most common coins referring to Actium was struck at the Roman Colony in Nîmes where veterans of Agrippa were settled in 16 BC (Fig.6.) and a few examples have been found in Britain.

Fig.4. Plated contemporary copy of a *denarius* of Augustus (Octavian), struck after c.29 BC. The prototype was struck in Italy and shows Victory on the prow of a ship and Octavian in a triumphal chariot. Found in Monmouthshire. © PAS NMGW-54F4C3; RIC I, c.f. 264 (19mm)

Fig.3. Silver *denarius* of Augustus struck in Spain in c.19 BC showing the Temple of Mars Ultor. Found in Cheshire. © PAS LVPL2418; RIC I, 69a (19mm)

Fig.2. Silver *denarius* of Augustus struck at Rome in c.17 BC showing a comet over Caesar's head, and recording Augustus as a son of a god – DIVI F(ilius). Found in Lincolnshire. © PAS LIN-82BAC1; RIC I, 338 (19mm)

Fig.5. Silver *denarius* of Augustus (Octavian), struck c.29-27 BC in Italy, showing a crocodile which refers to the defeat of Cleopatra and capture of Egypt. © British Museum; RIC I, 275a (19mm)

Fig.6. Copper alloy *as* of Augustus and Agrippa from the mint of Nîmes in Gaul, c.20 BC-AD 10, showing a chained crocodile referring to the conquest of Egypt in 30 BC. © PAS ESS-55F4F2; RIC I, 155ff (25mm)

Octavian Becomes Augustus 27 BC

Octavian became the undisputed ruler of the Roman Empire and in 27 BC was granted supreme power by the Senate and given the honorary title Augustus ("revered", "majestic", "venerable", "worthy of honour", hence the English word "august") (Fig.2.). (For most of the Roman Imperial period, senior emperors would be titled "Augustus", junior ones "Caesar".)

Augustus effectively took control of the Roman Empire, but he was keen to uphold the traditional bodies, such as the Senate, and to portray himself as the protector of the Roman people (Fig.7.). Therefore, he maintained the Republican traditions as a façade to his autocratic rule.

Augustus' Coinage Reforms

He enacted major reforms of the Roman coinage which were to underpin the Roman imperial coinage for the next 250 years (see Table 1). Gold coins (*aurei*) had been struck occasionally under the Republic, but the aureus now became a standard issue, struck in pure gold at 40 to the pound (c.7.9 grams) (Fig.7.); a rarer gold coin of half the weight, the *quinarius* was also struck.

The backbone of the imperial currency remained the silver *denarius*, struck from 96-98% silver at about 3.85 grams; the half-weight silver *quinarius* is very rare. The most important reforms concerned the base metal coins, coins which had

Fig.7. This extremely rare gold *aureus* of Octavian was struck in 28 BC just before he was made Augustus. He declares that he has restored to the people their laws and their rights. © British Museum (18mm)

Fig.8. *Orichalcum* (brass) *sestertius* of Augustus, struck by the moneyer P. Licinius Stolo at Rome c.17 BC. It shows the oak-wreath and laurel branches that Augustus displayed outside his house, signifying he had saved the lives of Roman citizens. Found in Oxfordshire. © PAS BERK-B0C026; RIC I, 346 (34mm)

only been issued sporadically in the late Republic. The *sestertius* was struck in *orichalcum* (brass: 80% copper and 20% zinc) at about 25 grams (Fig.8.). The *dupondius* was also struck in brass at

Fig.9. *Orichalcum* (brass) *dupondius* of Augustus, struck by the moneyer M. Sanquinius at Rome c.17 BC. This coin states that Augustus had the "Power of the Tribune". Found in building works in Taunton in the 1930s. © PAS-SOMDOR-C6ED32 (27mm)

Fig.10. Copper *as* of Augustus, struck by the moneyer C. Asinius Gallus at Rome in 16 BC. This coin was found in the foundations of a building in Chester in the 1950s – it might be an ancient loss from the legionary fortress. © PAS LVPL-99A704; RIC I, 373 (26mm)

Fig.11. Brass *semis* of Augustus, struck at Lugdunum in Gaul, AD 9-14. Augustus is titled *Pater Patriae*, "father of his country". © BM (BMC 569) (19mm)

Fig.12. Copper *quadrans* of Augustus, struck by the moneyers Galus, Messalla Apronius and Sisenna at Rome in 5 BC. © British Museum; BMC 257 (17mm)

Fig.13. The Temple of Saturn in the Roman Forum in Rome. It acted as the treasury for the metal to be coined just up the slope in the Mint of Juno Moneta on the Capitoline Hill. © Sam Moorhead

about 12.5 grams (Fig.9.). The most common base-metal coin was the copper *as* of about 11 grams (Fig.10.) with two other lesser denominations, the *semis* (Fig.11.) and the *quadrans* (Fig.12.). These base metal coins all bore S C, standing for *Senatus Consulto* ("by decree of the Senate") (e.g.

Figs.8-10.). This probably referred to the Senate's authority to draw base metal for coining from the Treasury (*Aerarium Saturni*: housed in the Temple of Saturn in the Roman Forum; Fig.13.). It was not long, however, before the emperor had control of base-metal coinage as well as the gold and silver,

Fig.14. Silver *denarius* of Augustus struck in Spain at Colonia Patricia (Cordoba) in 19 BC. It celebrates the return of legionary standards in 20 BC, which had been captured by the Parthians after their great victory over Crassus at Carrhae in 53 BC. Found in Leicestershire. © PAS LEIC-1368C1; RIC I, 86a (19mm)

Fig.15. Silver *denarius* of Augustus struck in Spain at Emerita by P. Carisius, c.25-23 BC. Carisius was Augustus' legate who led a successful campaign against Spanish tribes and founded a new Roman colony at Emerita in 25 BC. Found in Hertfordshire. © PAS BH-6EAFA6; RIC I, 7a (18mm)

Fig.16. Silver *denarius* of Augustus struck at Lugdunum (Lyon) in Gaul, 15-13 BC. Found in Cambridgeshire. © PAS LANCUM-15C602; RIC I, 167a (16.5mm)

Fig.17. Silver *denarius* of Augustus, struck at Rome by the moneyer L. Vinicius in 16 BC. This coin celebrated the road building programme that Augustus had initiated, and also shows an equestrian statue of the emperor. © PAS LIN-F32178; RIC I, 362 (18mm)

Fig.18. Silver *denarius* of Augustus struck at Rome, 2 BC-AD 4 (and possibly later). This coin honoured Augustus' grandsons, Caius and Lucius Caesar, who were nominated his heirs, but who both died by AD 4. It is the most common issue and many of this type are on the PAS database. Found in Suffolk. © PAS SF-A05047; RIC I, 207 (18mm)

Fig.21. An incomplete, extremely rare, silver *denarius* of Augustus, possibly struck at Lugdunum, after 27 BC. Augustus was born when the moon was in Capricorn. © PAS-IOW-0D5931; RIC I, 542 (17mm)

Fig.19. Copper *as* of Tiberius Caesar, struck under Augustus, at Lugdunum (Lyon) in Gaul, AD 9-14. The reverse shows the Altar of Roma and Augustus at Lyon which was dedicated in 10 BC. © British Museum; (BMC 576) (26mm)

Fig.20. Orichalcum *sestertius* struck in the reign of Tiberius (AD 14-37) at Rome in AD 22-23 to commemorate Augustus who is titled "divine father" of Rome: *Divus Augustus Pater*. © British Museum; BMC 130 (34mm)

although from now onwards it was traditional to add S C onto all base metal coins (down to the AD 260s). The most common source of metal for the coinage at this time was Spain where the imperial mines produced gold, silver, copper and zinc. Augustus effectively took control of the mines and the coinage, personally depositing 2,400 million *sestercii* in the state treasury.

Mints & Mint Organisation

In the last years of the Republic, the mint by the Temple of Juno Moneta at Rome had been closed, but it was re-opened by Augustus as early as 28-27 BC. Here, he continued to use the Republican system of the "College of Moneyers", the *Triumviri aere argento auro flando feriundo* ("the board of three men, responsible for casting and striking gold, silver and bronze"). Their names were to appear on coins until 14 BC (Figs.9, 10 & 12.), after which only the emperor's titles were recorded. Rome struck gold, silver and bronze, but was supplemented by a number of other mints across the Empire, notably at *Colonia Patricia* (Cordoba; Fig.14.) and at *Emerita* (Fig.15.) in Spain, at *Lugdunum* (Fig.16.) and *Nîmes* (Fig.6.) in Gaul, and at Eastern mints such as Ephesus and Pergamum.

Augustus' Titles

Augustus adopted a number of titles that had been used under the Republic. In 23 BC, he assumed the Power of the Tribune (*Tribunicia Potestas*; often abbreviated TR P or POT), giving him the power of veto and of convening the Senate (Fig.9.). Like several late Republican leaders, he (and later in his reign, Tiberius) assumed the title *Imperator* (commander in chief or victorious general) (Figs.7 & 19.). He had already been a Consul in the Republican period, but it was to be common for emperors to hold the consulship, the most senior magistracy of the Republic (often abbreviated COS) (Fig.5.). He was declared *Pontifex Maximus* (chief priest) in 13 BC and held the title until his death (often abbreviated PONT MAX or P M). Finally, in 2 BC, he was declared *Pater Patriae* (Father of his country), a title given in future years to particularly popular emperors (Fig.11).

Augustus' Coin Types

Augustus was keen to promote his activities on his coinage. Many of his coins referred to him "saving the state". He was allowed to decorate the door of his house with laurel branches and an oak-wreath, awards for those who had saved the lives of citizens (Fig.8.). One gold coin spelt out how he had given the Roman people back peace and their rights (Fig.7.).

In his autobiography, the *Res Gestae*, Augustus tells us that he found Rome a city of brick but left it a city of marble. Some of his building projects were celebrated on his coins, notably the building of the temples of Mars Ultor and Apollo (Figs.1 & 3.). However, he also recorded his major road-building schemes (Fig.17.). Events, such as the return of the lost legionary standards from Parthia, taken from the defeated army of Crassus in 53 BC, were also commemorated (Fig.14.).

In later years, there was more concentration on the succession. In 2 BC, an enormous issue of *denarii* was struck to honour Augustus' grandsons, and nominated heirs, Gaius and Lucius Caesar (although both died well before Augustus) (Fig.18.). These are the most plentiful Augustan *denarii* struck, being found in large numbers as far away as India and being the single most common type amongst detector finds in Britain.

By the time of his death, Augustus had acknowledged Tiberius as his successor, the son of the notorious Livia (Fig.19.). Augustus was revered as a god in the eastern part of the empire, but resisted the honour in the west; however, he allowed the building of an altar to Roma and Augustus at *Lugdunum* (Lyon in Gaul), a feature which was figure prominently on many base metal coins from the last years of his reign (Figs.11 & 19.). He was openly declared a god (Divus) after his death (Fig.20.).

Denomination	Gold Quinarius	Silver Denarius	Silver Quinarius	Brass Sestertius	Brass Dupondius	Copper As	Copper Semis	Copper Quadrans
Gold Aureus	2	25	50	100	200	400	800	1600
Gold Quinarius		12.5	25	50	100	200	400	800
Silver Denarius			2	4	8	16	32	64
Silver Quinarius				2	4	8	16	32
Brass Sestertius					2	4	8	16
Brass Dupondius						2	4	8
Copper As							2	4
Brass Semis								2

Table 1. The coin denominations used in the coinage of Augustus. They were to provide the model for the Roman Imperial coinage for around 250 years.

Augustan Coins Found in Britain

The most common denomination of Augustus found in Britain is the *denarius*, especially the coin depicting Gaius and Lucius Caesars (Fig.18.). This type is found in over a dozen early Roman coin hoards, notably ones from East Anglia. As site-finds, they are scarce, but are beginning to be found in significant numbers with over 170 on the Portable Antiquities Scheme database (www. finds.org.uk) (see Map). The majority are found south of the River Trent, reflecting their use before and in the early years of the Roman Occupation. Because of their high silver content, they began to be withdrawn after Nero's debasement of the coinage in AD 64; any surviving this event would have certainly been withdrawn as a result of Trajan's debasement (AD 98-117). Amongst the PAS coins, there is one extremely rare *denarius* which was retrieved from a "grot box" and identified by the National Finds Advisor (Fig.21.). The only other example of this coin is in the Bibliothèque nationale. There is also a large number of plated copies showing that the forging of silver coins in Roman Britain started soon after the conquest (Fig.4.). Gold coins of Augustus are extremely rare in Britain. Base metal coins are also rare and there are only a couple on the PAS database which are probably ancient losses (Figs.6 & 8.). Because base metal coins had little intrinsic value, they would not have arrived in Britain prior to AD 43, and by this time Augustan coins would have been that much scarcer.

Map 1. Sites in Britain where coins of Augustus have been recorded on the Portable Antiquities Scheme database. (© Dan Pett)

Chapter IX
Coinage of Tiberius, Gaius Caligula and Claudius
(AD 14-54)

Fig.1. The "Sword of Tiberius", found at Mainz in Germany, was probably given to a senior Roman officer after a series of bloody wars against the Germans in the last years of Augustus' reign (27 BC-AD 14). © British Museum

Fig.3. Gold *aureus* of Tiberius struck at Lugdunum, AD 14-37. It bears the same reverse type as the common silver *denarii* (see Fig.5.) (RIC 27). This is one of seven *aurei* of Tiberius recorded with the PAS. Found in Hampshire. © Portable Antiquities Scheme: HAMP-CC27E5 (19mm)

Fig.2. Close up of the "Sword of Tiberius" showing Tiberius offering Victory to Augustus who is seated in the guise of Jupiter. Right is a gold *aureus* of Augustus, struck at Lugdunum (Lyon), 15-12 BC, that shows two soldiers offering Augustus two olive branches (BMC 443). © British Museum (18mm)

Tiberius (AD 14-37)

In the previous chapter, I showed how Tiberius had been acknowledged by Augustus as his successor, Tiberius even appearing on coins in the last years of his step-father's reign. Tiberius was 54 when he came to the throne and was much more reclusive than Augustus, retiring to the island of Capri in the Bay of Naples in AD 27. He had spent much of his active career as a soldier in the East, in the Balkans and in Germany (Figs.1 & 2. sword of Tiberius); he had also been exiled to the island of Rhodes for eight years.

Court intrigues cost the lives of several of the imperial family and apparently even Tiberius was threatened by the commander of the praetorian guard, Sejanus. Tiberius realised the threat and had Sejanus killed. Tiberius died at Misenum, in AD 37, to the joy of Rome; he was never loved by the people. His son, Drusus, had already been poisoned by Sejanus, and the popular Germanicus (see Fig.12.) had died early in his reign. It was the only surviving son of Germanicus, Gaius Caligula, who was to succeed, "a viper for the Roman people" in the alleged words of Tiberius.

Coinage of Tiberius

The Greek writer Strabo tells us that Lugdunum (Lyon) was the main mint for the gold

Fig.4. Silver *denarius* of Tiberius struck at Lugdunum, AD 14-16. This type was only struck for the first couple of years of Tiberius' reign. It shows Tiberius in a four-horse chariot (RIC 2/4). Found in Staffordshire. © Portable Antiquities Scheme: WMID-BA4B62 (18mm)

Fig.5. Silver *denarius* of Tiberius struck at Lugdunum, AD 14-37. The inscription PONTIF MAXIM refers to Tiberius as being the Chief Priest. Many believe that the seated figure is his mother Livia (RIC 30). Found in Hampshire. © Portable Antiquities Scheme HAMP-569073 (19mm)

Fig.6. Silver *drachma* of Tiberius struck at the eastern imperial mint at Caesarea in Cappadocia (eastern Turkey). The reverse shows a famous local mountain, Mt. Argaeus. Eastern mint *drachmae* from Cappadocia and Lycia in Turkey are occasionally found in British hoards. © British Museum

Fig.7. Silver plated *denarius* copying the PONTIF MAXIM type of Tiberius (see Fig.5.). Found in Hampshire. © Portable Antiquities Scheme: SUR-99D5A6 (16.5mm)

Fig.8. Brass *sestertius* struck by Tiberius at Rome, AD 22-23, to commemorate Augustus: DIVVS AVGVSTVS PATER ("Our Father, the Divine Augustus") (BMC 34). © British Museum (34mm)

and silver of Tiberius in the west. It was protected by an "urban cohort". The *aureus* continued to be the main gold denomination (Fig.3.) although a number of gold *quinarii* were also struck.

Unlike the silver coinage for Augustus, there was little variety in the *denarii* of Tiberius. After a short early issue (Fig.4.), they all bore the reverse PONTIF MAXIM with a seated female figure (Fig.5.). Some people think that this represents Livia, the mother of Tiberius (now Pontifex Maximus – chief priest) and wife of the first imperial Pontifex Maximus (Augustus). Some, however, have suggested the figure is Pax or Justitia. This is the most common single type of *denarius* ever struck in the Roman world, the issue lasting throughout the reign. It is often called the "Tribute Penny" after its presumed use in the episode when Jesus told people to "render unto God what is God's and unto Caesar what is Caesar's" (Matthew 22, 17-21). However, the silver coin used was much more likely to have been a silver *drachma* from the imperial mint in Caesarea Cappadocia in western Turkey (Fig.6.).

Around 150 silver *denarii* of Tiberius have been recorded on the PAS database (www.finds.org. uk). Furthermore, a significant number of these coins are plated copies (Fig.7.). It is quite possible

that some of these *denarii* arrived in Britain before the conquest of AD 43, but it is certain that the military pay-chests of Claudius' army would have been full of Tiberian coins. The distribution map of Tiberius' coins shows where official and copied *denarii* have been found (Map.1.). The pieces from Lincolnshire probably show the use of these coins in the region from the AD 60s when the fort at Lincoln was built, and the ones in Cheshire probably show their circulation slightly later in the 70s.

The base metal coinage of Tiberius was struck at Rome, probably from four workshops, and had a much greater variety of types than for Augustus. Because Britain was not part of the Roman Empire in Tiberius' reign, these coins are very rarely found in Britain. Amongst his issues were ones which honoured his dead stepfather Augustus (Fig.8.).

The "Credit Crunch" of AD 33

The Roman historian Tacitus tells us in his Annals (vi.16) that there had been much illegal lending of money and that lenders finally were forced to call in many of their loans so as to come in line with the law. Lenders demanded payment from borrowers in cash and then hoarded gold and silver coins so as to buy land when it suited

Map.1. Distribution of coins of Tiberius (AD 14-37) recorded with the Portable Antiquities Scheme. (© Dan Pett)

them. This resulted in a massive shortage of currency in Italy and Tiberius had to inject 100 million *sestertii* (25 million *denarii*) into the economy in the form of interest-free loans so as to re-float the economy. Although this restored credit, the lenders failed to adhere to new regulations about land purchases which Tiberius laid down. This has a very strong resonance with the world of 2009 – Tacitus tells us that "patriotism comes second to private profits"!

Gaius Caligula (AD 37-41)

Initially, the 24 year old Caligula was very popular, abolishing treason trials, making generous payments to the people and rewarding the Praetorian Guard handsomely. However, he quickly fell out with his grandmother Antonia (see Fig.20.) and possibly forced her to commit suicide; he later exiled two of his sisters, Agrippina and Livilla (see Fig.17.). He certainly appears to have gone mad, even threatening to make his horse Incitatus a consul! His extravagant lifestyle meant that the 3,000 million *sestertii* he had inherited from Tiberius were soon squandered.

Furthermore, his military campaign in Germany was a failure and he aborted his invasion of Britain. He was finally assassinated at the Palatine Games in AD 41.

Coinage of Caligula

There is a debate over where Caligula's gold and silver was struck, but it is generally agreed that the mint was in Lugdunum at the start of the reign, but after two issues moved to Rome. Gold *aurei* and *denarii* were struck honouring his dead father Germanicus as well as his mother Agrippina the Elder (Fig.9.). His base metal coins were struck at Rome, one of the most common coins of his reign commemorating his grandfather, Marcus Agrippa, the general who won the battle of Actium for Augustus in 31 BC (Fig.10.). The PAS has also recorded a *dupondius* that honoured Caligula's dead brothers, Nero and Drusus Caesars (Fig.11.).

Coins of Caligula are generally scarce and it is possible that this is because they were demonetised after his death (according to the writers Dio Cassius and Suetonius). However, they are extremely

Fig.9. Gold *aureus* of Caligula, struck at Rome in AD 40. It honours Agrippina the Elder who died in AD 33 having been exiled by Sejanus (BMC 22). The cut mark on the reverse was possibly to ensure the coin was not plated. This coin was apparently found in South India where such cut marks are common on Roman gold and silver coins. © British Museum (19mm)

Fig.10. Copper-alloy *as* of Agrippa struck by his grandson Gaius Caligula (AD 37-41) at Rome. The coin shows Neptune on the reverse, alluding to Agrippa's naval victory at Actium in 31 BC. It is possible that this is a contemporary copy. There are two of these coins on the PAS database. Found in Hertfordshire. © Portable Antiquities Scheme: BH-07EF41; RIC 58 (26.6mm)

Fig.11. Copper-alloy *dupondius* of Caligula honouring Nero and Drusus Caesars, the sons of Germanicus, and brothers of Caligula, who died in AD 31 and 33. Found in Essex. © Portable Antiquities Scheme: ESS-8B8D77; RIC 34 (30mm)

Map.2. Distribution of coins of Caligula (AD 37-41) recorded with the Portable Antiquities Scheme in 2009. (© Dan Pett)

rare in Britain, normally only being found in hoards or very large assemblages (four *asses* were found in the Sacred Spring at Bath, out of around 12,000 coins). Therefore, we should not be that surprised that there are only around 29 coins of Caligula on the PAS database (see Map.2.).

Claudius (AD 41-54)

Claudius was the brother of Germanicus (Fig.12.) and the uncle of Caligula (Figs.9-11.). He was proclaimed emperor by the Praetorian Guard after the assassination of Caligula. Although he was portrayed as being a bit of a buffoon, he was

Fig.12. Copper alloy *as* of Claudius, struck for Germanicus (died AD 19) at Rome, c.AD 50-4 (RIC 106). Germanicus was the brother of Claudius and father of Caligula. Found in Leicestershire. © Portbable Antiquities Scheme: LEIC-536101 (29mm)

Fig.13. Gold *aureus* of Claudius, struck at Rome in AD 46-7 to celebrate the conquest of Britain. The reverse shows Claudius on horseback between two trophies on top of a triumphal arch inscribed DE BRITANN (BMC 32). © British Museum (19mm)

Fig.15. Gold *aureus* of Claudius, struck at Rome in AD 46-47 (RIC 40). It is one of three *aurei* of Claudius on the PAS database. Found in Staffordshire. © Portable Antiquities Scheme: WMID-626B77 (19mm)

Fig.16. Silver *denarius* of Claudius, struck at Rome, c.AD 46-52 (RIC 41). This splendid coin is one of 30 Claudian *denarii* on the PAS Database. Found in Leicestershire. © Portable Antiquities Scheme: LEIC-9F20A1 (18mm)

Fig.14. Silver *didrachm* of Claudius, struck at Caesarea, Cappadocia (eastern Turkey), c.AD 46. This coin shows Claudius riding in a chariot, over the inscription DE BRITANNIS, thus celebrating the conquest of Britain (BMC 237). © British Museum (27mm)

in fact highly intelligent and ruthless: he removed many potential political opponents. His reign saw the conquest of Mauretania (north-west Africa), and Britain in AD 43. Claudius actually participated in the British campaign and dedicated an arch in Rome in celebration (Figs.13 & 14.); he even named his son Britannicus after the new province.

Coinage of Claudius

With the exception of an issue of *quadrantes* from Lugdunum, all of the coinage of the Western Roman Empire was struck at Rome. He issued a large number of *aurei* and *denarii* throughout his reign (Figs.13 & 15-17.). He honoured his wife Agrippina the Younger and her son Nero who he adopted as his successor (Fig.17.). It is possible that one copper quadrans commemorates the restoring of the weights of gold and silver coins (Fig.18.). Claudius struck a large base metal coinage, including *sestertii* honouring his father Nero Drusus Claudius (Fig.19.) and *dupondii* for his mother Antonia, the daughter of Mark Antony (Fig.20.).

Claudian Coins in Britain

Gold and silver coins of Claudius are rarely found in Britain (Figs.15 & 16.). As with coins of earlier emperors, they are mostly found in hoards and large assemblages. However, a large hoard of plated copies of Claudian *denarii* was found in

Fig.17. Silver *denarius* of Claudius, honouring his wife Agrippina the Younger and her son Nero who was to succeed Claudius in AD 54 (BMC 82). © British Museum (19mm)

Fig.18. Copper *quadrans* of Claudius, struck at Rome in AD 41. The PNR under the scales might stand for Pondus Nummi Restitutum ("weight of the coins restored") (BMC 174). © British Museum (18mm)

Suffolk and is on display in the Roman Britain gallery at the British Museum. Likewise, official base metal coins of Claudius are also rare in Britain. It does seem that there was a massive shortage of small change when the Roman army (of up to 50,000 men) invaded. The response was to issue an enormous number of "Claudian copies", mostly

Fig.19. Brass *sestertius* of Claudius, struck at Rome in honour of his father Nero Claudius Drusus (died AD 9). Although worn, I am confident about the identification of this coin (RIC 93). Found on the Isle of Wight. © Portable Antiquities Scheme: AS IOW-0D4331.

Fig.20. Brass *dupondius* of Claudius, struck for his mother Antonia (died AD 37). Although this specimen is poorly preserved, I believe it to be official rather than a copy (RIC 104). Found in Hertfordshire. © Portable Antiquities Scheme: AS BH-8046A1.

Fig.21. Brass *dupondius* of Claudius, struck at Rome, c.AD 41-50. The reverse shows Ceres the goddess of harvest and grain. Found in North Yorkshire. © Portable Antiquities Scheme: AS SWYOR-24D027 (28mm)

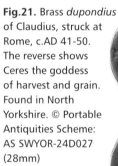

Fig.22. Contemporary copy of a copper *as* of Claudius of the common "Minerva" type. The tell-tale points are the left-facing head, the linear Minerva and the pronounced S C. Found in Buckinghamshire. © Portable Antiquities Scheme: AS NARC-41E2C5 (25mm)

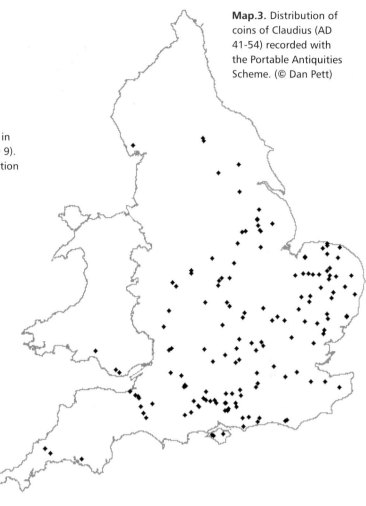

Map.3. Distribution of coins of Claudius (AD 41-54) recorded with the Portable Antiquities Scheme. (© Dan Pett)

of Antonia (as Fig.20.). Research has shown that these copies were probably mostly struck by the Roman army, probably under official licence. One can assume that the "mints" were in legionary fortresses at, for example, Colchester, Exeter, Kingsholm and Usk. However, it is probable that other people also created these copies, there being an enormous variation in their quality. If you have an *as*-sized coin with a left-facing head the chances are that is a Claudian copy; when you turn it over, you will probably find signs of a large S C (sometimes reversed) and a stick figure of Minerva with a shield.

The vast majority of the 404 or so Claudian coins recorded with the Portable Antiquities Scheme are "Claudian copies" of the Minerva type (Map.3.). These coins are mostly found to the east of the Fosse Way (that runs from Exeter to Lincoln). This reflects the extent of Roman occupation of Britain until the mid AD 60s. In AD 64, Nero began to strike an enormous number of base metal coins that started to alleviate the shortage of small change. However, we know that some Claudian copies remained in circulation until the 2nd century AD to be thrown into Coventina's Well on Hadrian's Wall.

asses of the Minerva type (Fig.22), but also of other types including copies of *asses* in the name of Agrippa (as Fig.10.) and the *dupondii* in the name

Chapter X
Coinage of Nero, Galba, Otho, Vitellius and The Civil Wars
(AD 54-69)

Fig.2. Gold *aureus* struck under Nero at Rome in AD 55. The obverse shows Nero and his mother Agrippina; the reverse shows the "divine" emperors Augustus and Claudius in a chariot drawn by elephants. © British Museum. BMC 7 (20mm)

Fig.1. Silver *denarius* struck under Claudius at Rome for Nero as Caesar (AD 50-4). The inscription tells us that Nero is the prince in charge of the "equestrian" class cavalrymen. © British Museum. BMC 93 (19mm)

Fig.3. Silver *denarius* struck under Nero at Rome in AD 54 showing Nero and his mother Agrippina. © British Museum. BMC 3 (19mm)

Fig.4. Brass *sestertius* of Nero struck at Rome c.AD 64-66. The triumphal arch celebrates the victories of the Roman general Corbulo in Armenia in AD 58. © British Museum. BMC 189 (35mm)

Nero AD 54-68

Nero, born in AD 37, was the step-son of Claudius (AD 41-54) who had married his mother Agrippina the Younger in AD 49 (Fig.3.). Nero was appointed "Caesar" (junior emperor) by Claudius in AD 50 and was soon honoured as consul-designate, given the tribunician power and made *Princeps Iuventutis* (Prince of the young "equestrian" rank cavalry who paraded for the emperor annually – the equestrian class was one down from the senatorial class) (Fig.1.). After Claudius' death in AD 54, Nero became emperor without any dispute.

Early Years & Military Successes

One of Nero's first acts when he came to the throne was to deify his stepfather Claudius, honouring him alongside Augustus (Fig.2.). At this time, Nero was heavily under the influence of his mother Agrippina (who also appeared on the coins – Fig.3.) the philosopher Seneca and commander of the Praetorian Guard, Afranius Burrus.

In the east, Nero's armies under Domitius Corbulo won great victories over the Parthians and in Armenia. In Britain, in AD 60-1, the Boudican Revolt was suppressed (Fig.4.). In AD 65,

Fig.6. Brass *sestertius* of Nero struck in Rome c.AD 65 – same type as Fig.5. Found in Buckinghamshire. © Portable Antiquities Scheme: BUC-6AE9F0 (31mm)

Fig.7. Copper *as* of Nero, struck in Rome, AD 62-8. The reverse shows Apollo, or Nero as Apollo, playing the lyre. Nero's recitals were famous for the wrong reasons – people even feigned death so as to be carried out! © British Museum. BMC 236 (30mm)

Fig.5. Brass *sestertius* of Nero struck in Rome c.AD 65. The reverse shows the Temple of Janus with closed doors. The doors were only closed when there were no wars anywhere in the Roman Empire – a rare event. © British Museum. BMC 162 (35mm)

Fig.8. Gold *aureus* of Nero struck in Rome, AD 64-5, possibly to celebrate Corbulo's victories in Armenia in AD 63. Found in Warwickshire. RIC 46. © Portable Antiquities Scheme: WMID-66DEC6 (20mm)

Fig.9. Gold *aureus* of Nero, struck in Rome, AD 64-5. The reverse shows Jupiter "the guardian". RIC 52. This coin was a chance find from a garden in Kent. © Portable Antiquities Scheme: FAIL-C77B04 (19mm)

Fig.10. Gold *aureus*, similar to Fig.9. Found in Cornwall. RIC 63. © Portable Antiquities Scheme: CORN-DE6541 (19mm)

Fig.11. Silver *denarius* of Nero struck in Rome AD 67-8. The reverse shows the personification of good health, Salus. This is a good example of a post-reform *denarius* of Nero, struck at lighter weight. RIC 72. Found in Hertfordshire. © Portable Antiquities Scheme: BH-008CA6 (18mm)

there was no war anywhere in the Empire meaning that the doors of the Temple of Janus could be closed (Figs.5 & 6.).

The Later Years: Nero the Monster

In AD 62, Burrus died and Seneca retired, later to be forced to commit suicide by Nero. From now on Nero became increasingly autocratic and ruthless. Early in his reign, in AD 55, he had already ordered Britannicus, Claudius' son, to be poisoned. Furthermore, after Nero's mother, Agrippina, fell from favour she was murdered upon his orders in AD 59. Nero had his first wife, Octavia, murdered in AD 62, and in AD 65 he accidentally killed his second wife Poppaea with a kick. After the Great Fire in Rome in AD 64, when Nero allegedly "fiddled while Rome burnt" the emperor began a grandiose scheme of rebuilding, including the construction of his massive Golden Palace. He also became

pre-occupied with the arts and spectacles, and even participated in musical events (Fig.7.). Nero became increasingly unpopular and when the legions of Gaul, Spain and Africa rebelled, and the Praetorian Guard deserted, Nero had little choice but to commit suicide in June AD 68.

Post-Reform Coinages of AD 64-8

In AD 64 there was a major debasement of the gold and silver coinages. Nero reduced the weight of coins in each metal, the *aureus* falling to about 7.25-40 grams (losing about 2% in weight) (Figs.8-10.) and the *denarius* to 3.2-50 grams

Fig.12. Silver *denarius* of Nero, struck in Rome, AD 67-8. It shows a legionary eagle between two standards. RIC 68. Found in Hampshire, it is the first coin of Nero to be recorded with the PAS. © Portable Antiquities Scheme: HAMP1389 (17mm)

Fig.13. Silver *denarius* of Nero, struck in Rome, AD 64-5. The reverse shows Concordia. RIC 49. Found in East Yorkshire. © Portable Antiquities Scheme: YORYM-A10CA3 (17mm)

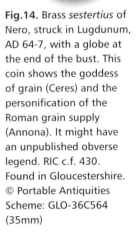

Fig.15. Brass *sestertius* of Nero, struck in Lugdunum, AD 64-7. This coin also has the globe at the front of the bust denoting the mint of Lugdunum. RIC 378-9. Found in Sussex. © Portable Antiquities Scheme: SUSS-6A0B14 (28.5mm)

Fig.16. Copper alloy *as* of Nero, struck in Lugdunum, AD 64-7. The reverse shows Genius sacrificing. RIC 467. This wonderful coin was found in a garden in Surrey. © Portable Antiquities Scheme: SUR-001DD2 (28mm)

Fig.14. Brass *sestertius* of Nero, struck in Lugdunum, AD 64-7, with a globe at the end of the bust. This coin shows the goddess of grain (Ceres) and the personification of the Roman grain supply (Annona). It might have an unpublished obverse legend. RIC c.f. 430. Found in Gloucestershire. © Portable Antiquities Scheme: GLO-36C564 (35mm)

Fig.17. Copper alloy *as* of Nero struck in Lugdunum (Lyon), AD 64-7. Note the globe at the base of the bust (by the inscription); this denotes the mint of Lugdunum. The reverse shows the *Ara Pacis* (Altar of Peace) which was built in Rome by Augustus and can still be seen today in a museum by the Mausoleum of Augustus. RIC 458. Found in Surrey. © Portable Antiquities Scheme: SUR-72ACF2 (29.5mm)

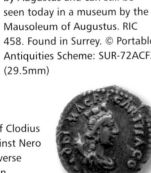

Fig.18. Silver *denarius* of Clodius Macer who rebelled against Nero in Africa, AD 68. The obverse shows the personification of Carthage and the reverse Medusa's head on a three-legged symbol called the *triskelis*. This was the symbol of Sicily, Rome's first province. © British Museum. BMC 5 (19mm)

(losing about 7%) (Figs.11-13.). Especially in the case of silver *denarii*, this weight reduction caused the rapid removal of earlier coins from circulation, making them very rare. This partly explains why *denarii* of Caligula, Claudius and the early years of Nero are hardly found in Britain. Many silver hoards buried in the 2nd and early 3rd centuries AD often start with worn post-reform coins of Nero; this shows that Nero's *denarii* circulated until well into the 3rd century.

Although Nero started to issue base metal coins in AD 62-3, it was after AD 64 that they were minted in enormous quantities. They were struck at Rome and Lugdunum (Gaul), coins of the latter mint being distinguished by a globe at the point of the bust on the obverse (Figs.14-17.). These coins of Nero flooded into Britain: wonderful large module *sestertii* (Figs.4, 6, 7, 14-15.), *dupondii* and *asses* (Figs.7 & 16-17.). The *asses* are by far the most numerous coins and are the first official Roman base metal coins to circulate in large numbers in Britain. Until this time, the Claudian *as* copies (covered in the last chapter) were the most numerous copper-alloy coins circulating in Britain. Overall, about 289 coins of Nero have been recorded with the PAS.

Fig.20. Silver *denarius* of the Civil War, struck at the start of Galba's rebellion in Spain in AD 68. The coin is copied from a Republican coin and shows "Good Happening" on the obverse and clasped hands (showing unity and harmony) on the reverse. This is the finest example that I have seen. RIC 6. Found in Lincolnshire: LIN-898441 (18.5mm)

Fig.21. Silver *denarius* of Galba, struck in Gaul, possibly at Vienna, AD 68. It shows Galba on horseback and Victory. The obverse inscription is a new variety. RIC 88var. Found in Northamptonshire. © Portable Antiquities Scheme: NARC-2D3504 (17mm)

Fig.19. Silver *denarius* of the Civil War, struck during the revolt of Vindex against Nero in Gaul, AD 68. The obverse shows Victory and the inscription "for the good of the human race". The reverse reads *Senatus Populus Que Romanus* – the Senate and People of Rome. RIC 73a. Found in Derbyshire: DENO-6BE2C2 (19mm). Another example of this coin has been found in North Yorkshire: PAS SWYOR-2C3EC0.

Fig.22. Brass *sestertius* of Galba, struck at Rome, AD 68-9. The reverse shows Roma, the personification of Rome. © British Museum. BMC 92 (36mm)

Fig.23. Silver *denarius* of Galba, struck in Rome, AD 68-9. SPQR on the reverse stands for *Senatus Populusque Romanus* – The Senate and People of Rome. RIC 167. Found in Glamorgan. © Portable Antiquities Scheme: NMGW-E16807 (18mm)

The Civil Wars AD 68-9
The Revolt of Vindex, March-May 68

C. Julius Vindex, governor of Gallia Lugdunensis (Southern France), rebelled against Nero in March AD 68. His revolt was suppressed in May 68 by Verginius Rufus, but by then Galba had supported the rebellion in Spain, and Clodius Macer (Fig.18.) was in open revolt in Africa, leading to the suicide of Nero on 9 June. A significant coinage of silver *denarii* was struck by Vindex in Gaul, some of the coins suggesting a better future for Rome and even a return to Republican government (Fig.19.). Only two coins of Vindex's revolt have been recorded from Britain on the PAS database.

Galba July 68-15 January 69

Galba, the governor of Spain, supported the revolt of Vindex against Nero and on 2 April was declared Imperator by his troops in Spain. However, he was very careful not to assume the title of emperor until invited to be Augustus by the Senate after the death of Nero in June AD 68, probably in July. Anonymous "Civil War" coins had already been struck for Galba in Spain and a few have been found in Britain (Fig.20.); he also appears to have struck coins at Vienna

Fig.24. Silver *denarius* of Galba, struck in Rome, AD 68-9. The reverse has the inscription DIVA AVGVSTA and shows Livia, the wife of Augustus, who was made a goddess by Claudius. RIC 186/224. Found in Hertfordshire. © Portable Antiquities Scheme: BH-1746A5 (17mm)

(Fig.21.). He arrived in Rome and quickly dealt with a contender for the throne, Clodius Macer, the governor of Africa. Macer's coins, probably struck at Carthage, are rare and none have been recorded with the PAS (Fig.18.).

At Rome, Galba struck a large number of gold, silver and base metal coins (Fig.22.). However, it is the silver *denarii* that tend to travel furthest and around 31 have been recorded with the PAS. Galba's coin designs try to forge links with the people (Fig.23.) and he even tried to

Fig.26. Silver *denarius* of Otho, struck in Rome, AD 69. The reverse shows Victory with the inscription "The Victory of Otho". RIC 14. Found in Cambridgeshire. © Portable Antiquities Scheme: PAS-DA0BB1 (18mm)

Fig.27. Silver *denarius* of the Civil War, struck for Vitellius in Gaul, AD 69. The coin honours the army (*exercitus*) and the Praetorian Guard in Rome who Vitellius wanted to attract away from his rival Otho. RIC 118. Found in Cambridgeshire: SF-E12920 (18mm)

Fig.25. Silver *denarius* of Otho, struck in Rome, AD 69. The reverse has the inscription PONT(ifex) MAX(imus) (Chief Priest) with Ceres the goddess of harvests standing. The only other coin known of this particular variety is in Paris. RIC 20var. Found in Hertfordshire. © Portable Antiquities Scheme: BH-F5BD67 (18mm)

Fig.28. Silver *denarius* of the Civil War, struck by pro-Vitellian supporters in Gaul, AD 69. The obverse shows Vesta, the goddess of the hearth whose flame burnt eternally in the Forum. The reverse shows Jupiter Optimus Maximus (Jupiter the Best and Great) whose temple was on the Capitoline Hill. RIC 128a. Found in Derbyshire: DENO-340DE5 (18mm)

Fig.29. Silver *denarius* of Vitellius, struck at Rome, AD 69. On this coin, Vitellius is proclaiming that he has "restored liberty". RIC 105. Found in Leicestershire. © Portable Antiquities Scheme: LEIC-53FBC6 (17mm)

Fig.31. Silver *denarius* of Vitellius, struck in Rome, AD 69. The reverse shows a tripod, raven and dolphin and probably commemorates Vitellius' election into the college of senior priests. RIC 109. Found in Lincolnshire: NLM-3F2F40 (17.5mm)

Fig.30. Silver *denarius* of Vitellius, struck at Rome, AD 69. The reverse shows Concordia. RIC 66/73. Found in Hampshire. © Portable Antiquities Scheme: SUR-9ADB81 (17mm)

Fig.32. Silver *denarius* of Vitellius, struck at Tarraco(?) in Spain, AD 69. The coin shows Victory holding a shield inscribed SPQR (see Fig.23. for explanation). This mint struck many coins for Vitellius whilst Otho had control of the mint in Rome. RIC 14. Found in Staffordshire. © Portable Antiquities Scheme: WMID-E8E056 (18mm)

associate himself closely with Augustus' family (Fig.24.). However, Galba's strict measures concerning the army led to the German legions declaring their general, Vitellius (Figs.29-31.) emperor in January 69. But before Vitellius could march on Rome, Galba was assassinated on 15 January AD 69 by the followers of Otho who declared himself emperor at Rome.

Otho 15 January-17 April 69

Otho was disgruntled with Galba for not giving him a higher position in Rome. After the assassination of Galba, Otho was only able to hold onto the throne for three months, all the time under pressure from Vitellius and his supporters in Gaul and Germany. In the east, he was losing support to the future emperor Vespasian.

Map 1. Find spots for the coins of Nero, Galba, Otho, Vitellius and the "Civil Wars" which are recorded on the PAS database. (© Dan Pett)

After Otho's army was defeated by Vitellius' forces at Bedriacum, Otho committed suicide on 17 April. He only issued gold *aurei* and silver *denarii*, and his coins are the rarest of the three Civil War emperors. However, 22 *denarii* are recorded on the PAS database, some of them very rare varieties (Figs.25 & 6.).

Vitellius 1 January-20 December 69

Vitellius was the commander of the German legions which had rebelled against Galba, but he was unable to rule from Rome because of Otho. However, he put increasing pressure on Otho: it is thought that some coins, apparently struck by a Vitellian supporter in southern Gaul, were an attempt to win over the Praetorian Guard at Rome (Fig.27.). Another Civil War issue of Vitellius honours Jupiter Optimus Maximus and Vesta, both prominent deities in Rome (Fig.28.).

After he won the Battle of Bedriacum against Otho, Vitellius was finally installed emperor at Rome on 19 April where his coins declared he had "restored liberty" and "Concordia" (harmony) and had been made a senior priest (Figs.29-31.). He also struck coins in Spain, one of which is recorded on the PAS database (Fig.32.).

Overall, Vitellius is the most common emperor of the three civil war rulers on the database with 65 coins, all *denarii*, although he did strike in gold and base metal as well. Vespasian was declared emperor by the soldiers at Alexandria (Egypt) on 1 July AD 69 and then gained the support of the Danube legions. He finally invaded Italy and defeated Vitellius, who was assassinated and thrown into the River Tiber. In the next chapter I will discuss the coinages of Vespasian and his sons Titus and Domitian.

Distribution of Coins of Nero and the Civil Wars in Britain

By the time that the coinage of Nero reached Britain, the province had been under Roman control for over a decade and there was Roman activity in the south-west (Devon and Cornwall), Wales and the North Midlands. However, this distribution map also shows that Neronian and Civil War period coins continued to circulate for at least a century – the coins in Yorkshire, Cumbria and near to Hadrian's Wall were probably lost much later, mostly in the 2nd century AD.

Chapter XI
Coinage of The Flavian Dynasty – Vespasian, Titus and Domitian
(AD 69-96)

Vespasian, as I explained in the last chapter, was the emperor who finally triumphed after the Civil Wars of AD 68-9. A native of Falacrinae in Sabine country, north-east of Rome, Vespasian was from a middle-class background; his generation of the family were the first to be made senators. Before he became emperor, Vespasian had served in many parts of the Empire: as a soldier in Thrace (northern Greece); as *quaestor* (financial official) in Crete and North Africa; and as commander of Legio II Augusta during the Claudian invasion of

Britain (AD 43) with whom he won many battles on his way down to Devon. He was made a Consul and later became Governor of Africa. He even accompanied Nero on an imperial trip to Greece. In fact, Vespasian was lucky to survive Nero's reign, having fallen asleep during one of Nero's infamous recitals, an offence that could lead to execution!

When news of Nero's death reached Vespasian, he was in the process of suppressing the Jewish Revolt (AD 66-74) with his son Titus (see Figs.4 & 18.). Vespasian left Titus to capture

Fig.1. Silver *denarius* of Vespasian struck at an unknown mint, possibly in Spain, c.AD 69-79. It shows "Victorious Fortune". This is the only example of this type known and now has its very own entry in the new volume of *Roman Imperial Coinage* for the Flavians – RIC II (2nd ed) no.1366. Found in Northamptonshire – NARC 9EAB50. © The Portable Antiquities Scheme (19mm)

Fig.2. Silver *denarius* of Vespasian struck at an uncertain mint, possibly Tarraco in Spain. The reverse type is unclear, but shows a person seated left; it is apparently unpublished. This coin was found quite recently at a rally in Hampshire and the National Finds Advisor, and the world authority on Flavian coins (Ian Carradice) would like to have a chance to study the coin further. HAMP-5F3E60. © The Portable Antiquities Scheme (18.5mm)

Fig.3. Silver *denarius* of Vespasian, struck at Rome in AD 70, proclaiming Vespasian's new dynasty by showing his two sons, Titus and Domitian, as Caesars. RIC II (2nd ed) 16. Found in North Lincolnshire – NLM-3D98A2. © The Portable Antiquities Scheme (18mm)

Jerusalem and went to Alexandria where he prepared his claim on the empire. The troops of Syria and the Danube declared for him and by the time he arrived in Rome his son Domitian was already ruling in Vespasian's name.

Vespasian's Coinage

In the first couple of years, coins were struck at a variety of mints in Spain, Egypt (probably Alexandria), Judaea and Syria (Antioch). The PAS has already recorded at least one previously unknown coin from a Spanish mint, and another recent find might also be a new type from Spain (Figs.1 & 2.). Rome, however, was to be the most prolific mint. At the outset of his reign, Vespasian declared his sons Titus and Domitian as Caesars, his junior colleagues. This is shown on early *denarii* and *sestertii* of Rome where his two sons are shown on the reverse (Fig.3).

Throughout the reign, coins are also struck for the two Caesars in their own name (see Figs. 4, 12, 19 & 26). The suppression of the Jewish Revolt is celebrated on coins of most denominations of Vespasian and of Titus from early in the reign – examples found in Britain are often poorly preserved (Figs.4 &18.).

Other types show traditional scenes: one *denarius* depicts sacrificial implements which reflects the emperor's piety to the gods (Fig.5.), and an *aureus* the Temple of Vesta (Fig.11.); another *denarius* shows two yoked oxen, alluding to the foundation of Rome by Romulus (Fig.6.); finally a *sestertius* shows the personification of Rome, Roma, herself (Fig.7.). One *denarius* makes a reference to the corn supply sent to Rome from Africa to be handed out to the people of Rome (Fig.8.), an act that would maintain the "Faith of the People" (Fig.9.).

Fig.4. Orichalcum (brass) *sestertius* of Titus as Caesar, struck at Lugdunum (Lyon) in AD 77-8. The reverse proclaims that Judaea has been captured (IVDAEA CAPTA). RIC II (2nd ed) 1245. © The British Museum (34mm). Note that a poorly preserved *sestertius* of similar type has been found in County Durham (NCL-BDEF01)

Fig.8. Silver *denarius* of Vespasian, struck at Rome in AD 77-8. The reverse shows a *modius* (corn measure) which alludes to the grain supply of Rome. RIC II (2nd ed) 981. Found in Sussex – SUSS-92E8E5. © The Portable Antiquities Scheme (19mm)

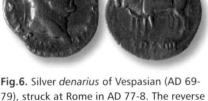

Fig.6. Silver *denarius* of Vespasian (AD 69-79), struck at Rome in AD 77-8. The reverse shows two yoked oxen. RIC II (2nd ed) 943. Found in Suffolk – SF-060777. © The Portable Antiquities Scheme (17mm)

Fig.5. Silver *denarius* of Vespasian, struck at Rome in AD 72-3. AVGVR TRI POT and sacrificial implements. An augur predicted the future through the flight of the birds. RIC II (2nd ed) 356. Found in Surrey – SUR-32F604. © The Portable Antiquities Scheme (17mm)

Fig.7. Brass *sestertius* of Vespasian, probably struck at Lugdunum (Lyon) in AD 77-8. The reverse shows Roma standing. RIC II (2nd ed) c.f. 1136/83. Found in Essex – ESS-C621D6. © The Portable Antiquities Scheme (34mm)

Fig.9. Brass *dupondius* of Vespasian, struck at Lugdunum (Lyon) in AD 77-78. The globe on the front of the bust, denoting Lugdunum, is clear. The reverse refers to the "Faith of the People". RIC II (2nd ed) 1210. Found in Buckinghamshire – SOM-55E500. © The Portable Antiquities Scheme (29mm)

Fig.10. Copper-alloy *as* of Vespasian, struck in AD 72 at Lugdunum (Lyon). It is claimed that this coin with an eagle on the reverse is most commonly found in the military zones of the north-western empire. RIC II (2nd ed) 1202. Found in Berkshire – BERK-8A1BF5. © The Portable Antiquities Scheme (26mm)

Fig.11. Gold *aureus* of Vespasian, struck at Rome in AD 72-3. The reverse shows the ancient temple of Vesta that was sited in the Roman Forum. It is possible that this coin celebrates the rebuilding of the temple after it was damaged by fire in AD 69. BMC 372. © The British Museum (19mm)

Fig.12. Silver *denarius* of Titus as Caesar, under Vespasian, struck at Rome in AD 73. The reverse shows Titus in a *quadriga* (four horse chariot) riding right. RIC II (2nd ed) 531. Found in Buckinghamshire – BH-4251D6. © The Portable Antiquities Scheme (18.5mm)

Fig.13. Silver *denarius* of Titus, struck at Rome in AD 80-1 to commemorate Vespasian. The reverse shows two Capricorns and a globe inscribed S C. RIC II (2nd ed) 357. Found in Leicestershire – LEIC-0975F5. © The Portable Antiquities Scheme (18mm)

Fig.14. Brass *sestertius* of Titus, struck at Rome in AD 80-1, to celebrate the completion of the Flavian Amphitheatre, better known as the Colosseum. BMC 190. © The British Museum (31mm)

Fig.15. Silver *denarius* of Titus, struck at Rome in AD 80. The reverse shows a dolphin entwined around an anchor. RIC II (2nd ed) 113. Found in Leicestershire – LEIC-188874. © The Portable Antiquities Scheme (17mm)

Fig.16. Brass *sestertius* of Titus (79-81), struck at Rome in AD 80-1. The reverse shows Vespasian and Titus standing together. RIC II (2nd ed) 161. Found in Hampshire – HAMP-424315 © The Portable Antiquities Scheme (32mm). This coin is one of only six *sestertii* of Titus recorded with the PAS.

Fig.17. Brass *dupondius* of Titus (79-81), struck at Rome in AD 80-1. It is a revival of a coin struck, possibly in honour of Livia, by Tiberius. It might be Livia's portrait on the obverse. RIC II (2nd ed) 427. Found in Sussex – SUSS-E72134 © The Portable Antiquities Scheme (29mm). This is one of only two *dupondii* from Titus' reign recorded with the PAS.

Fig.18. Gold *aureus* of Titus as Caesar, struck at Rome under Vespasian in AD 72-3. It shows Titus standing over the personification of Judaea. BMC 84. © The British Museum (19mm)

Mint of Lugdunum

After Rome, the most important mint of Vespasian's reign was at Lugdunum (Lyon) where Nero had already issued a massive base metal coinage. As with Nero, coins of Lugdunum can normally be identified by the globe at the base of the bust (Fig.9.). Lugdunum operated in two phases, striking gold, silver and base metals in AD 70-72 and base metal only in AD 77-8 (Fig.10.). In the first phase, the coins were only issued in Vespasian's name, in the second phase for his sons as well. It is reckoned from the large numbers of coins of 77-8 found in North-West Europe that these coins were struck to satisfy local demand.

Volume of Coinage in Britain

Vespasian struck an enormous number of coins, reflected by the 974 or more recorded on the PAS database (see Table 1). It is interesting that there is only one gold coin of Vespasian on the database, sadly without an image. I illustrate a British Museum coin instead (Fig.11.). Silver *denarii* are particularly common, with 468 on the database (Figs.1-3, 5-6 & 8.).

Many of these are worn and we know that they circulated until the early 3rd century, many such specimens being found in coin hoards. Of the base metal coins, *asses* are the most common (355), with *sestertii* (64) and *dupondii* (85) being much scarcer (Figs.7 & 9-10.). We can assume that the lion's share of coins being sent to Britain was to finance two major elements of Roman policy. Firstly, there was a military thrust into Wales, Brigantia and finally Scotland, under the governors Vettius Bolanus, Petilius Cerealis, Julius Frontinus and Gnaeus Agricola. This culminated in the Roman victory at Mons Graupius in c.AD 83 over the Caledonians under the command of Calgacus. The result was a short-lived frontier just south of the Grampian

Fig.19. Silver *denarius* of Domitian as Caesar, struck at Rome under Vespasian, AD 77-8. The reverse shows Romulus and Remus with the wolf, and also informs us that Domitian has been made Consul for the fifth time. RIC II (2nd ed) 961. Found in Hertfordshire – BH-F63DC7. © The Portable Antiquities Scheme (18mm)

Mountains, based on the legionary fortress at Inchtuthil. Secondly, there were urban development programmes in the south at towns such as Verulamium and London. There is even an inscription at Verulamium that tells us the forum was completed in the governorship of Agricola (c.AD 77-83).

I believe it was all this military activity and urban building that caused the massive influx of *denarii* and *asses* during Vespasian's reign. When Vespasian died, he left the state's finances in much better shape. Being the son of a tax-collector, he maximised tax revenue, even incurring the wrath of his son Titus for taxing the urinals!

Titus AD 79-81

Titus was long seen as Vespasian's designated heir having been declared Caesar; he also shared the consulship with his father seven times. Quite a copious coinage was struck for Titus under his father (Fig.12.).

Vespasian had made Titus the commander of the Praetorian Guard and it is probable that Titus' activities in this role led to his becoming very unpopular. However, when he became emperor, he quickly honoured his father on the coinage (Fig.13.) and swiftly gained popularity with the people of Rome. This was probably partly because he was generous in financing relief after a disastrous plague and fire in Rome, and for the help he provided to people of the Bay of Naples after the eruption of Vesuvius had destroyed Pompeii, Herculaneum and other towns in AD 79. However, I think he was most popular because it was in his reign that the Colosseum was finally opened – he provided many gladiatorial games which, along with free bread, kept the urban masses happy (Fig.14.).

Titus' Coinage

Nearly all of Titus' coins were struck at Rome and he continued to strike for his brother Domitian, as Caesar. His coins are much rarer than those of Vespasian, unsurprisingly since he only reigned for two years (Figs.13-19.). His *denarii* are generally more common than base metal issues, there being very few good condition *sestertii*, *dupondii* or *asses* on the database (see Table) (Figs.16-17.). However, Titus did strike some interesting issues in honour of previous rulers or members of the imperial family, one fine *dupondius* on the database being a good example (Fig.17.). There are no gold coins of Titus recorded on the database, but again I illustrate a British Museum coin (Fig.18.).

Domitian AD 81-96

Domitian was the second son of Vespasian who was Caesar under his father and Titus (Fig.20.). He is normally thought of as being a bad emperor, and there is no doubt in later years he became a paranoid megalomaniac. However, the senatorial writers have left a biased account of his reign. One of the most famous character assassinations comes in *The Agricola* by Tacitus. In this work, Tacitus writes a eulogy of his father-in-law Agricola who was governor of Britain from c.77 to 83, and who won the Battle of Mons Graupius against the Caledonians in Scotland, c.AD 83 (which I mentioned above).

Domitian did gain the support of the army, raising their pay significantly from 225 to 300 *denarii* per annum. There were serious problems on the Rhine and Danube frontiers which occupied Domitian for much of his reign – he defeated the barbarians on several occasions (Fig.26.).

It is perhaps appropriate that his favourite deity was the warlike Minerva who appears continuously on his silver coins (Figs.20 & 21.). One fine *sestertius* shows Domitian sacrificing with the army (Fig.22.) and an *as* shows Domitian wearing Minerva's protective aegis (Fig.24.). However, back in Rome Domitian unleashed a "reign of terror" in the last four years of his reign, senators and imperial staff being executed or exiled in great numbers. Finally, he was assassinated by conspirators including the Praetorian Guard; only the army mourned his death.

Domitian's Coinage

Most of Domitian's coinage was struck at Rome, but he moved the mint from the Capitoline Hill to next to the Church of San Clemente (just east of the Colosseum), an event probably celebrated by an issue of *asses* showing MONETA AVGVSTI, struck from AD 84 (Fig.23.).

Domitian's coinage is quite commonly found in Britain, although it is not as abundant as

Fig.20. Silver *denarius* of Domitian (81-96) struck at Rome in AD 89. The reverse shows Minerva in warlike fashion. RIC II (2nd ed) 685. Found in Shropshire – HESH-927906. © The Portable Antiquities Scheme (17mm)

Fig.21. Silver *denarius* of Domitian (81-96) struck at Rome in AD 88-9. RIC II (2nd ed) 661. The reverse of this coin also shows his favourite goddess, Minerva. Found in Lincolnshire – LIN-2EB138. © The Portable Antiquities Scheme (18mm)

Fig.22. Copper alloy *sestertius* of Domitian (81-96) struck at Rome c.AD 86. This fine coin shows Domitian sacrificing with his army. RIC II (2nd ed) 471. Found in Yorkshire – YORYM-EDC9B4 © The Portable Antiquities Scheme (34mm). There are other examples of this rare coin in Paris and Oxford.

Fig.23. Copper alloy *as* of Domitian, struck at Rome in AD 90-1. The honouring of *Moneta Augusti* probably celebrates the move of the mint in Rome from the Capitoline Hill to next to San Clemente. RIC II (2nd ed) 488. Found in North Yorkshire – SWYOR-71E577. © The Portable Antiquities Scheme (29mm)

Fig.24. Copper alloy *as* of Domitian, struck in Rome in AD 86. The reverse refers to the good fortune of the emperor. The obverse shows Domitian wearing the *aegis*, the protective shawl of Minerva (Domitian's favourite goddess). Found in Lincolnshire – LVPL-5677E0. The finder supplied the image with a scale that suggests that this coin is well over 30mm in diameter. However, *sestertii* were not struck with this type, so it is probably a very large *as*.

Vespasian's. Again, however, *denarii* and *asses* predominate (see Table 1) (Figs.20 & 21; 23 & 24), although there are some good examples of *sestertii* and *dupondii* on the database (Figs.22 & 25.). Again, as for Titus, there are no gold coins for Domitian on the database, so I illustrate a British Museum coin (Fig.27.).

Quadrantes From Domitian's Reign

There is one *quadrans* of Domitian which is not illustrated on the database (WMID2874). However, there was a large number of anonymous *quadrantes* struck between about AD 81 and 161. This small denomination was not issued

for use in Britain, although a few examples do reach the Province. One has to assume that these coins arrived in private purses, rather than in official pay chests. The Portable Antiquities Scheme has three examples, mostly found in the military zone of Britain (Fig.28.).

Flavian Coinage in Britain

Urban and military sites in Britain show a marked increase in the proportion of Flavian coins found. As I have already stated, I believe this is due to military activity and urban development. However, there are relatively fewer Flavian coins on rural sites which is where most metal

Fig.25. Copper alloy *dupondius* of Domitian (81-96) struck at Rome in AD 86. The reverse shows the personification of the grain supply, Annona, with the prow of a ship in the background. RIC II (2nd ed) 477. Found in Kent – KENT-1855A5. © The Portable Antiquities Scheme (30mm)

Fig.26. Gold *aureus* of Domitian, struck at Rome in AD 86. The reverse shows the personification of Germany, defeated, seated on a shield with a broken spear. Domitian won major victories over the Germans. BMC 91. © The British Museum (19mm)

Fig.27. Copper alloy *quadrans* struck between c.AD 81 and c.AD 161. The obverse shows Mercury's winged hat, and the reverse his wand known as the caduceus. RIC II (1st ed) 32. Found in Cheshire – LVPL-05B7D1. © The Portable Antiquities Scheme (15mm)

Emperor	Aureus	Denarius	Sestertius	Dupondius	As	Total
Vespasian	2	468	64	85	355	974
Titus	2	90	6	2	22	122
Domitian	2	285	55	75	199	616
Total	6	843	125	162	576	1712

Table 1. Flavian coins recorded on the Portable Antiquities Scheme Database. (Note: there are a number of uncertain Flavian coins not included in this table.)

detecting takes place. Indeed, the PAS database has relatively fewer Flavian coins than have been found on excavations of military and urban sites. Because Flavian coins could stay in circulation until the 3rd century AD they are not only often worn, but also had a chance to circulate widely as shown by the map. Finally, it is interesting to note that the 843 Flavian *denarii* recorded on the PAS would almost cover three years of pay for a legionary soldier in Domitian's reign, as he increased their annual salary to 300 *denarii*.

Map 1. The distribution of Flavian coins across Britain. (© Dan Pett)

Chapter XII
Coinage of Nerva and Trajan
(AD 96-117)

Fig.2. Brass *dupondius* of Nerva (96-8), struck at Rome. The reverse declares the "Liberty of the People", probably referring to the end of Domitian's regime. RIC II, 87. Found in Suffolk. © Portable Antiquities Scheme SF-F1B5DB (26.5mm)

Fig.1. Brass *dupondius* of Nerva (96-8), struck at Rome in honour of the "Divine" emperor Augustus (27 BC-AD 14). This rare coin was probably struck in an attempt by Nerva to claim legitimacy as emperor. The reverse shows a rudder and globe. Found in Somerset. © Portable Antiquities Scheme SOMDOR-C65865

Fig.4. Silver *denarius* of Nerva (96-8), struck at Rome in AD 97. Same reverse as Fig.3. RIC II, 26. Found in North Yorkshire. © Portable Antiquities Scheme NCL-1CEEE5 (19mm)

Fig.3. Gold *aureus* of Nerva (96-8), struck at Rome in c.AD 97. The reverse shows Nerva's attempt to gain the favour of the soldiers, claiming "Concord with the Army" with clasped hands. RIC 14 © British Museum (17.5mm)

Nerva AD 96-98

After Domitian's death on 18 September 96, the elderly senator Nerva immediately acceded to the throne at the age of 60. Nerva had been close to several emperors for many years, serving as consul under Vespasian and Domitian; Nerva even honoured Augustus on his coinage in an attempt to legitimise his regime (Fig.1.). There was an enormous backlash against Domitian in Rome: many of his close colleagues were killed, statues were destroyed and buildings desecrated. Although Nerva was a popular alternative to Domitian in Rome (Fig.2.), he found it hard to

contain these demonstrations. He faced an even harder task in placating the army who were still supportive of Domitian, the first emperor to have given them a pay rise in about 100 years (Figs.3 & 4).

The Praetorian Guard mutinied and Nerva was forced to adopt a successor who would be more popular. He chose the governor of Germania Superior, Marcus Ulpius Traianus (who we call Trajan), who was already a successful military commander. Trajan succeeded on Nerva's death in 98. However, Nerva did pass some popular laws including providing charity for the poor and

Fig.5. Brass *sestertius* of Nerva (96-98), struck at Rome, AD 97. The reverse shows two mules in front of a harness and cart shafts – this coin celebrates Nerva taking on the costs of running the imperial post in Italy. BMC 119 © British Museum (35mm)

Fig.6. Silver *denarius* of Nerva (96-8), struck at Rome in AD 97. The reverse shows the personification of good fortune, Fortuna. RIC II, 16. Found in Lincolnshire. © Portable Antiquities Scheme LIN-4FEED8 (c.18mm)

Fig.8. Copper-alloy *as* of Nerva (96-8), struck at Rome. The reverse probably shows Fortuna. The coin was pierced to be suspended. Found in Cambridgeshire. © Portable Antiquities Scheme CAM-49DD14 (28mm)

Fig.9. Copper-alloy *as* of Trajan (98-117) struck in Rome, AD 98-9. This coin was struck very early in Trajan's reign before the coin engravers had an official portrait. Hence, the portrait looks similar to Nerva. RIC II, 395. Found in Buckinghamshire. © Portable Antiquities Scheme, SOM-562F13 (27.5mm)

Fig.7. Brass *sestertius* of Nerva (96-8), struck at Rome, AD 96-7. The reverse shows Fortuna. RIC II, 60, 73, or 83. Found in Surrey. © Portable Antiquities Scheme SUR-3D6BD0 (c.30mm)

relieving the people of the burden of funding the imperial postal service in Italy (Fig.5.).

Nerva's Coinage

Nerva struck all his coins at Rome. Quite large numbers were issued, his coins only being scarce because he reigned for only about 18 months. In total 160 of his coins have been recorded with the PAS. No gold *aurei* are on the database, the one illustrated being from the British Museum (Fig.3.). The most common denomination recorded is the *denarius* with 88 specimens (Figs.4 & 6.). Brass *sestertii* (Figs.5 & 7.) and *dupondii* (42) (Figs.1 & 2.) outnumber the copper *asses* (29) (Fig.8.).

Trajan AD 98-117

Trajan came from a distinguished provincial family that was based at Italica in Spain. His father had been a successful general and politician, serving in the suppression of the Jewish Revolt and as Governor of Syria. Trajan was to start his military career with his father before commanding Legio VII Gemina in Spain. He was Governor in Germany when he received his letter of adoption from Nerva; on Nerva's death, Trajan swiftly had the Praetorian Guards who had mutinied against Domitian put to death. Trajan's early

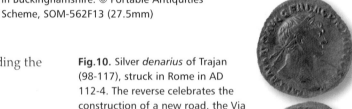

Fig.10. Silver *denarius* of Trajan (98-117), struck in Rome in AD 112-4. The reverse celebrates the construction of a new road, the Via Traiana from Benevento to Brindisi in Italy. RIC II, 266. Found on the Isle of Wight. © Portable Antiquities Scheme IOW-9B8D34 (19mm)

coins were struck before his official portrait was available to the mint engravers (Fig.9.)

Trajan was received warmly in Rome and won over the Senate. He undertook a series of works projects across the empire, notably the construction and repair of roads, and provided charity for the poor (Figs.10 & 11.). In the Senate House today, there are reliefs on display showing tax bills being burnt in the Forum, an act which relieved many from the burden of payment.

Conquest of Dacia AD 101-6

Since the AD 80s, the Dacians (of modern Romania) had been causing problems on the Danube frontier. After a successful campaign against Decebalus of Dacia in 101-2, the Dacians were still not brought to heel in the longer term

Fig.13. Brass *dupondius* of Trajan (98-117), struck in Rome, AD 104-11. The reverse of the coin shows a schematic representation of the famous bridge of Apollodorus which was built across the Danube. BMC 914 © British Museum (28mm)

Fig.14. Brass *sestertius* of Trajan (98-117), struck in Rome, AD 103-11. Trajan is shown on horseback spearing a Dacian. RIC II, 534. Found on the Isle of Wight. © Portable Antiquities Scheme IOW-9F63D1 (32mm)

Fig.11. Brass *dupondius* of Trajan (98-117) struck in Rome, AD 114-7. This coin also celebrates the new road, the Via Traiana, built between Benevento and Brindisi. RIC II, 641. Found in Cheshire. © Portable Antiquities Scheme, LVPL-89BE90 (23.5mm)

Fig.15. Silver *denarius* of Trajan (98-117), struck in Rome, AD 104-111. The reverse shows a Dacian captive seated right; this coin celebrates Trajan's conquest of Dacia in AD 106. RIC II, 218. Found in Leicestershire. © Portable Antiquities Scheme LEIC-99D086 (18mm)

Fig.16. Brass *sestertius* of Trajan (98-117), struck in Rome, AD 103-11. Victory is shown attaching a shield, inscribed VIC DAC, to a tree, celebrating Trajan's conquest of Dacia in AD 106. RIC II, 527. Found in Essex. © Portable Antiquities Scheme ESS-B92131 (33mm)

Fig.12. Silver *denarius* of Trajan (98-117), struck in Rome, AD 101-2. This coin, struck early in Trajan's reign shows Mars carrying a trophy, celebrating Trajan's initial victory in Dacia. The name of Nerva in the obverse inscription makes it clear that Trajan was legitimately adopted by his successor. Found in Suffolk. © Portable Antiquities Scheme SF-99DB60 (18mm)

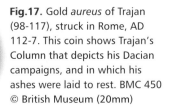

Fig.17. Gold *aureus* of Trajan (98-117), struck in Rome, AD 112-7. This coin shows Trajan's Column that depicts his Dacian campaigns, and in which his ashes were laid to rest. BMC 450 © British Museum (20mm)

Fig.18. Brass *sestertius* of Trajan (98-117), struck in Rome, probably c.AD 112-4. The reverse shows the Basilica Ulpia, which was part of Trajan's massive new forum complex. BMC 983 © British Museum

(Fig.12.). Trajan had to start a fresh campaign in 105, this time involving the building of a massive bridge across the Danube, designed by the architect Apollodorus (Fig.13.).

A year later, after fierce fighting, the Dacian capital Sarmizegethusa had been taken and Decebalus was dead (Figs.14-16.). Today, you can still follow the course of Trajan's campaign by looking at the wonderful reliefs on Trajan's Column in Rome, constructed to house his ashes (Fig.17.).

Trajan's Forum & A New Port

To the north of Forum of Caesar, Trajan built the most magnificent series of buildings. There was an enormous hall or basilica with rows of massive columns, a series of markets, and even a Greek and Latin library. Pliny tells us that this was the most wonderful of all Roman buildings – the remains of Trajan's Forum has recently been opened to the public and is well worth a visit (Fig.18.).

Trajan also built a new harbour at Portus,

Fig.19. Brass *sestertius* of Trajan (98-117), struck in Rome, AD 104-11. This coin shows Trajan's new harbour built at Portus, near Ostia. BMC 770A. © British Museum (34mm)

Fig.20. Gold *aureus* of Trajan (98-117), struck in Rome, AD 103-111. This coin celebrates Trajan's annexation of the Kingdom of Nabataea (capital at Petra) in AD 106 – it became the Roman province of Arabia. This coin is one of many that calls Trajan the "Best Prince" (*Optimo Princ*). RIC II, 142. © British Museum (19mm)

Fig.21. Brass *semis* of Trajan (98-117), probably struck in Antioch in AD 116. These coins seem to have travelled west in large numbers, there being 20 in the Bath Spring finds. The bull's head countermark is associated with Antioch; one of the Bath coins also had this countermark. Found in Northamptonshire. © Portable Antiquities Scheme, NARC-B683C2 (24mm)

Fig.22. Brass *sestertius* of Trajan (98-117), struck in Rome, AD 114-7. The reverse shows Trajan standing over personifications of Armenia, Euphrates and Tigris; this coin celebrates Trajan's victory over the Parthians. RIC II, 642. Found in Sussex. © Portable Antiquities Scheme, SUSS-977223 (33mm)

Rome's second port, built just north of Ostia. Claudius had already built a harbour at Portus; Trajan's harbour was built further inland and would have enabled more efficient import of grain and other foodstuffs for Rome (Fig.19.). Also through this port would have arrived thousands of animals destined for the Colosseum where Trajan held lavish games.

Arabia (AD 106) & the Eastern War (AD 114-7)

In 106, Trajan annexed the kingdom of Nabataea (based in modern Jordan, with its capital at Petra) and created the new province of Arabia. This was to become one of the most important frontier provinces in the eastern part of the Empire, the borders being patrolled by troops using camels (Fig.20.).

To the east of the Roman Empire, the Parthians ruled over modern Iraq and Iran. Rome and Parthia often came into conflict over the small kingdom of Armenia that lay between their territories. The Parthians had just put a ruler on the throne of Armenia; Trajan was not having this and quickly moved to Antioch (Fig.21.). He made Armenia a Roman Province and then, in AD 115,

advanced down into Mesopotamia (modern Iraq) taking the Parthian capital at Ctesiphon (Figs.22 & 23.). However, in 116, the Parthians took the offensive and Trajan was forced to retreat. It was ultimately left to his successor Hadrian (117-38) to make peace with the Parthians.

Trajan's Death

Trajan's last year on the throne was marred by momentous Jewish rebellions in North Africa, Egypt and Cyprus. Trajan's health was deteriorating and on 9 August 117, he died at Selinus in Cilicia (in south-east Turkey). Trajan was an extremely popular emperor and his reputation lived on for centuries (Fig.24.).

Even in his life time he was known as the "Best Prince" (*Optimus Princeps*); after his death, the senate would pray that a new emperor would be "more fortunate than Augustus, better than Trajan". His ashes were laid under his column which stood at the end of his new Forum in Rome (Fig.17.).

Trajan's Coinage

Trajan's coins are very common, the PAS database having about 1,452 specimens. There

Fig.24. Brass *sestertius* of Trajan (98-117), struck in Rome, AD 114-7. The coin celebrates the foresight (*Providentia*) of the emperor. RIC II, 663. Found in Somerset. © Portable Antiquities Scheme SOMDOR-85FD63 (34mm)

Fig.25. Brass *sestertius* of Trajan (98-117), struck in Rome, AD 114-7. This wonderful coin honours the Senate and People of Rome, showing Felicity. RIC II, 672. Found in Cambridgeshire. © Portable Antiquities Scheme BH-D556B5 (33mm)

Fig.23. Brass *sestertius* of Trajan (98-117), struck in Rome, AD 116. The reverse shows Trajan seated on a platform with a Prefect. Trajan is crowning the new ruler of Parthia, King Parthamaspates, who is being presented to a kneeling Parthia. RIC II, 667. Found in Surrey. © Portable Antiquities Scheme SUR-91AB23 (34mm)

Fig.26. Brass *dupondius* of Trajan (98-117), struck in Rome, AD 103-11. The obverse shows the distinctive radiate crown used to distinguish the dupondius. RIC II, 516. Found in Somerset. © Portable Antiquities Scheme, SOMDOR-D73207 (27.5mm)

Fig.27. Silver *denarius* of Plotina (died AD 129), wife of Trajan, struck in Rome during Trajan's reign, c.AD 112-7. This rare coin shows an altar with a figure of Pudicitia (modesty), a fitting image for this respected lady. RIC II, 733. Found in North Yorkshire. © Portable Antiquities Scheme, LANCUM-CA5EA2 (20mm)

are two gold *aurei* on the database, but I show two pieces from the British Museum collection here (Figs.17 & 20.). There is a higher number of silver *denarii* (653, some plated; Figs.,10, 12 & 14.) to *sestertii* (436, Figs.13, 15, 16, 18, 19, 22-5.).

Sestertii (436) also outnumber the combined total for *dupondii* (166, Figs.11 & 26.) and *asses* (177, Fig.9.).

Semisses of Trajan also have been found in small numbers in Britain, the denomination not normally being used in this province (Fig.21.).

Trajan's Female Relatives

Trajan struck coins for three empresses. His wife Plotina was a pious and highly respected woman, although she had no children (Fig.27.). Hadrian, under Trajan's guardianship from an early age, was Plotina's favourite and it is thought by some that she engineered his succession.

Marciana, Trajan's sister, is commemorated with a wonderful *sestertius* on which she rides on a chariot pulled by two elephants (Fig.29.). Matidia was the daughter of Marciana and the mother of Sabina. Sabina was to become the wife of Hadrian. Coins of these women are rare, there

Fig.28. Brass commemorative *sestertius* of Marciana (died AD 114), sister of Trajan, struck at Rome, c.AD 114-7. The reverse shows Marciana being drawn in a cart by two elephants. RIC II 750. Found in Cambridgeshire. © Portable Antiquities Scheme, CAM-7766F5 (32mm). A similar coin was found in Devon (DEV-FA2637)

Fig.29. Silver *denarius* of Matidia, daughter of Marciana and mother-in-law of Hadrian, made Augusta in AD 113. This coin was struck under Trajan in Rome, c.AD 113-7. RIC 759. Found in Cornwall. © Portable Antiquities Scheme, CORN-1AB9D8 (21mm)

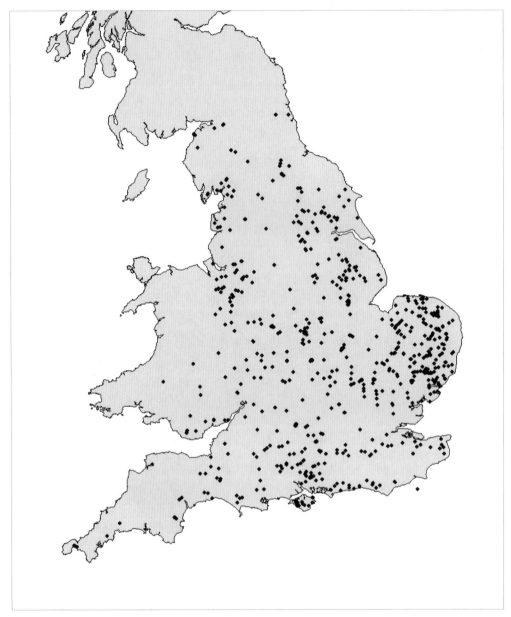

Map 1. Distribution of coins of Nerva and Trajan recorded with the Portable Antiquities Scheme. (© Dan Pett)

only being one for Plotina and Matidia on the database and two for Marciana.

Coin Distribution in Britain

In Trajan's reign there was a general consolidation of the province. The Roman armies retreated from their Scottish gains to a new frontier based on the Stanegate Road across northern England, which was garrisoned by troops at forts like Vindolanda. To the south, York, Chester and Caerleon legionary fortresses were being transformed from turf and timber to stone. Given this situation, it comes as no surprise that coins of Nerva and Trajan are found throughout the province. (See Map 1)

Chapter XIII
Coinage of Hadrian, Sabina and Aelius Caesar
(AD 117-38)

Section of Hadrian's Wall at Walton Crags.

Hadrian's Early Years & Accession

Hadrian came from a Roman family that had originally been settled at Italica in Spain at the end of the 2nd Punic War with Carthage (217-201 BC) (Fig.1.). He was born in AD 76 and was only nine when his father died. One of his guardians was Trajan, who was later to become emperor (AD 98-117 – see previous chapter). Hadrian learnt much about military life and statecraft from Trajan and became a favourite of Plotina, Trajan's wife. Some have suggested that Plotina staged the "death-bed declaration" by Trajan that stated that Hadrian should be his heir.

Fig.1. Silver *denarius* of Hadrian (117-38), struck at Rome, AD 134-8. The reverse shows Hadrian raising the personification of Spain (Hispania). Between them is a rabbit, a species native to Spain. RIC II, 327. Found in Hertfordshire, BH-0FB3B1. © Portable Antiquities Scheme. (17mm)

Fig.4. Gold *aureus* of Hadrian (117-38), struck in Rome, AD 125-8. The reverse denotes that Hadrian is Consul for the third time, and he is shown riding his favourite horse Borysthenes. RIC 187d. Found in the Didcot Hoard, 1995. © British Museum. (19mm)

Fig.2. Brass *dupondius* of Hadrian (117-38), struck at Rome, AD 119-21. The obverse inscription declares the emperor as "Caesar Traianus Hadrianus Aug[ustus]", making it clear that Hadrian has been adopted by Trajan. The reverse shows Moneta. RIC II, 600b. Found in Hampshire, HAMP-FD8BB6. © Portable Antiquities Scheme. (26mm)

Fig.3. Silver *denarius* of Hadrian (117-38), struck at Rome, AD 134-8. The reverse shows Germania – Hadrian initiated a major new fortified frontier in Germany, just before he came to Britain to build his wall. RIC II, 302. Found in Nottinghamshire, DENO-F24A33. © Portable Antiquities Scheme. (18mm)

Fig.5. Stone milestone erected 8 miles from the Roman fort of Kanovium in North Wales in the early years of Hadrian's reign, AD 120-1. © British Museum

Whatever the truth, Hadrian acted swiftly and gained lifelong dislike from the Senate for having four ex-Consuls from their number executed at the start of his reign – they were potential rivals and Hadrian was already the master of "realpolitik". His coins were also used to strengthen his grip on the throne, declaring that he was "Caesar Traianus Hadrianus Augustus" (Fig.2.).

Withdrawal from Mesopotamia & Securing the Frontiers (AD 117-21)

Hadrian quickly withdrew from Mesopotamia (modern Iraq) and gave up the conquests made by Trajan in the region. However, he managed to negotiate a very favourable peace with the Parthians. He then consolidated Rome's grip on Dacia (Romania) which had been conquered by Trajan. In Germany, Hadrian decided to build a linear frontier (the "limes"), which consisted of a turf rampart with timber palisade (Fig.3.). This was supported by large forts. A similar stone frontier was erected in southern Algeria and Tunisia, called the *Fossatum Africae*. This was probably to keep the nomads and their goats out at crucial times of the year when crops were being sown and grown. On all his early travels, Hadrian was to ride his faithful horse Borysthenes (Fig.4.).

Hadrian in Britain (AD 122)

"...Hadrian set out for Britain, and there he corrected many abuses and was the first to construct a wall, eighty miles in length, which was to separate the barbarians from the Romans." (*The Augustan History*)

It appears that Hadrian did more than just start the building of his wall across the north of England when he arrived in the province in AD 122. He probably encouraged further urban development – the forum at Wroxeter was built in his reign. There was also work on the roads, for example in North Wales, which might have been associated with silver, lead and copper mining (Fig.5.).

Fig.6. Brass *sestertius* of Hadrian (117-38), struck at Rome, AD 119. This is one of the few coins of Hadrian which have been found relatively near to Hadrian's Wall. RIC II c.f. 563b. Found in Northumberland, NCL-44A517. © Portable Antiquities Scheme. (32mm)

Fig.7. Copper-alloy *as* of Hadrian (117-38), struck at Rome, AD 119. This is the first time that Britannia appears on the coinage of Britain. It is thought that this coin was struck to celebrate a victory in northern Britain. RIC 577b. Found on the Isle of Wight, IOW-072A43. (25mm)

Fig.8. Copper-alloy *as* of Hadrian (117-38), struck at Rome, AD 119. The reverse shows Britannia seated – this type was struck exclusively for use in Britain. RIC II, c.f. 577a. Found in Surrey, SUR-E0D5E1. © Portable Antiquities Scheme. (25mm)

Fig.9. Brass *sestertius* of Hadrian (117-38), struck at Rome, AD 118. The reverse shows Hadrian handing out largesse to citizens. RIC II, 552. Found in Leicestershire, LEIC-05EBF6. © Portable Antiquities Scheme. (34mm)

Fig.10. Silver *denarius* of Hadrian (117-38), struck at Rome, AD 125-8. The reverse shows implements used in pagan sacrifices. RIC II, 198. Found in Hampshire, HAMP3036. © Portable Antiquities Scheme. (18.5mm)

Fig.11. Gold *aureus* of Sabina (wife of Hadrian, 117-38), struck at Rome, AD 128-37. The reverse shows Vesta holding a sceptre and the Palladium (statuette of Athena taken from Troy). BMC 922. © British Museum. (19mm)

It has also been suggested that he drained the Fens, providing land that could grow more food, quite possibly for the garrison of his new wall to the north. Hadrian's Wall was 80 Roman miles long, with outpost forts, turrets, mile-castles, and auxiliary forts. It must have generated much activity in the north and would have brought more money into the region (Fig.6.). Hadrian's most famous coin type for Britain was the first ever depiction of Britannia on a coin. These coins are quite commonly found in Britain; they were struck in Rome especially for use in this province (Figs.7-8.).

Rome & Tivoli

Back in Italy, Hadrian decided not to reside in Rome. I believe that this was partly due to the fact that he was not popular with the Senate, although he must have been more popular with the citizens who received hand-outs! (Fig.9.). Instead, he built a massive palace complex at Tivoli (larger than any town in Roman Britain). This palace consisted of many exotic elements, including one part which was based on Egyptian sites. However, when he did visit Rome, he held court in his marvellous new domed temple, the Pantheon, which is still marvelled at by thousands of tourists every day (Fig.10.).

The Empress Sabina (died AD 137)

Hadrian married Trajan's niece Sabina in AD 100, but it was not a happy marriage. It is even alleged that while Hadrian was in Britain she had improper relationships with two of his senior officials, one of them being the famous historian Suetonius (who wrote the *Twelve Caesars*).

Coins were struck for Sabina from AD 128 showing her with two major hairstyles. The earlier hairstyle shows her hair dressed on top of her head (Figs.11-12.). The later coins, struck after the trip to Egypt in AD 130, show her with a

Fig.12. Brass *sestertius* of Sabina, struck under Hadrian at Rome, c.AD 128-37. The reverse shows Ceres, the goddess of grain and the harvest. RIC II, 1019. Found in Hertfordshire, BH-5D5863. © Portable Antiquities Scheme. (29mm)

Fig.13. Silver *denarius* of Sabina, struck under Hadrian at Rome, c.AD 128-37. The reverse shows Venus, the goddess of love. RIC II, 396. Found in Buckinghamshire, BH-8E97E7. © Portable Antiquities Scheme. (20mm)

Fig.14. Silver *denarius* of Sabina, struck under Hadrian at Rome, c.AD 128-37. The reverse shows Juno, the Queen of the Gods. RIC II 395a. Found in Hampshire, HAMP-BEE193. © Portable Antiquities Scheme. (18mm)

Fig.15. Silver *denarius* of Sabina, struck under Hadrian at Rome, c.AD 128-37. The reverse shows Concordia; however, there was not great concord between Hadrian and Sabina. RIC II, 398. Found in Hampshire, HAMP-937F42). © Portable Antiquities Scheme. (18mm)

Fig.16. Brass *sestertius* of Sabina, struck under Hadrian at Rome, c.AD 128-37. The reverse shows Pudicitia, the personification of modesty. RIC II, 1032. Found in Nottinghamshire, DENO-1E9CB5. © Portable Antiquities Scheme. (32mm)

twisted plait – these coins are the more common (Figs.13-16.).

Although Hadrian did not have a good relationship with his wife, she had the first major issue of coins for an empress; earlier empresses only receiving sporadic coinages, if any at all. Furthermore, when Sabina died in AD 137, commemorative coins were struck for her by Hadrian (Fig.17.).

Fig.17. Gold *aureus*, struck by Hadrian to commemorate Sabina, Rome, AD 137-8. The reverse shows the empress being taken to heaven by an eagle. BMC 955. © British Museum. (18mm)

Egypt & Antinous (AD 130)

Hadrian visited Egypt in AD 130 (Figs.18-19.). It does seem that Hadrian was homosexual and we know that he was heartbroken when his young companion Antinous was drowned in the Nile (Fig.20.). Only a small number of provincial coins were ever struck for Antinous and they are not found in Britain (Fig.21.).

The Jewish Revolt (AD 132-5)

Hadrian's reign was marred by a catastrophic war in Judaea. The Jews continued to have real grievances with Rome and rebelled under Simon bar Kockba in AD 132. After three years of fighting, the loss of at least three Roman legions and over 600,000 dead on the Jewish side, the rebellion was put down. Hadrian renamed Jerusalem *Aelia Capitolina* (after his family name) and

Fig.18. Brass *sestertius* of Hadrian (117-38), struck at Rome, AD 132-4. The reverse shows the imperial galley which Hadrian used on his voyages. RIC II 706. Found in Surrey, SUR-A600A3. © Portable Antiquities Scheme. (30mm)

Judaea was renamed Syria-Palestina. During the revolt, the Jews issued their own coinage, some pieces being over-struck on *denarii* of Hadrian (Fig.22.). At this time it appears that some worn earlier coins were countermarked for use at

Fig.19. Copper-alloy *as* of Hadrian (117-38), struck at Rome, AD 134-8. The reverse shows the personification of Egypt reclining. RIC II, 839. Found on the Isle of Wight, IOW-139D56. © Portable Antiquities Scheme. (25mm)

Fig.20. Plated copy of a silver *denarius* of Hadrian (117-38), struck at Rome, AD 134-8. The reverse shows the personification of the River Nile, the river in which Hadrian's boyfriend Antinous drowned. RIC II, 310. Found in Hampshire, HAMP-802A46. © Portable Antiquities Scheme. (16mm)

Fig.21. Copper-alloy coin of Antinous, struck at Alexandria, c.AD 130. The reverse shows Antinuos riding as Hermes (Mercury). BM 2932. © British Museum. (27mm)

Fig.22. Silver quarter shekel of the second Jewish Revolt over-struck on a *denarius* of Hadrian in AD 133-5. The inscriptions name Simon bar Kockba and Jerusalem. BMC 61. © British Museum. (19mm)

Fig.24. Gold *aureus* of Aelius (136-8), struck in Rome. The reverse shows Concordia. BMC 998. © British Museum. (19mm)

Fig.23. Brass *dupondius* of Trajan (AD 98-117), struck at Rome. It is countermarked in front of the head with a laureate pattern which was apparently applied at Antioch just before the Jewish Revolt (AD 132-5). The second countermark behind the head is unclear. The reverse is not illustrated because it is worn flat. The coin was found in Cornwall so it might have travelled by sea from the eastern Mediterranean around Spain and Gaul to Britain. CORN-5E39D1. © Portable Antiquities Scheme. (25mm)

Fig.25. Silver *denarius* of Aelius (136-8), struck at Rome, AD 137. The reverse shows Concordia. RIC II, 436a. Found in Wiltshire, WILT-B0E164. © Portable Antiquities Scheme. (18mm)

Fig.26. Brass *sestertius* of Aelius (136-8), struck at Rome, AD 137. The reverse shows the personification of Pannonia, the province where Aelius served as governor after he had been nominated Hadrian's successor. RIC II, 1059. Found in Essex, ESS-1AD453. © Portable Antiquities Scheme. (31mm)

Fig.27. Silver *denarius* of Hadrian (117-38), struck at Rome, AD 125-8. The reverse shows seven stars above a crescent. RIC II, 202. Found on the Isle of Wight, IOW-4DBE03. © Portable Antiquities Scheme. (18mm)

Antioch, probably to indicate that they were legal tender (Fig.23.).

Aelius, the Succession & Hadrian's Death (AD 136-8)

In AD 136, the ageing Hadrian turned his mind to the succession. His first choice was a young man called L. Ceionius Commodus who came from a distinguished senatorial family. He was nominated Hadrian's heir and renamed Lucius Aelius Caesar (Figs.24-25.).

In 137, Aelius was sent to govern the province of Pannonia on the River Danube – much of Hungary and parts of Austria and Balkan

Fig.28. The Didcot Hoard of 126 *aurei*, ranging from the reign of Nero (AD 54-68) to Antoninus Pius (AD 138-61). A total of 35 coins of Hadrian and 3 of Sabina were in the hoard which was found in 1995. All of the coins have been acquired by the British Museum. © British Museum

countries (Fig.26.). However, he fell ill on his return to Rome and died in January 138. Hadrian was obviously upset, not the least because of the large amount of money that had been wasted on "donatives" given to the army at the accession of the young emperor! Hadrian only survived a few more months, dying in July 138. He was to be succeeded by Antoninus Pius (138-61) who will be the subject of the next chapter.

Hadrian's Coinage

Hadrian struck an enormous imperial coinage at Rome, in gold, silver and base metal, reflected by over 1,588 coins of Hadrian on the PAS database. Four gold *aurei* have been found in Welsh hoards. There are around 604 silver *denarii* (Figs.1, 3, 10, 20 & 27.), 585 brass *sestertii*

(Figs.6, 9 & 18.), 128 *dupondii* (Fig.2.), and 264 *asses* (Figs.7, 8 & 19.).

Sabina has 89 coins on the database. There are no gold coins recorded for her, but 59 silver *denarii* (Figs.13-15.), 17 brass *sestertii* (Figs.12 & 16.), two *dupondii*, and 7 *asses*.

Although few gold coins of Hadrian and Sabina have been recorded with the PAS, 38 *aurei* of theirs were found in the Didcot Hoard, discovered in 1995 (Figs.28 & 4.). The distribution of the coins of Hadrian and Sabina is nationwide (see Map), but it is interesting to note that there is not an enormous number in the north of England near Hadrian's Wall. Coins of Aelius are rare in Britain, although they were struck in all denominations. The PAS has records for 8 *denarii* (Fig.25.) and 11 base metal coins (Fig.26.).

Map 1. Distribution of coins of Hadrian and Sabina recorded with the Portable Antiquities Scheme.
(© Dan Pett)

Chapter XIV

Coinage of Antoninus Pius, Faustina I, Aurelius Caesar and Faustina II

(AD 138-161)

Antoninus Pius' Accession (AD 138)

As mentioned previously, Hadrian initially chose Aelius Caesar as his successor. However, after the premature death of Aelius, Hadrian adopted Antoninus Pius as his successor. (Fig.1.). At 52 years old, Antoninus was a respected and seasoned member of Hadrian's government who had a reputation for fairness and moderation. Early in his reign, he made two important decisions. Firstly, he insisted, against senatorial opinion, that Hadrian should be made a god, even threatening to give up the throne if he should be thwarted (Fig.2.). Secondly, he promoted his adopted son (a favourite of Hadrian), Marcus Aurelius, to the rank of Caesar (junior emperor) (Fig.3.).

Faustina I (died AD 141)

Antoninus Pius' wife, Faustina, a woman of "excessive frankness and levity in her way of life" was declared Augusta (empress) by the Senate and coins were struck for her early in Pius' reign (Figs.4 & 23.), before she died in AD 141. This resulted in an enormous commemoration coinage (unprecedented in scale and duration) which might have lasted at least a decade – because she was made a goddess, the inscription reads *Diva Faustina* (Figs.5-9.). In addition to this coinage, a temple was built in her (and later Pius') honour in the Roman Forum (Figs.9 & 10.).

Fig.2. Gold *aureus* struck by Antoninus Pius (AD 138-61) to commemorate the deified Hadrian, Rome, c.AD 138. The reverse shows Hadrian being flown to heaven on an eagle – the eagle was believed to represent the soul of the dead emperor. BMC IV, 32. © British Museum (20mm)

Fig.1. Silver *denarius* of Antoninus Pius as Caesar (Feb-July, AD 138), struck at Rome. The head of Antoninus is depicted in the style of his successor, Hadrian. BMC III, 1005. © British Museum (18mm)

Fig.3. Silver *denarius* of Antoninus Pius (AD 138-61) with a portrait of Marcus Aurelius as Caesar (junior emperor) on the reverse. Struck in Rome in AD 140. RIC III, 415a. Found on the Isle of Wight, IOW-9BD0B7. © Portable Antiquities Scheme (18mm)

Fig.4. Brass *sestertius* of Faustina I, struck at Rome, AD 138-41. The reverse shows a peacock (bird of Juno, queen of the gods) under a throne. BMC 1118. © British Museum (35mm)

Fig.5. Silver *denarius* struck under Antoninus Pius (AD 138-61), commemorating Faustina I, Rome, c.AD 141-50. The obverse type, with unveiled head, is not recorded for this reverse type of Ceres in RIC. RIC III, 382b variant. Found in Hertfordshire, BH-897157. © Portable Antiquities Scheme (19mm)

Fig.6. Brass *sestertius* of Faustina I, struck after her death by Antoninus Pius (138-61), Rome, c.AD 141-50. The reverse inscription would have read AVGVSTA; Vesta is shown holding a sceptre. RIC III, 1124. Found in Essex, ESS-560CA3. © Portable Antiquities Scheme (31mm)

Fig.7. Brass *dupondius* of Faustina I, struck after her death by Antoninus Pius (138-61), Rome, c.AD 141-50. The reverse inscription read AETERNITAS; Juno stands left, holding a sceptre. RIC III, 1155. Found in Derby, DENO-C22F36. © Portable Antiquities Scheme (25mm)

Fig.8. Copper-alloy *as* of Faustina I, struck after her death by Antoninus Pius (138-61), Rome, c.AD 141-50. The reverse is AETERNITAS with Pietas standing; this is a "Coin of British Association", struck in Rome for use in Britain. RIC III, 1162. Found in Wiltshire, WILT-C58E77. © Portable Antiquities Scheme (23mm)

Fig.9. Silver *denarius* struck to commemorate Faustina I (DIVA FAVSTINA; died AD 141) by Antoninus Pius, Rome, c.141-50. This scarce coin shows the Temple of the Deified Faustina (and later Antoninus) which is still visible in the Roman Forum (see Fig.10.). RIC III, 343. Found in Lincolnshire, LIN-2E7675 (18mm)

Fig.10. Temple of Diva Faustina and Divus Antoninus in Rome, constructed in the reign of Antoninus Pius. Construction began after the death of Faustina in AD 141. © Sam Moorhead

Pax Romana

Antoninus Pius did not need to conduct many serious wars. There was a major insurrection in Mauretania and a few minor revolts in Germany, Dacia, Greece, Judea, and Egypt. (He did initiate a new advance into Scotland – see below). Pius did not need to lead armies as "no one had so much authority among foreign nations as he". He was able to concentrate on the government and administration of the empire: "He ordered his procurators (financial officials) to levy tribute in moderation…and he did not take pleasure in any profit as a result of which a provincial was oppressed." He was so fair in his dealings that "He brought down the eminence of the imperial position completely to the level of the ordinary citizen." There can be no doubt that in Pius' peaceful reign we can witness the height of the Golden Age of the Roman Empire (Fig.11.).

Advance Against the Caledonians (AD 142)

One campaign, which was celebrated on the coinage of Pius, was against the Caledonians of

Fig.11. Brass *sestertius* of Antoninus Pius, struck at Rome, 145-61. The reverse shows Pax (Peace) setting fire to arms, an entirely appropriate type for Antoninus Pius whose reign was generally peaceful. RIC III, 777. Found in Cheshire, LIN-8E4974. © Portable Antiquities Scheme (30mm)

Fig.12. Brass *sestertius* of Antoninus Pius (AD 138-61), struck in Rome, c.AD 143-4. The reverse mentions celebrates Pius' advance into Scotland, with Victory and BRITAN[NIA] visible on the coin. BMC 1613. © British Museum (35mm)

Fig.13. The Antonine Wall, built c.AD 142-8, showing the rampart and the berm to the left (south) and the ditch and the view to the north. The wall ran for 37 miles between the Clyde Isthmus and the Firth of Forth; it was built of turf and timber on a stone foundation, with a selection of forts along its course. Much of the wall is still visible today and it is a World Heritage Site.

Scotland (Fig.12.). Under the governor of Britain, Lollius Urbicus, the Roman legions advanced to central Scotland in c.AD 139-40 where they constructed the Antonine Wall, a turf and timber structure that can still be seen in many places over its course of 37 miles between the Clyde and the Forth (Fig.13.). It is thought that the major reason for this advance was to provide Pius with a victory that would gain praise in Rome – Britannia was regarded as one of the most dangerous provinces, the Caledonians as the wildest of its occupants.

Unrest in Britain (AD 150s?)

It is possible that there was unrest in northern Britain in the AD 150s although there is no conclusive evidence. Probably the most common coin of Antoninus Pius found in Britain is a copper-alloy *as* which shows a "mournful" Britannia on the reverse (Figs.14 & 15.). It was struck in Rome in AD 154-5, and some scholars have suggested that it commemorates the suppression of a rebellion in northern Britain. It is one of a series of coins struck only for issue in Britain (see Coins of British Association, below).

Aurelius Caesar & Faustina II

Marcus Aurelius was to spend almost his entire life at Antoninus Pius' side (Figs.3, 16 & 24.). The young prince fervently studied philosophy, but developed a keen sense of duty to the empire. He married Pius' daughter, Faustina II, in AD 145 and coins were also struck for her in her father's reign (Fig.17.).

Coins of British Association

In the reign of Hadrian, there were a few coin types which were apparently struck for use only in Britain (see the Britannia *as* in the previous chapter). This has been made clear from research into the 12,000+ coins excavated from the Sacred Spring at Bath in 1979-80 by the late David Walker. He showed that particular issues of *dupondii* and *asses* were extremely common in the reign of Antoninus Pius as well, notably ones struck in the year AD 154-5 when Pius held the Tribunician Power for the 18th time and Marcus Aurelius held it for the 9th time.

Records on the Portable Antiquities scheme are showing that, as we would expect, such coins are common across the whole Province of

Fig.14. Copper-alloy *as* of Antoninus Pius (AD 138-61), struck at Rome, AD 154-5. The reverse shows Britannia. This coin is a "Coin of British Association", being struck in Rome for exclusive use in Britain. RIC III, 934. Found in Wiltshire, WILT-0824F2 (25mm)

Fig.15. Copper-alloy *as* of Antoninus Pius (AD 138-61), struck at Rome, AD 154-5. This coin has quite a distinctive oval flan, common for this issue. RIC III, 934. Found in Cambridgeshire, BH-642FA1 (25mm)

Fig.18. Brass *dupondius* of Antoninus Pius (138-61), struck at Rome, AD 154-5. This coin has the inscription LIBERTAS COS IIII S C on the reverse and shows Libertas holding the cap of liberty. It is a "Coin of British Association", this type being struck exclusively for use in Britain. RIC III, 933. Found on the Isle of Wight, IOW-09A766 (26.5mm)

Fig.16. Silver *denarius* of Marcus Aurelius as Caesar (138-61), struck at Rome, AD 147-8. The reverse shows Minerva. RIC III, 438a. Found in Essex, ESS-C70DA3. © Portable Antiquities Scheme (17.5mm)

Fig.17. Brass *sestertius* of Faustina II, struck under Antoninus Pius (138-61), Rome, c.AD 145-61. The obverse inscription tells us that she is the daughter of Antoninus Pius. RIC 1379. Found in Northamptonshire, NARC-36F3C3. © Portable Antiquities Scheme (32mm)

Britannia (Figs.8, 14, 15 & 18). What this tells us is that at the Mint in Rome, a particular workshop (*officina*) was tasked with striking batches of coins intended to supply Britain, sometimes choosing appropriate designs like Britannia. The Roman administration was such that these bags of coin were efficiently transported from the mint to Britain – it would be fascinating to identify the route and means of transport used.

Antonine Peak for Coin Loss in Britain

When we record Roman coins on the Portable Antiquities Scheme database, we assign them to particular periods, as determined by the coin expert Richard Reece. This enables us to compare particular sites and regions in Britain, and is now enabling us to compare Britannia with other provinces in the Roman Empire. Coins from the reign of Antoninus Pius fall into Reece Period 7 (AD 138-61). Whereas on urban and military sites the first major peak in coin loss tends to be in Period 4 (Flavian emperors, AD 69-96) (Fig.19.). Rural sites (as recorded with the Portable Antiquities Scheme) normally show the first major peak in Period 7 with the coinage of Antoninus Pius (Fig.20.). This probably reflects

the large quantity of coins of Pius and his family arriving in Britain, but probably also shows how the monetary economy was now reaching rural regions. This is yet another important contribution that the PAS data has made to our study of Roman coin use in Britain.

Antoninus' Death

Antoninus died at the age of 75. On his death-bed, he bequeathed the empire to Marcus Aurelius and instructed that the gold statue of Fortuna, which used to be placed in the imperial bedchamber, should be given to the new emperor. He then gave the watchword "equanimity" to the tribune, rolled over and died. "The Senate deified him, everyone competing in their efforts, for all praised his dutifulness, clemency, intelligence and purity." Marcus Aurelius honoured his adoptive father with an issue of commemorative coins at the start of his reign in AD 161. (Figs.21 & 22.).

Antoninus Pius' Coinage

Antoninus Pius struck coins in all metals for his family. Pieces for Pius, Faustina I, Marcus Aurelius as Caesar and Faustina II are commonly

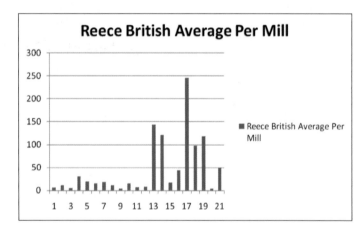

Fig.19. This graph shows the breakdown of about 150,000 Roman coins by period, carried out by Richard Reece in the 1990s. You will see that there are more coins in Period 4 (AD 69-96: the Flavians) than in Period 7 (AD 138-161: Antoninus Pius). Most of these coins came from Roman towns and forts. (Note: for convenience sake, we use Per Mill rather than percent in our calculations – the numbers are easier to work with!)

Fig.20. This graph shows the breakdown of about 50,000 PAS coins (from sites with more than 20 coins recorded) by period, carried out by Philippa Walton (National Finds Advisor at the British Museum). You will see that there are more coins in Period 7 (AD 138-161: Antoninus Pius) than in Period 4 (AD 69-96: the Flavians). Most of these coins come from rural sites such as farmsteads, villas and villages. This shows how larger quantities of coin arrived in the countryside later than in towns and villas.

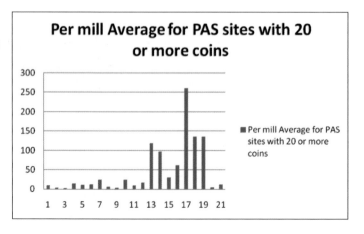

Fig.21. Silver *denarius* struck under Marcus Aurelius (161-80) to commemorate Antoninus Pius, Rome, c.AD 161. The reverse shows the funeral pyre. RIC III, 436. Found in Derbyshire, DENO-0429F6. © Portable Antiquities Scheme (17mm)

Fig.22. Silver *denarius* struck under Marcus Aurelius (161-80) to commemorate Antoninus Pius, Rome, c.AD 161. The reverse shows an eagle (the symbol of the dead emperor's soul) standing on an altar. RIC III, 431. Found in Suffolk, SF-0D5143. © Portable Antiquities Scheme (18mm)

Fig.23. Gold *aureus* of Faustina I, struck in AD 138-9 at Rome. The reverse shows Concordia. RIC III, 327. Found in the Didcot Hoard in 1995. © British Museum (18mm)

Fig.24. Gold *aureus* of Marcus Aurelius as Caesar, struck in Rome in AD 146/7. The reverse shows Minerva and that Marcus holds the Tribunician Power and is Consul for the second time. RIC III, 435b. Found in the Didcot Hoard in 1995. © British Museum (20mm)

Fig.25. Copper-alloy *as* of Antoninus Pius (AD 138-61), struck at Rome, probably in AD 140-1. This coin appears to be unpublished. The reverse inscription TR POT III COS III dates the coin to AD 140-1 for Antoninus Pius. Found in Cambridgeshire, PAS-83F9C1. © Portable Antiquities Scheme (23mm)

Fig.26. Copper-alloy contemporary copy of an *as* of Faustina I, probably struck in Britain, c.AD 141-61. The obverse inscription reads DIVA FAVSTINA; the reverse shows an uncertain woman standing. A few copies of Faustina were found in the Sacred Spring at Bath. Found in Suffolk, SF-FD8527. © Portable Antiquities Scheme (26mm)

Map 1. The distribution of coins of Antoninus Pius and Faustina I recorded with the PAS. (© Philippa Walton)

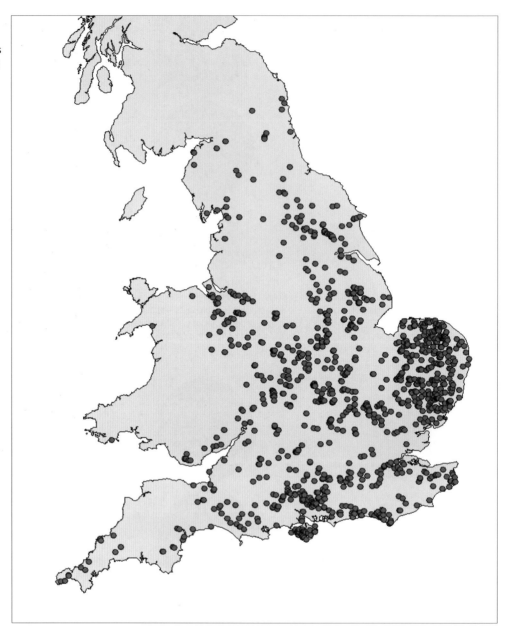

found in Britain. There are 1,567 coins recorded for Antoninus Pius on the PAS database, 518 *denarii*, 624 *sestertii*, 181 *dupondii* and 235 *asses*. For Faustina I there are 507 coins, 239 *denarii*, 234 *sestertii*, 181 *dupondii* and 238 *asses*. Gold coins of this period, however, are rarely found, although the recent Didcot hoard did contain 18 *aurei* from the reign of Antoninus Pius (Figs.23 & 24.). The map shows the widespread distribution of coins of Antoninus Pius and Faustina I across Britain (see Map 1).

Amongst the PAS coins are some unpublished pieces (Fig.25.) and some hitherto unknown contemporary copies (Fig.26.) which underlines the importance of recording with the Portable Antiquities Scheme.

Antoninus Pius.

Chapter XV
Coinage of Marcus Aurelius, Faustina II, Lucius Verus, Lucilla, Commodus and Crispina
(AD 161-192)

Fig.1. Gold *aureus* of Marcus Aurelius (AD 161-80), struck at Rome, AD 176-7. The reverse refers to further victories over the barbarians on the Danube. BMC IV, 737. © British Museum (20mm)

Fig.2. Silver *denarius* of Marcus Aurelius (AD 161-80), struck at Rome in AD 179. This coin was struck in the last year of his reign and shows Mars. RIC III, 406. Found in Hampshire, HAMP-BECE61. © Portable Antiquities Scheme (18mm)

Fig.4. Copper-alloy *sestertius* of Marcus Aurelius (AD 161-80), struck at Rome in AD 173-4. The reverse shows Jupiter seated left. RIC III, 1098. Found in Hampshire, SUR-A5C1D2. © Portable Antiquities Scheme (32mm)

Fig.5. Gold *aureus* of Lucius Verus (AD 161-9), struck at Rome, AD 165-6. The coin shows Verus riding down an enemy, referring to his victories in Mesopotamia (Iraq). BMC IV, 415. © British Museum (20mm)

Fig.3. Copper-alloy *sestertius* of Marcus Aurelius (AD 161-80), struck at Rome in AD 171-4. The reverse shows Roma seated holding Victory. RIC III, cf. 1033. Found in Hampshire, SUR-A62A53. © Portable Antiquities Scheme (32mm)

Accession of Marcus Aurelius and Lucius Verus (AD 161)

Marcus Aurelius had been designated as a future emperor by Hadrian (AD 117-38) and was adopted as a junior emperor (Caesar) during the reign of Antoninus Pius (AD 138-61); Marcus also married Pius' daughter Faustina II – the previous chapter covered the coinage of Marcus as Caesar under Pius.

Upon the death of Pius, Marcus Aurelius became senior emperor (Augustus) (Figs.1-4.). However, Marcus chose to share the throne with

Fig.6. Silver *denarius* of Lucius Verus (AD 161-9), struck at Rome in AD 162-3. The reverse shows Providentia (foresight) standing with a globe and horn of plenty. RIC III, 491. Found in Staffordshire, WMID-D9A1B7. © Portable Antiquities Scheme (17.5mm)

Fig.7. Silver *denarius* of Lucius Verus (AD 161-9), struck at Rome in AD 163-4. The reverse shows Mars, referring to the Parthian War. RIC III, 514. Found in Shropshire, HESH-4EA604. © Portable Antiquties Scheme (18mm)

Fig.9. Silver *denarius* of Lucius Verus (AD 161-9), struck at Rome in AD 165. The reverse shows a Parthian seated, his hands bound behind his back amongst weapons. This coin celebrates Verus successes against the Parthians in Mesopotamia. RIC III, 540. Found in Yorkshire, YORYM-8FC205. © Portable Antiquities Scheme (18.5mm)

Fig.8. Brass *sestertius* of Lucius Verus (AD 161-9), struck at Rome in AD 163-5. This coin shows Mars and was struck during the campaigns of Verus in Mesopotamia (Iraq). RIC III, c.f. 1379/1420. Found in Warwickshire, LEIC-F1CBE5. © Portable Antiquities Scheme (31mm)

Fig.10. Brass *sestertius* of Lucius Verus (AD 161-9), struck at Rome in AD 166. This coin was struck to celebrate Verus' victory over the Parthians in Mesopotamia (Iraq). RIC III, c.f. 1456. Found on the Isle of Wight, IOW-0916F7. © Portable Antiquities Scheme (31mm)

Lucius Verus (the son of Aelius Caesar) who had also been adopted by Antoninus Pius – this was the first joint reign of the later Roman Empire.

Marcus Aurelius was to rule from 161 to 180 and was based mostly at Rome and on the Danube frontiers. Lucius Verus ruled from 161 to 169 and was based for much of his reign in the eastern part of the empire (Figs.5-10.). Marcus struck coins for his empress Faustina II (Figs.11-15.) and for his daughter Lucilla who married Lucius Verus in AD 164. (Figs.16-21.).

War in the East (AD 161-6)

In AD 161, the Parthians (ruling in Mesopotamia, modern Iraq), invaded Armenia and put a pro-Parthian ruler on the throne. They also defeated the Roman army of Syria in the process. Lucius Verus went East in 162 to lead a campaign against the Parthians and in 163 had retaken Armenia, putting a new pro-Roman king on the throne (Figs.7-8.).

In 165, the Romans reached the Parthian capital at Ctesiphon (in Iraq) where they sacked the Parthian king's palace. In the autumn of 166 Verus and Marcus shared a triumph in Rome, also taking the titles Armeniacus, Parthicus Maximus and Medicus, the last title referring to the region of Media in northern Mesopotamia (Figs.9-10.). One unfortunate effect of the Parthian War was that the soldiers brought back plague with them which broke out into a major epidemic in AD 167, killing many in Rome and the western empire.

War on the Danube Frontier (AD 166-80) & death of Lucius Verus (AD 169)

In 166-7, Germanic barbarians had begun to invade over the Danube. It required Marcus and Lucius to go north in 168 to help resolve the problem. However, Verus died in early 169; he was buried in Hadrian's mausoleum in Rome. However, Marcus had to go back to the Danube frontier where he fought bitter campaigns against the Quadi and the Marcomanni tribes until AD 175 when the tribes had been defeated (Fig.1.).

Marcus' army had to endure horrible conditions, ranging from scorching summers in Hungary to cold and wet winters. The brutality of this war is depicted on the Column of Marcus Aurelius which still stands in Rome. It was now

Fig.11. Silver *denarius* of Faustina II, struck under Marcus Aurelius at Rome, c.AD 161-75. The reverse shows Juno, queen of the gods, with her peacock. RIC III, 688. Found in Leicestershire, LEIC-B51791. © Portable Antiquities Scheme (18mm)

Fig.12. Silver *denarius* of Faustina II, struck under Marcus Aurelius at Rome, c.AD 161-75. The reverse shows Juno seated. RIC III, 698. Found in Bedfordshire, CAM-5E8162. © Portable Antiquities Scheme (15mm)

Fig.14. Copper-alloy *sestertius* of Faustina II, struck under Marcus Aurelius at Rome, c.AD 61-75. The reverse of this scarce coin shows Cybele the "Great Mother" goddess seated holding a drum with two lions by her throne. RIC III, 1663. Found in Leicestershire, LIEC-D1F687. © Portable Antiquities Scheme (31mm)

Fig.13. Copper-alloy *sestertius* of Faustina II, struck under Marcus Aurelius at Rome, c.AD 161-75. The reverse shows Juno or Faustina holding an infant between two children. RIC III, 1649. Found in Hampshire, HAMP-CE9F37. © Portable Antiquities Scheme (32mm)

Fig.15. Gold *aureus* struck for the deified Faustina II by Marcus Aurelius, Rome, AD 176-180. Faustina is shown as the "Mother of the Camp", holding a Phoenix with three legionary standards nearby. BMC IV, 704. © British Museum (20mm)

that Marcus Aurelius started to write his *Meditations* which show a stoic and resolute emperor who was determined to do his duty in adverse circumstances. Although Marcus celebrated his Danubian victories in a triumph in Rome in 176, he and his son Commodus had to return to fight again in the region in 178-9 (Fig.2.)

Revolt of Cassius and Promotion of Commodus (AD 175)

In 175, the governor of Syria, Gaius Avidius Cassius rebelled against Marcus. It is said that Cassius thought that Marcus had died; and less credibly that Marcus' wife, Faustina II (Figs.11-14.), had even supported Cassius. However, although he gained support in the eastern provinces, Cassius was assassinated by soldiers loyal to Marcus. So as to ensure the succession, Marcus made his son Commodus Caesar in AD 175 (Fig.22.); two years later, in AD 177, Commodus was promoted to junior Augustus (Fig.23.). Meanwhile, Faustina II had died in south-east Turkey in 176 while touring the empire with Marcus. Although she had apparently been disloyal, Marcus paid her great respect and a large commemorative coinage was struck (Fig.15.).

Death of Marcus Aurelius (AD 180)

Cassius' mistake over Marcus' "premature" demise seems understandable given that Marcus had been ill for several years before he died. It is suggested that he had cancer and that he became addicted to an opium-based drug. He finally died in Vienna in March 180. He was buried in Hadrian's Mausoleum and was declared a god by the Senate. He was to become one of the most famous Roman emperors in late Roman, medieval and Renaissance times, his *Meditations* inspiring many to live honourable and dutiful lives:

"For everything I do, whether by myself of with another, must have as its sole aim the service and harmony of all." (Bk 7.5)

Commodus (AD 177-92)

Commodus had gone through much experience of warfare on the Danube with his father and had also accompanied Marcus to the east (Figs.24-25.). However, he was not cut in his father's mould and soon slipped into a life of debauchery. There were attempts on his life early in his reign; his elder sister (and widow of Lucius Verus) Lucilla being implicated and subsequently executed (Figs.16-21.).

Fig.16. Gold *aureus* of Lucilla (AD 164-9), struck at Rome. The reverse shows "Modesty" (Pudicitia). BMC IV, 347. © British Museum (20mm)

Fig.17. Silver *denarius* of Lucilla, struck at Rome, AD 164-9. The reverse shows Juno, Queen of the Gods, with her peacock. RIC III, 772. Found in Northamptonshire, NARC-2B4055. © Portable Antiquities Scheme (19mm)

Fig.19. Brass *sestertius* of Lucilla, struck at Rome, AD 164-9. The reverse is worn, but might show Venus. RIC III, c.f. 1763/9. Found in Surrey, SUR-B01364. © Portable Antiquities Scheme (30mm)

Fig.20. Brass *sestertius* of Lucilla, struck at Rome, AD 164-9. The reverse shows Vesta (Goddess of the Hearth) holding a ladle and a statuette of Athena (Palladium). RIC III, 1779. Found in Surrey, SUR-F8A521. © Portable Antiquities Scheme (30mm)

Fig.18. Probably a contemporary copy of a *denarius* of Lucilla. The prototype was struck at Rome, c.AD 164-9. The coin is of crude style and might be plated. Furthermore, the reverse type of VENVS VICTRIX is only recorded for a gold *aureus*. RIC III, c.f. 736. Found in Leicestershire, LEIC-C23096. © Portable Antiquities Scheme (15.5mm)

Fig.21. Brass *sestertius* of Lucilla, struck at Rome, AD 164-9. The reverse shows Venus holding a small Victory. RIC III, 1776. Found in Bedfordshire, NARC-135FF6. © Portable Antiquities Scheme (29mm)

Fig.22. Copper-alloy *as* of Commodus as Caesar (under Marcus Aurelius), struck at Rome, AD 175-6. The reverse proclaims that Commodus is the "Hope of the People". Found in Derbyshire, DENO-D3ACE6. © Portable Antiquities Scheme (27mm)

His wife, Crispina, whom he married in AD 177, was also banished early in his reign and was executed in exile in 183 (Figs.31-33.).

Commodus ruled through various powerful individuals while he led a life of depravity. The first of these ministers, Perennis, was executed in AD 185 after 1500 disaffected soldiers marched from Britain to Rome (it is possible that Perennis had acted unjustly in suppressing a mutiny in Britain earlier in the year). Whatever the exact details of the events, coins were struck celebrating victory in Britain in AD 184-5, and Commodus took the title "Britannicus" in AD 184. (Figs.26-27.). The emperor's second minister, Cleander, died in 190 after the people of Rome rose in rebellion over the price of grain.

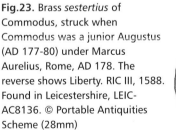

Fig.23. Brass *sestertius* of Commodus, struck when Commodus was a junior Augustus (AD 177-80) under Marcus Aurelius, Rome, AD 178. The reverse shows Liberty. RIC III, 1588. Found in Leicestershire, LEIC-AC8136. © Portable Antiquities Scheme (28mm)

Commodus as Hercules and as a Gladiator (AD 190-2)

After Cleander's death, Commodus became more unhinged and associated himself with the demigod Hercules (Figs.28-29.). He even regarded himself as being the son of Jupiter (c.f. Fig.25.).

Fig.24. Brass *dupondius* of Commodus, struck at Rome in AD 179-80. The reverse shows Mars. RIC III, 292a/296. Found on the Isle of Wight, IOW-822203. © Portable Antiquities Scheme (22mm)

Fig.25. Brass *sestertius* of Commodus (AD 180-92), struck at Rome in AD 181-2. The reverse shows Jupiter. RIC III, 322/343. Found in Somerset, SOM-29B083. © Portable Antiquities Scheme (29mm)

Fig.27. Brass *sestertius* of Commodus (AD 180-92), struck at Rome, AD 184-5. The reverse shows Victory seated – the inscription below has worn away, but once read VICT BRIT, celebrating a victory in Britain. RIC III, 440/451-2. Found in Hertfordshire, BH-E50103. © Portable Antiquities Scheme (30mm)

Fig.28. Gold *aureus* of Commodus (AD 180-92), struck at Rome, AD 191. The reverse shows Commodus, in the guise of Hercules, with the personification of Africa. BMC IV, 355. © British Museum (20mm)

Fig.26. Silver *denarius* of Commodus (AD 180-92), struck at Rome, AD 187-88. The coin shows Liberty (Libertas); on the obverse, Commodus is titled BRIT[annicus] as a result of military victories in Britain during his reign. RIC III, 168. Found in Shropshire, WMID-8A8E02. © Portable Antiquities Scheme (18mm)

Fig.30. Silver *denarius* of Commodus (180-92), struck at Rome, AD 192. The reverse shows Victory. This coin was struck in the last year of Commodus' reign. RIC III, 237. Found in Essex, ESS-47B0D2. © Portable Antiquities Scheme (16mm)

Fig.31. Silver *denarius* of Crispina, struck under Commodus, Rome, c.AD 180-2. The reverse proclaims Concord, but there was little between Crispina and Commodus – he exiled her early in his reign and had her executed. RIC III, 278. Found in Cambridgeshire, BH A41C92. © Portable Antiquities Scheme (17mm)

Fig.29. Silver *denarius* of Commodus (AD 180-92), struck at Rome, AD 191-2. The reverse shows Hercules, the demi-god with whom Commodus associated himself. RIC III, 254a. Found in Cambridgeshire, CAM-9C1B66. © Portable Antiquities Scheme (17mm)

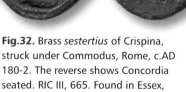

Fig.32. Brass *sestertius* of Crispina, struck under Commodus, Rome, c.AD 180-2. The reverse shows Concordia seated. RIC III, 665. Found in Essex, ESS-7BA853. © Portable Antiquities Scheme (33mm)

Fig.33. Copper-alloy *dupondius* or *as* of Crispina, struck under Commodus, Rome, c.AD 180-2. The reverse shows Juno, Queen of the Gods, with her peacock. RIC III, 681. Found in Hertfordshire, BH-324273. © Portable Antiquities Scheme (25mm)

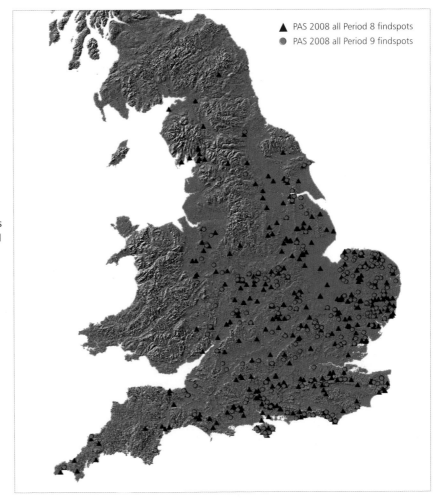

Map 1. Distribution of coins in Britain from the reigns of Marcus Aurelius and Lucius Verus (Period 8) and Commodus (Period 9), as recorded on the Portable Antiquities Scheme database. (© Philippa Walton)

▲ PAS 2008 all Period 8 findspots
● PAS 2008 all Period 9 findspots

After a fire that destroyed much of the centre of Rome, Commodus proclaimed himself the re-founder of Rome, but called the city "The Colony of Commodus". However, Commodus became increasingly obsessed with the gladiatorial games, even entering the arena and killing wild (although tame in many cases) animals (as shown in Ridley Scott's blockbuster film "Gladiator" which does play with the truth somewhat!).

It was while he was planning more extravagant games (in which it was rumoured he would kill two consuls) that his staff decided he had to go. After an attempt to poison him failed, he was strangled by an athlete. Although he was initially buried quickly, four years later his remains were placed in Hadrian's Mausoleum. However, his reputation was never good: "More savage than Domitian, more foul than Nero". (Fig.30.)

Coins from the reigns of Marcus Aurelius, Lucius Verus and Commodus in Britain

The PAS Database (www.finds.org.uk) has recorded 1,195 coins of Marcus Aurelius and 122 for Lucius Verus. Coins of Verus are quite scarce, not only because he ruled for eight years, but also because it does seem that fewer were struck. There are 601 coins of Faustina II, but much more interestingly 221 for Lucilla.

Lucilla only became an empress in 164, but she has double the number of coins as her husband Lucius Verus. It does seem possible that coins continued to be struck for her after Verus' death in AD 169, but much more research is needed.

With 624 coins, Commodus is on a par with Faustina II. Crispina's short marriage to Commodus (177 to early 180s) is reflected by only 72 coins on the database.

So far as denominations are concerned, *sestertii* are the dominant coin in this period with 1,822 on the database; there are only 645 *denarii* and 546 *dupondii/asses*. However, this is the last great period for the *sestertius*, the denomination becoming much rarer under the Severan emperors who are to follow. Gold *aurei* of these rulers are rarely found in Britain and there are none on the database – all those shown in this chapter are from the British Museum's collection.

Coins of this period, AD 161-92, are found across the entire province (see Map 1).

Chapter XVI

Roman Coinage AD 193-217

Pertinax (193), Didius Julianus (193), Pescennius Niger (193-4), Clodius Albinus (193-7), Septimius Severus (193-211), Julia Domna, Caracalla (198-217), Plautilla and Geta (209-11)

Fig.1. Silver *denarius* of Pertinax (AD 193), struck in Rome. The reverse shows the emperor sacrificing. RIC IV, 13a. Found in Oxfordshire, BERK-DF2625 (16mm)

Fig.2. Brass *sestertius* of Pertinax (AD 193), struck in Rome. This is one of only four *sestertii* of Pertinax recorded on the PAS Database. Found in Surrey, SUR-F8C763. © Portable Antiquities Scheme (27mm)

Death of Commodus & the Ensuing Civil Wars

Commodus was assassinated by Laetus, the Prefect of the Praetorian Guard, along with Eclectus, Commodus' chamberlain (New Year's Eve, 192). They prompty asked Pertinax to become the next emperor. He was only to last 87 days before Didius Julianus bought the empire; he survived only 66 days. By then, three other contenders had emerged: Clodius Albinus in Britain, Pescennius Niger in Syria, and Septimius Severus in Illyricum. In 193, Severus deposed Didius Julianus and took Rome; the following year he defeated and killed Niger; Severus tolerated Albinus until finally defeating and killing him at Lyon in 197. This left Severus the sole ruler of the Roman Empire; he was to elevate his two sons, Caracalla and Geta, as co-emperors to ensure the succession. Many of these people had long and varied careers before becoming emperors.

Pertinax (1 January-28 March, 193)

Pertinax started his career as a teacher of grammar, but then decided to follow a career in the imperial service. In the reign of Marcus Aurelius (161-80), he served in the Parthian War and then in Britain. He was to command a cavalry unit in Moesia, the German fleet (in the North Sea and on the Rhine) and then Legio I in Rhaetia and Noricum. He was also a procurator (financial official), promoted to the Senate and was nominated as Consul twice. He was made governor of Moesia and Dacia and then Syria and Africa (two of the richest provinces in the empire). He therefore knew a great deal about the empire.

Pertinax pledged 12,000 *sestertii* (3,000

Fig.3. An incomplete silver *denarius* of Didius Julianus (AD 193), struck at Rome. This is one of only two coins of Didius Julianus on the PAS Database. RIC IV, c.f. 2. Found in Essex, ESS-091A22 (14mm)

Fig.4. Brass *sestertius* of Didius Julianus (AD 193), struck at Rome. There is one *sestertius* of Didius Julianus on the PAS Database, but without a photograph. BMC V, 25. © British Museum (30mm)

Fig.5. Silver *denarius* of Manlia Scantilla, wife of Didius Julianus (AD 193), struck at Rome. There are two coins of Manlia Scantilla on the PAS Database, but without photographs. BMC V, 11. © British Museum (17mm)

Fig.6. Brass *sestertius* of Didia Clara, daughter of Didius Julianus (AD 193), struck at Rome. Her coins are very rare and there are none on the PAS Database. BMC V, 40. © British Museum (33mm)

Fig.7. Silver *denarius* of Pescennius Niger (AD 193-4), struck at Antioch. All coins of Niger were struck in the East and are very rare in western provinces. There are none on the PAS Database. BMC V, 304. © British Museum (19mm)

denarii) to each of the Praetorian guards, but then attempted to instil more discipline in their ranks. He also tried to stop corruption amongst the palace staff. He was very popular with the people of Rome because of this, but creating enemies amongst his palace officials and the army was a mistake. The former allowed 300 of the latter to storm the palace and kill Pertinax after a reign of only 87 days. However, he had been respected by the people of Rome and Septimius Severus later added the name Pertinax to his title on his early coins (Fig.10.).

Pertinax struck coins at Rome in gold, silver and copper, but they are generally rare with only 14 on the PAS database (Figs.1 & 2.)

Didius Julianus (28 March-1 June, 193)

Didius Julianus was another man with a lengthy career in the imperial service. He had held the offices of *quaestor* (financial official), *aedile* (official for public works and games) and *praetor* (legal official) in Rome; he was once even in charge of child welfare in Italy. He commanded Legio XXII in Germany and defeated the barbarian tribes of the Chauci and Chatti. He was made a consul and survived a charge of treason against Commodus. He was governor of Bithynia

and Africa and was made joint consul with Pertinax in AD 175.

On the death of Pertinax, Didius Julianus found himself in a bidding game with Titus Flavius Sulpicianus. Julianus finally gained the throne by promising the Praetorian Guards 25,000 *sestertii* each; he eventually gave them 30,000! However, he was loathed by the people who abused him in the forum and at the games. It was during his reign that three other claimants to the throne emerged: Clodius Albinus, Pescennius Niger, and Septimius Severus. Severus swiftly marched his legions from Illyricum to Italy, taking the naval base at Ravenna en route. Everyone began to desert Julianus who was finally murdered by a soldier in the palace on 1 June after a reign of only 66 days. Septimius Severus arrived in Rome shortly afterwards.

Didius Julianus struck coins in all metals. There were also coins struck for his wife Manlia Scantilla and daughter Didia Clara. Coins of all of these rulers are very rare. Scantilla and Clara did survive the death of Julianus (Figs.3-6.).

Pescennius Niger (193-4)

Born of humble parents, Pescennius Niger worked his way up through the ranks. He held

Fig.8. Silver *denarius* of Clodius Albinus, as Caesar under Septimius Severus (AD 193-5), struck at Rome. The coin follows the convention of showing junior emperors bare-headed. RIC IV, 7. Found in Hampshire, HAMP-ADB647. © Portable Antiquities Scheme (18mm)

Fig.9. Copper-alloy *sestertius* of Clodius Albinus, as Caesar under Septimius Severus (AD 193-5), struck at Rome. The reverse probably shows Felicitas. RIC IV, c.f. 52. Found in East Yorkshire, YORYM-CE8D95. © Portable Antiquities Scheme (28mm)

Fig.10. Brass *sestertius* of Septimius Severus (AD 193-211), struck at Rome in AD 194. The reverse shows the three "Monetae" personifications of money and the mint. In Severus' reign the mint began to be run by military officials. RIC IV, 678. Found in Sussex, SUSS-730F01. © Portable Antiquities Scheme (32mm)

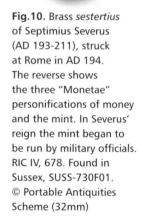

Fig.11. Silver *denarius* of Septimius Severus (AD 193-211), struck at Rome in AD 196-7. The reverse celebrates Severus' arrival in Rome in late AD 196 after stabilising the Eastern Empire. RIC IV, 74. Found in Leicestershire, LEIC-7DA794. © Portable Antiquities Scheme (18mm)

Fig.12. Silver *denarius* of Septimius Severus (AD 193-211), struck at Rome in AD 200. The reverse shows Victory and celebrates Severus' victory over Parthia in AD 198. RIC IV, 150. Found in Staffordshire, DENO-994581. © Portable Antiquities Scheme (17mm)

the rank of centurion before ultimately commanding the Syria army under Commodus (180-92). He was to become a Consul and was even held in high regard by Severus under whom he had served in Gaul. After the execution of Niger, he did receive the support of some people in Rome for his disciplined and honest character; furthermore, as governor of Syria, Niger did have command of a powerful army. Severus advanced east against Niger and won decisive victories at Cyzicus and Nicaea in western Turkey. He offered to make terms with Niger but to no avail. After a further battle at Issus in south-eastern Turkey, Niger fled on horseback, but was killed near Antioch.

Niger struck coins at Antioch, his capital in Syria. There were a few gold *aurei* but the great bulk of his coinage was silver *denarii*. No base metal coins were issued. His silver coins often proclaim the "justice" of his regime. Coins proclaiming his military prowess were, however, premature in their declarations. Coins of Niger are extremely rare in Britain, none being recorded on the database (Fig.7.).

Clodius Albinus (193-7)

Albinus came from an old Roman family that had settled in Hadrumetum in Africa (modern Sousse in Tunisia). Albinus commanded a Dalmatian cavalry unit before becoming a legionary commander. He defeated the barbarians on the Rhine frontier, before he was made a legal magistrate (Praetor) and finally Consul. It is even written that Commodus had asked him to become his Caesar, but Albinus declined, being aware of Commodus' poor reputation; many doubt this story.

When he declared himself a candidate for supreme power, he was governor of Britain where he had command over a substantial force, including three legions. Initially, Severus acknowledged Albinus as a junior colleague (Caesar) in the west. However, Severus decided that his sons, Caracalla and Geta, should succeed him so started to make moves against Albinus. Albinus declared himself Augustus in 195 or early 196, probably when he realised that Severus had no intention of accommodating another emperor.

On 19 February 197, after a bloody showdown near Lyon, Albinus' body was decapitated and

Fig.13. Arch of Septimius Severus in the Roman Forum at Rome. It was built to celebrate Severus' victory over the Parthians in AD 197. © Sam Moorhead

the head sent to Rome. Severus rode over his body before it was thrown into the River Rhone. With the defeat of Albinus, Severus was now supreme in the Roman world.

In the first two years of his reign, AD 193-5, coins were struck for Albinus as Caesar at Rome, alongside coins of Septimius Severus (Figs.8-9.). They were struck in all metals, but gold is rare. After Albinus realised that Severus did not have good intentions, a new mint was set up in Gaul, probably at Lyon. Here Albinus had gold and silver struck proclaiming him Augustus. Only one base metal issue, of *asses*, is known from Lyon for Albinus.

Septimius Severus (AD 193-211)

Severus was the first African to become a Roman emperor. A native of Leptis Magna on the coast of modern Libya, Severus was probably of Punic or Berber stock, keeping his African accent throughout his life. He was from a prominent provincial family and two relatives had become Consuls. He went to Rome when he was 18 and embarked on his career. He was a *quaestor* (financial magistrate) in Rome before serving in Sardinia. He then served as a military commander in Africa, Spain and Syria before he was made a governor in Gaul and then Sicily. Finally,

he was made Consul in the reign of Commodus before becoming governor of Upper Pannonia.

Severus had one eye on the throne after the death of Commodus and after the demise of Pertinax Severus' legions at Carnuntum declared him emperor on 19 April 193. He then moved against Didius Julianus in Rome and, as recounted above, took residence in Rome before dispatching his other rivals Pescennius Niger and Clodius Albinus (Fig.11.). Severus did deify Pertinax, striking commemorative coins and adding Pertinax's name on his early coins (Fig.10.).

Severus was a ruthless ruler. When he arrived in Rome he had many of the Praetorian Guard executed; the rest were disbanded. After the demise of Niger and Clodius Albinus, 29 senators who had been their supporters were executed. Severus maintained control of the empire by gaining the support of the army. He improved soldiers pay, and allowed them to marry and to live with their wives. He also put on lavish games in Rome to gain the support of the people.

The Parthian War (AD 197)

In 195, Severus had conducted a minor campaign in the East, but in 197 he led a major offensive against the Parthians. He took his army

Fig.14. Silver *denarius* of Julia Domna, struck under Septimius Severus (AD 193-211) at Rome, AD 193-6. The reverse shows Venus. RIC IV, 536. Found in Dorset, SOMDOR-151946. © Portable Antiquities Scheme (19mm)

Fig.15. Silver *denarius* of Julia Domna, struck under Septimius Severus (AD 193-211) at Rome, AD 196-211. The reverse shows Pudicitia (Modesty). RIC IV, 576. Found in Staffordshire, WMID-9B32B5. © Portable Antiquities Scheme (19mm)

Fig.17. Brass *sestertius* of Caracalla as Caesar (AD 196-8) under Septimius Severus, struck at Rome in AD 196-7. The reverse announces that the young Caracalla is the "perpetual hope" for the future of Rome. This rare coin is one of only three *sestertii* of Caracalla recorded on the PAS database. Found on the Isle of Wight, IOW-5ACA82. © Portable Antiquities Scheme (28mm)

Fig.18. Silver *denarius* of Caracalla as joint Augustus (198-211) with Septimius Severus, struck at Rome in AD 207. Note that Caracalla took the name Antoninus Pius – as a result a number of his coins are sometimes mistakenly attributed to the earlier Antoninus Pius (AD 138-61). Found in Hampshire, HAMP-F01245. © Portable Antiquities Scheme (17.5mm)

Fig.16. Silver *denarius* of Caracalla as Caesar (AD 196-8) under Septimius Severus, struck at Rome in AD 196-8. The increasing amount of copper used in silver coins is apparent from the green verdigris on this coin. RIC IV, 9. Found in Cornwall, CORN-DB8307. © Portable Antiquities Scheme (17mm)

down the Euphrates and then sacked the capital at Ctesiphon – all men were killed and 100,000 women and children sold into slavery. Severus was to remain in the East for five years. His Parthian successes were to be celebrated by the building of a triumphal arch in the Roman Forum and on coins (Figs.12-13.). His second wife, Julia Domna, was a native of Syria. She was a well-educated lady and was to play an important role in the careers of her sons Caracalla and Geta (Figs.14-15.).

Caracalla, Geta & Plautilla

With the fall of Albinus, Severus was able to nominate his own sons as his successors. In AD 196, Caracalla was made Caesar (Fig.16.); two years later he was promoted to Augustus (Fig.18.). His younger brother, Geta, was made Caesar in 198 (Fig.19.) and Augustus in 209 (Fig.20.). In 202, Caracalla was married to Plautilla, the daughter of Gaius Fulvius Plautianus, the commander of the Praetorian Guard. Plautianus was not popular with many and Caracalla disliked him and his daughter (Figs.21-22.). Plautianus was implicated in plot, real or fabricated we are not sure, and was executed in 205.

Caracalla immediately banished Plautilla to the island of Lipari; he had her killed when he came to power in AD 211. However, relations between Caracalla and Geta were growing worse, fuelled by the machinations of their supporters.

The British Campaign (AD 208-11)

There had been trouble on the northern frontier in Britain since the AD 190s, the Caledonian and Maeatae tribes of Scotland being bought off by the Roman governor. However, it seems that there were still problems which led to an appeal to Severus in c.207. Severus probably used this as a pretext to take his sons away from Rome on a military campaign. In 208 Severus (suffering from gout) and his family arrived at York. Caracalla led the invasion of Scotland (alongside Severus) whilst Geta saw to imperial affairs at York. The Roman army did advance at least as far as Carpow-on-Tay where a fort was built, but the campaigns came to an end with the death of Severus at York in AD 211; Caracalla quickly signed a treaty with the Scottish barbarians and rushed back to Rome with Geta. On his deathbed, Severus said, "When I took over the state chaos reigned everywhere; I am leaving it at

Fig.19. Silver *denarius* of Geta as Caesar (AD 198-209) under Septimius Severus, struck at Rome in AD 200-2. The reverse shows Castor, one of the two Heavenly Twins. RIC IV, 6. Found in Staffordshire, WMID-792AB8. © Portable Antiquities Scheme (18mm)

Fig.20. Silver *denarius* of Geta as Augustus (AD 209-212), struck at Rome, AD 212. Coins of Geta as Augustus are much rarer than his coins as Caesar. Found in Leicestershire, LEIC-543491. © Portable Antiquities Scheme (17mm)

Fig.22. Silver *denarius* of Plautilla (wife of Caracalla, AD 202-5), struck at Rome, c. 202-4. The reverse shows Concordia. RIC IV, 359. Found in Dorset, SOMDOR-6BF2F7. © Portable Antiquities Scheme (19mm)

Fig.21. Silver *denarius* of Plautilla (wife of Caracalla, AD 202-5), struck at Rome, c. 202-4. The reverse shows Plautilla and Caracalla clasping hands, a scene rather stretching the truth of their relationship! RIC IV, 362. Found in Lincolnshire, LIN-493661. © Portable Antiquities Scheme (18mm)

Fig.23. Gold *aureus* struck under Caracalla and Geta to commemorate Septimius Severus, Rome, AD 211. Severus died at York, where he was probably cremated. BMC V, 19. © British Museum (21mm)

peace, even Britain...the empire which I am leaving [my sons] is a strong one..." (Fig.24.).

Caracalla & Geta (AD 211-212)

Severus told his sons to "Work in harmony, pay the soldiers and scorn everyone else". However, Caracalla and Geta fell at the first hurdle – they could not work together and their supporters were at loggerheads. In the end, after only 10 months of joint rule, Caracalla murdered Geta who died in the arms of his mother (Julia Domna). Caracalla was now sole emperor.

Caracalla (AD 212-217)

Caracalla did follow his father's advice with regards to the army (Fig.25.). Severus had increased military pay, but we are not sure by how much. We do know that soldiers received a 50% pay rise under Caracalla, which might have raised a legionary's pay to as much as 900 *denarii* a year. The cost to the Roman treasury might have been 70 million *sestertii* (or 17.5 million *denarii*) a year. In AD 212 Caracalla passed a momentous law which gave Roman citizenship to all free-born men in the Roman Empire, thus breaking down the barriers between Romans and provincials.

Fig.24. Brass *sestertius* of Septimius Severus (AD 193-211). struck at Rome in AD 209-11. The reverse celebrates victories over the Britons, obviously relating to Severus' campaigns in Scotland. BMC V, 811. © British Museum (33mm)

Fig.25. Silver *denarius* of Caracalla as sole Augustus (AD 212-17), struck at Rome, AD 214. The reverse shows Jupiter holding a thunderbolt, his eagle to the left. Found in Oxfordshire, BERK-CECD82. © Portable Antiquities Scheme (19mm)

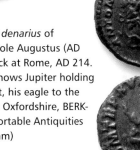

Fig.26. Base silver (probably a contemporary copy) *denarius* of Caracalla as joint Augustus with Geta (AD 211-12), struck at Rome in AD 212. The obverse inscription ends with BRIT[annicus], celebrating Caracalla's "victory" in Britain. RIC V, c.f. 192. Found in Somerset, SOM-9443B3. © Portable Antiquities Scheme (18.5mm)

Fig.27. Silver *denarius* of Julia Domna, struck under Caracalla (AD 211-17) at Rome. Coins of Julia Domna struck under Caracalla are much scarcer than those struck under Septimius Severus. RIC IV, 390. Found in Lincolnshire, LIN-804835. © Portable Antiquities Scheme (18mm)

Fig.28. Brass *sestertius* of Julia Domna, struck under Caracalla (AD 211-17), at Rome in AD 211-2. The reverse refers to Julia Domna as mother of Caracalla and Geta, of the Senate and of the State (fatherland). RIC IV, 588. Found in Essex, SOMDOR-9F8F80. © Portable Antiquities Scheme (33mm)

Fig.29. Silver *radiate* of Caracalla (AD 212-17), struck at Rome in AD 217. This coin is still often called the *antoninianus* by numismatists, but this is not an ancient name. The coin weighs 1.5 *denarii*. BMC V, 187. © British Museum (25mm)

Fig.30. Silver-plated contemporary copy of a *denarius* of Septimius Severus (AD 193-211). The prototype from which this coin was copied was struck in Rome in AD 207. The plating has chipped off just to the left of the shield on the reverse. See RIC IV, 211. Found in Sussex, SUSS-2CDF63. © Portable Antiquities Scheme (18mm)

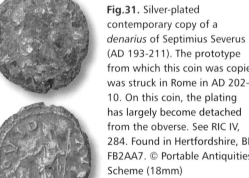

Fig.31. Silver-plated contemporary copy of a *denarius* of Septimius Severus (AD 193-211). The prototype from which this coin was copied was struck in Rome in AD 202-10. On this coin, the plating has largely become detached from the obverse. See RIC IV, 284. Found in Hertfordshire, BH-FB2AA7. © Portable Antiquities Scheme (18mm)

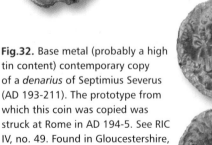

Fig.32. Base metal (probably a high tin content) contemporary copy of a *denarius* of Septimius Severus (AD 193-211). The prototype from which this coin was copied was struck at Rome in AD 194-5. See RIC IV, no. 49. Found in Gloucestershire, NMGW-8CD4C8. © Portable Antiquities Scheme (c. 16mm)

Caracalla won victories in Germany, earning the title Germanicus and then travelled east where he visited the site of Troy. However, in Alexandria, Caracalla's men massacred many unarmed citizens – the cause of this action is unknown. He was finally murdered by an assassin during the Parthian campaign of AD 217. His mother, Julia Domna, died soon afterwards, and the ashes of both were interred in the Mausoleum of Hadrian at Rome (Figs.27-28.).

Caracalla introduced the first silver "radiate" coin (traditionally called the *antoninianus* by numismatists, but with no authority) in AD 215. It has been suggested that this coin was a double-*denarius* although it only weighed one and a half *denarii*. It was used into the reign of Elagabalus (AD 218-222 – see next chapter), but did not then reappear until the joint reign of Balbinus and Pupienus in AD 238. From AD 238, the radiate became the standard denomination until c.AD 296 (Fig.29.).

Coins of the Severans

As one would expect, coins of Septimius Severus are the most common, there being 947 on the PAS Database. The vast majority (861)

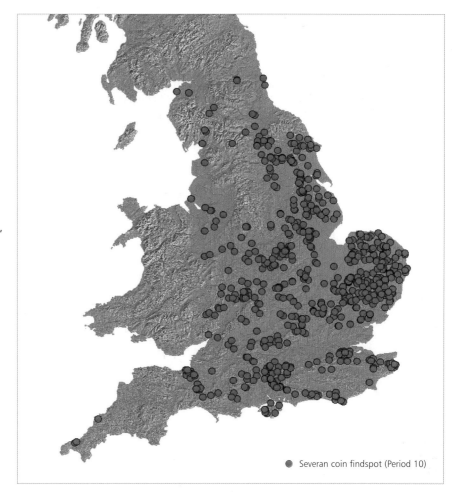

Map 1. Coins of the Severans, AD 193-211, recorded on the PAS database. (© Philippa Walton)

● Severan coin findspot (Period 10)

are *denarii*. There are also 88 *sestertii*, but these are scarce. There are also around 460 coins for Caracalla and around 179 for Geta. Julia Domna is also well represented with around 351 coins. Plautilla's swift fall from favour means that only 35 coins are recorded.

What is really interesting is the ratio of silver to base metal coins. For the period AD 161-92, 84% of the coins recorded are base metal coins. For the Severan Period, AD 193-217, it is quite the opposite with over 87% of coins recorded being silver *denarii*. There are several possible reasons for this. Firstly, more *denarii* were struck as a result of debasement. In AD 193, *denarii* contained about 80% silver; by AD 217, the silver content had dropped to almost 50%. This debasement was probably the result of the massive pay increases for the army, which required much new coin but from insufficient silver reserves. Secondly, there are a large number of contemporary copies although more research is needed to work out the exact proportions (see below). Thirdly, after c.AD 197, there was a marked decrease in the number of base metal coins produced – *sestertii* of Severus and his family are rare. Gold coins of this period are very

rarely found in Britain and there are no pieces on the database; I illustrate one coin from the British Museum collection (Fig.23.). Map 1 shows that Severan coins are found across Britain.

Copies of Severan Denarii

In the early 3rd century there started a spate of forging of Severan period silver coins. We know that this continued at least until the early AD 230s. Some are good quality plated coins (Fig.30.), others have a poorer quality silver wash (Fig.31.) and some are made from base silver (Figs.26 & 32.). Some are only copper-alloy cores for plated *denarii*. These coins are more common as site-finds (as opposed to hoard-finds) probably because they were more likely to be rejected in the market place and by savers. However, given the large quantity of such pieces, it is probable that they played a role in the economy, possibly substituted for *sestertii*, *dupondii* and *asses* which, as we have seen above, were not imported in large numbers to Britain at this time. The PAS Database is becoming a vital source of information for these copies and we are hoping that a major research project looking at Roman forgeries will be initiated by a major British university.

Chapter XVII
Roman Coinage
AD 217-238

Macrinus and Diadumenian (217-8), Elagabalus and his Empresses (218-22), Severus Alexander and Julia Mamaea (222-35), Maximinus I and Maximus (235-8), Gordian I and II (238), and Balbinus and Pupienus (238)

Macrinus & Diadumenian (AD 217-8)

I finished the last chapter with the assassination of Caracalla in Syria. One of the men implicated in the plot, Macrinus, was to succeed as emperor (Figs.1 & 2). He was a Moor (of the North African Mauri tribe) from Caesarea in Mauretania (Cherchel in Algeria). He was the first emperor who had not been a senator; he had risen through the ranks to be the commander of the Praetorian Guard. Because Caracalla had been so popular with the army, Macrinus had

to give a particularly high donative (money) to his troops upon the adoption of his son Diadumenian as Caesar (Figs.3 & 4). Then, in order to secure peace on the Eastern frontier, Macrinus had to pay 200 million *sestertii* (50 million *denarii*) to the Parthians.

Meanwhile, a plot was being hatched to replace Macrinus with another Severan. Varius Avitus (to be called Elagabalus) who was the grandson of Julia Maesa (the sister of Julia Domna, Severus' wife who died soon after Caracalla;

Fig.1. Silver plated contemporary copy of a *denarius* of Macrinus (AD 217-8), copied from a coin struck in Rome. This coin shows the emperor with a short beard and younger features. RIC IV, pt 2, c.f. no. 84. Found in Essex, ESS-8BD770. © Portable Antiquities Scheme (19mm)

Fig.2. Silver *denarius* of Macrinus (AD 217-8), struck at Rome. This coin shows the emperor with a long beard and older features. RIC IV, pt 2, no. 56. Found in Warwickshire, WAW-69E393. © Portable Antiquities Scheme (18mm)

Fig.3. Silver *denarius* of Diadumenian as Caesar (AD 217-8), struck at Rome. The reverse shows the young emperor with military standards. RIC IV, pt 2, no. 102. Found in Oxfordshire, BERK-175BF7. © Portable Antiquities Scheme (20.5mm)

Fig.11.). Elagabalus was only 14, but he was taken to the camp of Legio III Gallica near Emesa (Syria) where it was announced that he was in fact the illegitimate son of Caracalla (an emperor loved by the soldiers). The army turned against Macrinus and Diadumenian; both fled for their lives, but they failed and were killed leaving the young Elagabalus emperor (Fig.5.). Macrinus and Diadumenian had coins struck in all metals.

Elagabalus, Julia Maesa, Julia Soaemias, Julia Paula, Aquilia Severa & Annia Faustina (AD 218-222)

Elagabalus was one of the more bizarre Roman emperors. Although he only reigned for four years (between the age of 14 and 18) he was to leave an indelible mark on history (Figs.5-7.). Firstly, he was the High Priest of the Sun God of Emesa, Elagabal (Baal), after whom he is normally known (Fig.6.). His official name, linking him with Caracalla, was Marcus Aurelius Antoninus Pius and he is normally titled ANTONINVS PIVS on his coins (not to be confused with coins of Caracalla, 196-217, and Antoninus Pius, 138-61). Elagabalus took the worship of his Sun God very seriously and even took the cult stone (betel

stone) of the god from Emesa to Rome, in AD 219. There, two temples were built to Elagabal, one on the outskirts of the city and one close to the Colosseum (Fig.7.).

Elagabalus made the Sun God the senior deity in Rome and insisted on numerous sacrifices and a major festival in his honour; this did not go down well with the people of Rome. Throughout his reign, his mother Julia Soaemias was to be a powerful figure (Fig.8.)

Elagabalus also had a scandalous sex-life, having several wives (possibly five, but we know of Julia Paula, Aquilia Severa, and Annia Faustina) (Figs.9 & 10.). His marriage to Julia Aquilia Severa was particularly controversial as she was a Vestal Virgin, thus sworn to chastity. If this was not enough, Elagabalus also liked men and even wanted a sex-change! He "married" a male slave from Asia Minor, called Hierocles.

However, it was Elagabalus' failure to appoint experienced men to important posts that really angered his enemies – an actor was put in charge of the Praetorian Guard!

There had been some attempts to overthrow the emperor, but by AD 221 he was forced to adopt his cousin Bassianus Alexianus (the future

Fig.4. Silver *denarius* of Diadumenian as Caesar (AD 217-8), struck at Rome. The reverse proclaims Diadumenian as the "Hope of the State". RIC IV, pt 2, no. 117. Found in Essex, ESS-FFFC33. © Portable Antiquities Scheme (18mm)

Fig.5. Silver *denarius* of Elagabalus (AD 218-22), struck at Antioch. The mint of Antioch struck a significant number of coins for Elagabalus, who was of Syrian descent. RIC IV, pt 2, no. 60. Found in Hertfordshire, BH-C7E0B2. © Portable Antiquities Scheme (18mm)

Fig.6. Silver *denarius* of Elagabalus (AD 218-22), struck at Rome. The reverse shows Elagabalus sacrificing at an altar, and being proclaimed the "Invincible Priest" [of the Sun God Elagabal]. RIC IV, pt 2, no. 88. Found in Hampshire,aa SUR-349C64. © Portable Antiquities Scheme (19mm)

Fig.7. Gold *aureus* of Elagabalus (AD 218-22), struck at Antioch in 218-9. It shows the sacred conical stone that represented the Sun God Elagabal (Baal) on a triumphal car. BMC V, no. 273. © British Museum (22mm)

Fig.8. Silver *denarius* of Julia Soaemias, mother of Elagabalus (AD 218-22), struck at Rome. The reverse shows Venus seated with a child in front of her. RIC IV, pt 2, no. 243. Found in Cambridgeshire, SF-CE1752. © Portable Antiquities Scheme (20mm)

Severus Alexander) as Caesar. Elagabalus tried to get Severus Alexander murdered; instead the Praetorian Guard turned on him and killed him and his mother Julia Soaemias. But, his grand-mother, Julia Maesa (Fig.11.), survived to see another grandson, Severus Alexander, become emperor.

Coinage was struck in all metals for Elaga-balus and his empresses. Silver *denarii* (Figs.5-6 & 8-11) are commonly found in Britain, but radi-ates are much rarer (Fig.12.). Base metal is very scarce: hardly any *sestertii, dupondii* and *asses* being recorded on the database. However, there were a small number of Roman Provincial base metal coins arriving in Britain at this time, pos-sibly helping to alleviate the shortage of imperial coinage (Figs13 & 14.).

Severus Alexander, Julia Mamaea & Orbiana (AD 222-235)

At only 14, Severus Alexander (Figs.15-19.) was not able to run the Empire in person; for most of his reign, it was his mother, Julia Mamaea (Figs.20-23.), who was the power

behind the throne. During the reign, Severus was to grow increasingly frustrated by his mother's over-bearing presence. Severus married Orbiana (Figs.24 & 25.) in 225, but by 227 she had been thrown out of the imperial palace by Mamaea, against the wishes of Severus.

Eastern (AD 231-2) & German (AD 234-5) Campaigns

In AD 224 a major event occurred in the East. The old enemy of Rome, the Parthian Empire, was finally overthrown by a new Sasanian Empire under Ardashir. In 230, the Sasanians captured the Roman province of Mesopotamia (Iraq), forc-ing Severus Alexander to respond. Alexander did not lead a distinguished campaign, but a peace was made in the East in AD 232 (Fig.19.).

In Germany, Alexander was no more deci-sive, trying to pay-off the German barbarians. The soldiers did not take kindly to the emperor's lack of initiative and so began to plot against him. A career soldier called Maximinus, of Thra-cian stock, provided the focus for a rebellion and Severus Alexander was murdered at Vicus

Fig.9. Silver *denarius* of Julia Paula, first wife of Elagabalus (AD 218-22), struck in Rome in AD 219-220. The reverse shows Concordia. RIC IV, pt 2, no. 211. Found in Leicestershire, LEIC-B50412. © Portable Antiquities Scheme (18mm)

Fig.10. Silver *denarius* of Aquilia Severa, second wife of Elagabalus (AD 218-22), struck in Rome in AD 220. The coin shows Aquilia and Elagabalus clasping hands; Aquilia had been a Vestal Virgin and their marriage caused a scandal. RIC IV, pt 2, no. 228. Found in Northamptonshire, NARC-99D733. © Portable Antiquities Scheme (18.5mm)

Fig.11. Silver *denarius* of Julia Maesa, grandmother of Elagabalus (AD 218-222), struck at Rome. Maesa survived into the early years of the reign of Severus Alexander (AD 222-235). Found in Leicestershire, LEIC-03B121. © Portable Antiquities Scheme (21mm)

Fig.12. Silver "radiate" of Elagabalus (AD 218-222), struck at Rome. Radiates of Elagabalus are much rarer than *denarii*. RIC IV, pt 2, no. 155. Found in North Yorkshire, YORYM-476B46. © Portable Antiquities Scheme (22mm)

Fig.13. Copper-alloy Roman provincial coin struck for Elagabalus (AD 218-22) at Byblos (Lebanon). As papyrus for writing scrolls was imported from Egypt via Byblos, the city gave its name to the Bible. BMC Phoenicia no. 48ff. Found in West Sussex, HAMP-E0A9F0. © Portable Antiquities Scheme (25.5mm)

Britannicus (Town of the Britons; modern Bretzenheim) in March 235.

Coins were struck in all metals for Severus Alexander, Julia Mamaea and Orbiana. Silver *denarii* of Severus and Mamaea are commonly found in Britain (Figs.15, 19 & 20). Although rare, there are a few more base metal coins from this reign than for Elagabalus (Figs.16-18 & 22). We also start to get a small number of slightly undersized cast copies of base metal coins which probably mostly come from the Rhine Frontier where scholars call them *Limesfalsa* ("Frontier Forgeries") (Fig.23.). All coins of Orbiana are rare, there only being nine on the PAS database. (Figs.24 & 25.).

Maximinus I & Maximus Caesar (AD 235-8), Gordian I & II (AD 238), Balbinus & Pupienus (AD 238)

Maximinus Thrax ("The Thracian") was a giant; the Augustan History claims he was 8 feet 6 inches tall! (Figs.26-28.). His coins also show him with a formidable chin. He had risen through the ranks and in 234 was put in charge

Fig.14. Copper-alloy Roman provincial coin struck for Elagabalus (AD 218-22) at Cius (Bithynia, north-west Turkey). A coin of the same type was found in Kent in 2001, suggesting that a batch of these coins arrived together in Britain. BMC Pontus etc., no. 41. Found in Hertfordshire, BH-9909C7. © Portable Antiquities Scheme (23.5mm)

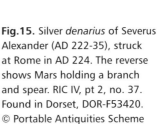

Fig.15. Silver *denarius* of Severus Alexander (AD 222-35), struck at Rome in AD 224. The reverse shows Mars holding a branch and spear. RIC IV, pt 2, no. 37. Found in Dorset, DOR-F53420. © Portable Antiquities Scheme (19mm)

Fig.16. Brass *sestertius* of Severus Alexander (AD 222-35), struck at Rome in AD 225. The reverse refers to the "Faith of the Army". RIC IV, pt 2, no. 552. Found on the Isle of Wight, IOW-9F88E1. © Portable Antiquities Scheme (30.2mm)

Fig.17. Brass *sestertius* of Severus Alexander (AD 222-35), struck at Rome in AD 229. The reverse shows the emperor giving out money to the people to celebrate his third Consulship. BMC VI, no. 564. Found in Hertfordshire, BH-C947C3. © The Portable Antiquities Scheme (30mm)

Fig.18. Brass *sestertius* of Severus Alexander (AD 222-35), struck at Rome in 231. The reverse shows Providentia holding corn ears over a corn measure, referring to the food supply of Rome. RIC IV, pt 2, no. 642. Found in Hampshire, SUR-A605A7. © The Portable Antiquities Scheme (31mm)

Fig.19. Silver *denarius* of Severus Alexander (AD 222-35), struck at Rome in AD 232. The reverse shows the sun god Sol and probably refers to the fact that Severus was campaigning in the East against the Persians. Found in Hampshire, HAMP-955F23. © The Portable Antiquities Scheme (21mm)

Fig.20. Silver *denarius* of Julia Mamaea, mother of Severus Alexander, struck at Rome in AD 222. This was one of the first coins to be struck for Julia Mamaea. RIC IV, pt 2, no. 343. Found in Oxfordshire, BERK-EFBAC8. © The Portable Antiquities Scheme (20mm)

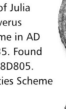

Fig.21. Silver *denarius* of Julia Mamaea, mother of Severus Alexander, struck at Rome in AD 228. RIC IV, pt 2, no. 335. Found in Leicestershire, LEIC-C8D805. © The Portable Antiquities Scheme (19mm)

Fig.22. Copper-alloy *as* of Julia Mamaea, struck at Rome in AD 226. The reverse shows Vesta (Goddess of the Hearth) holding a Palladium. Found in Shropshire, LVPL-C481E2. © The Portable Antiquities Scheme (23mm)

of new recruits for the German campaign. When he became emperor, it is likely he raised his son Maximus to the rank of Caesar (Fig.29.). He was also to issue commemorative coins for his wife Paulina who died around AD 235 (Fig.30.). He survived two early attempts on his life and then led a vigorous campaign against the Germans across the Rhine, receiving the title Germanicus Maximus. He then crossed the other great frontier river, the Danube, to fight against the Dacians and Sarmatians. However, these campaigns required much money to be raised in taxes which upset people across the Empire; he even took money ear-marked to provide free food for the poor in Rome.

In Africa, rich landowners were feeling the effects of Maximinus' fiscal policies and the elderly governor of the province, Marcus Antonius Gordianus Sempronianus (to be Gordian I) was encouraged to stand as emperor (Fig.31.). He was a distinguished senator (in contrast to Maximinus) and therefore popular in Rome; he declared his son (Gordian II) as joint emperor (Fig.32.). The rebellion failed because Legio III Augusta,

Fig.23. Copper-alloy "frontier forgery" of an *as* of Julia Mamaea, struck c.AD 220s to 240s. These cast coins were mostly made on the Rhine Frontier in Germany where they are called *Limesfalsa* = "Frontier Forgeries". They are found in Britain where the PAS is recording a small, but significant, number. Found in Wiltshire, SOM-CE12D5. © The Portable Antiquities Scheme (23.5mm)

Fig.24. Gold *aureus* of Orbiana, wife of Severus Alexander, struck in Rome in AD 225. BMC VI, 292. © The British Museum (21mm)

Fig.26. Silver *denarius* of Maximinus I (AD 235-8), struck at Rome in AD 236. The reverse shows Pax (Peace). RIC IV, pt 2, no. 12. Found in Leicestershire, LEIC-4E9DC2. © Portable Antiquities Scheme (18mm)

Fig.25. Fragment of a silver *denarius* of Orbiana, wife of Severus Alexander, struck in Rome in AD 225. This is one of only nine *denarii* of Orbiana on the PAS database. Found in Northamptonshire, LANCUM-8462A2. © Portable Antiquities Scheme (16mm)

Fig.27. Copper-alloy *as* of Maximinus I (AD 235-8), struck at Rome in AD 235-6. RIC IV, pt 2, no. 60. Found in Northamptonshire, NARC-E97105. © Portable Antiquities Scheme (23mm)

in neighbouring Numidia, was commanded by a man hostile to the Gordiani – both men died after the legion took Carthage in a swift action. They had ruled only 20 days.

The Senate still opposed Maximinus and nominated two more emperors from their ranks in Rome: the experienced and distinguished Pupienus and Balbinus (Figs.33-36). This was not a popular choice with the people who wanted another member of the Gordian family to rule; Gordian III (grandson of Gordian I and nephew of Gordian II) was declared Caesar. Meanwhile, Pupienus marched to the major city of Aquileia in northern Italy so as to block Maximinus' advance on Rome. In the ensuing actions, Maximinus and his son Maximus lost the support of their army and were assassinated. Although Pupienus was triumphant, he returned to a major squabble with Balbinus in Rome (Fig.36.); the Praetorian Guard decided that they wanted neither man so after a reign of 99 days both were murdered. It now fell to Gordian III (238-44) to pick up the pieces (see next chapter).

Coins in all metals were struck for Maximinus

Fig.28. Silver *denarius* of Maximinus I (AD 235-8), struck at Rome in AD 236. The reverse shows Salus (Health) feeding a snake. RIC IV, pt 2, no. 14. Found in Kent, LON-DB8FC4. © Portable Antiquities Scheme (21mm)

Fig.29. Copper-alloy *dupondius* of Maximus Caesar (AD 235-8), struck at Rome in AD 235-6. The reverse shows sacrificial implements, a common type for junior emperors. Found in Worcestershire, WAW-7A9418. © Portable Antiquities Scheme (29mm)

Fig.30. Silver *denarius* of Paulina (wife of Maximinus I (AD 235-8), struck at Rome. Paulina died just before or just after the accession of Maximinus. BMC VI, no. 127. © The British Museum (20mm)

Fig.31. Brass *sestertius* of Gordian I (AD 238), struck at Rome. This is one of only 18 coins of Gordian I in the British Museum collection. BMC VI, no. 13. © The British Museum (30mm)

Fig.32. Brass *sestertius* of Gordian II (AD 238), struck at Rome. This is one of only 16 coins of Gordian II in the British Museum collection. BMC VI, no. 23. © The British Museum (31mm)

Fig.33. Silver *denarius* of Balbinus (AD 238), struck at Rome. This is one of four *denarii* of Balbinus on the PAS database. RIC IV, pt 2, no. 7. Found in Hertfordshire, BH-EBA0F0. © Portable Antiquities Scheme (19mm)

Fig.34. Brass *sestertius* of Balbinus (AD 238), struck at Rome. This is the only base metal coin of Balbinus on the PAS database. RIC IV, pt 2, no. 19. Found in Flintshire, LVPL-91FAE4. © Portable Antiquities Scheme (29mm)

and Maximus. Silver *denarii* are the most common denomination found in Britain for Maximinus (Figs.26 & 28.), but base metal coins appear to be more common for Maximus (Fig.29.). The coins of Gordian I and II are extremely rare (Figs.31 & 32.). Although rare, the odd piece of Pupienus and Balbinus is found in Britain. They continued to strike silver *denarii* (Fig.33.), but also re-introduced the radiate (Fig.36.) which was to become the dominant silver coin from the reign of Gordian III (238-44). In fact, one can say, that the era of the *denarius* really comes to an end in 238, later *denarii* being struck in much smaller

numbers than radiates. As a whole, silver coins are much more common between AD 217 and 238, outnumbering base metal coins by well over ten to one. Plated copies of *denarii* continued to be issued in this period, mostly up to the end of the reign of Severus Alexander. There are many on the PAS database (see Fig.1.). Finally, Map 1 shows that coins of this period are found across England.

It is interesting to construct a league table of emperors and empresses for this period, as recorded on the PAS Database, so as to give an indication of relative rarity (see Table 1).

Fig.35. Brass *sestertius* of Pupienus (AD 238), struck at Rome. This is one of two *sestertii* of Pupienus on the PAS database. RIC IV, pt. 2, 23a. Found in Northamptonshire, NARC-6C6FE8. © Portable Antiquities Scheme (29mm)

Fig.36. Silver "radiate" of Pupienus (AD 238), struck at Rome. The reverse refers to the mutual love of Pupienus and Balbinus; nothing could have been further from the truth! BMC VI, no. 83. © The British Museum (25mm). A coin of this type has been recorded on the PAS Database (FASA-7B9118)

Emperor / Empress	Date	No. of Coins
Macrinus and Diadumenian	217-8	19
Elagabalus	218-22	260
Julia Soaemias	218-22	41
Julia Paula	219-20	14
Aquilia Severa	220-1	3
Julia Maesa	218-early 220s	80
Severus Alexander	222-35	535
Julia Mamaea	222-35	197
Orbiana	c.225-7	9
Maximinus I	235-8	84
Maximus Caesar	235-8	8
Balbinus	235-8	5
Pupienus	235-8	3

Table 1. League table of emperors and empresses for the period, as recorded on the PAS Database, giving an indication of relative rarity.

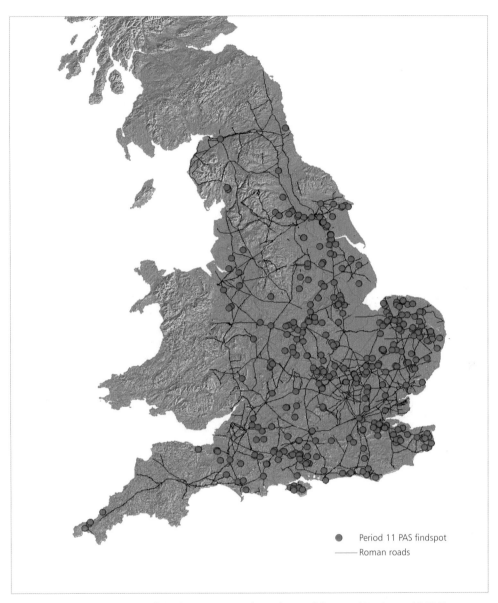

Map 1. Distribution of coins of the later Severans through to Balbinus and Pupienus. (© Philippa Walton)

Chapter XVIII
Roman Coinage AD 238-253/4
Gordian III to Uranius Antoninus

Fig.1. Gold *aureus* of Gordian III (AD 238-44), minted in Rome, AD 238-9. The reverse shows Jupiter holding a thunderbolt. RIC IV, pt 3, no. 8. Found in Leicestershire, LEIC-196037. © Portable Antiquities Scheme (19mm)

Fig.2. Silver "radiate" of Gordian III (238-44), minted in Rome, AD 243-4. The reverse shows Fortune "the home-bringer", probably represented in the hope that Gordian would return safely from the Persian campaign. RIC IV, pt 3, no. 144. Found in Hampshire, HAMP-2156D5. © Portable Antiquities Scheme (24mm)

Fig.4. Copper alloy *sestertius* of Gordian III (AD 238-44), minted in Rome, c.AD 240. The reverse shows "Abundance". RIC IV, pt 3, no. 274a. Found in Somerset, SOM-D42B31. © Portable Antiquities Scheme (30mm)

Fig.5. Copper alloy *sestertius* of Gordian III (AD 238-44), minted in Rome, AD 241-3. The reverse shows the sun god Sol. RIC IV, pt 3, no. 297a. Found in Hampshire, SUR-CD9766. © Portable Antiquities Scheme (29mm)

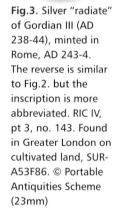

Fig.3. Silver "radiate" of Gordian III (AD 238-44), minted in Rome, AD 243-4. The reverse is similar to Fig.2. but the inscription is more abbreviated. RIC IV, pt 3, no. 143. Found in Greater London on cultivated land, SUR-A53F86. © Portable Antiquities Scheme (23mm)

In AD 238 there were no fewer than seven emperors ruling at one time or another (see last chapter). It was to herald a period in Roman history when numerous rulers came and went in quick succession. In this chapter, I will only cover 15 years, but in this period there were no fewer than 17 emperors and empresses represented on coins.

Gordian III (AD 238-44)

We saw in the last chapter how Gordian I and II only ruled for 20 days in AD 238. However, after the defeat of Maximinus and the deaths of Pupienus and Balbinus, the Senate chose the 13 year old Gordian III (grandson of Gordian I) to be the next emperor (Figs.1-7.). Gordian was heavily reliant on his faithful commander of the Praetorian Guard, Gaius Furius Sabinius Aquila Timesitheus, for ruling the empire. In 241, Gordian married Timesitheus' daughter, Tranquillina (Fig.8.). Gordian did manage to suppress a rebellion in Africa and to push the Goths back over the Danube, but it was in the East that the real danger lay.

Fig.7. Silver "radiate" of Gordian III (AD 238-44), minted in Antioch (Syria). The reverse shows Aequitas. RIC IV, pt 3, no. 177a. © British Museum (24mm)

Fig.8. Silver "radiate" of Tranquillina (AD 241-4), minted in Rome. This is one of only three "radiates" of Tranquillina in the British Museum. RIC IV, pt 3, 249. © British Museum (22mm)

Fig.6. Copper-alloy *as* of Gordian III (AD 238-44), minted in Rome, AD 240-2. The reverse shows the emperor holding a spear and globe. Found in Hampshire, HAMP-5F1953. © Portable Antiquities Scheme (21mm)

Fig.9. Silver *drachm* of Shapur I, King of the Sasanians (c.AD 240-70), minted in Persia. Shapur was the scourge of the Romans for most of his reign. The reverse shows a Sasanian fire altar. BM Reg. COC25859. © British Museum (25mm)

Fig.10. Silver "radiate" of Philip I (244-9), minted in Rome, AD 244-7. The reverse proclaims "Security in the World", but it had cost Philip much money to buy off the Persians. RIC IV, pt 3, no. 48b. Found in Northamptonshire, NARC-788972. © Portable Antiquities Scheme (23mm)

The Persian Threat

In the East, the old Parthian Empire had collapsed in AD 226, only to be replaced by a much more vigorous and aggressive Sasanian Empire. In 240, the Sasanian King Shapur I (Fig.9.) began to advance westwards, attacking the Roman Empire a year later. In 243, Gordian's army arrived in Syria and won some victories in Northern Mesopotamia. However, Timesitheus died, leaving Gordian without his major protector and adviser. The new commander of the Praetorian Guard, Philip "the Arab", plotted against Gordian, and when the young emperor asked the army to choose between the two men, they chose Philip. Gordian was killed and Philip succeeded as emperor.

Coinage of Gordian III

Gordian III struck in all metals. However, it was in his reign that the silver "radiate" (named after the radiate crown of the Sun God worn by the emperors; the coin is sometimes called the *antoninianus*) became the dominant denomination (Figs.2-3. & 7.), almost completely ousting the *denarius*. On coins of empresses, the bust is superimposed on the crescent of the moon (e.g. Figs.8., 15 & 34.). Of the 244 coins on the

database, over 150 are radiates. There was a brief revival in the supply of base-metal coins to Britain under Gordian – there are around 29 *sestertii* and 33 *dupondii* and *asses* (Figs.4-6.). Gold is rare, but one *aureus* is recorded (Fig.1.). Coins of Tranquillina are extremely rare and normally are only found in large hoards (Fig.8.). Rome was the main mint, but the occasional coin from Antioch does arrive in Britain (Fig.7.). It might interest you to know that Roger Bland, Head of the Portable Antiquities Scheme, is also the world authority on the coinage of Gordian!

Philip I, Philip II & Otacilia Severa (AD 244-9)

Philip I (Figs.10-13.) quickly made peace with the Sasanians, paying them half a million *denarii* (Fig.10.). He also made his young son, Philip II, Caesar, although he was only five or six (Fig.14.); his wife Otacilia was made empress (Figs.15-18.). Philip was from Syria and he patronised his hometown Philippopolis (modern Shahba) with grand buildings. However, he made a swift move to Rome to establish himself as emperor. In AD 248, Philip celebrated Rome's 1000th Anniversary (it was founded in 753 BC) and his coins and those of his empress Otacilia

Fig.11. Silver "radiate" of Philip I (244-9), minted in Rome, AD 248. The reverse shows the Wolf and Twins, referring to the legendary foundation of Rome by Romulus in 753 BC. RIC IV, pt 3, 15. © British Museum (23mm)

Fig.12. Silver "radiate" of Philip I (244-9), minted in Rome, AD 247-9. The reverse shows Fortune the "home-bringer". RIC IV, pt 3, no. 63b. Found in Cambridgeshire, CAM-8BF945. © Portable Antiquities Scheme (21mm)

Fig.14. Silver "radiate" of Philip II as Augustus (AD 247-9), struck at Rome. The reverse type is only recorded for Philip II as Caesar, so this coin is probably a new variety. RIC IV, pt 3, c.f. 213. Found in Hampshire, HAMP-35B3E1. © Portable Antiquities Scheme (23.5mm)

Fig.15. Silver "radiate" of Otacilia Severa, minted in Rome, AD 246-8. The reverse shows Concordia. RIC IV, pt 3, no. 125c. Found in Leicestershire, LEIC-8C9CF7. © Portable Antiquities Scheme (23mm)

Fig.13. Copper-alloy *as* of Philip I (AD 244-9), minted in Rome, AD 244-9. The reverse shows Annona, the personification of the food supply. RIC IV, pt 3, no. 168b. Found in Suffolk, SF-370FD2. © Portable Antiquities Scheme (21mm)

Severa publicise the celebratory games (Figs.11 & 16.). These games, however, were a shadow of those held 100 years earlier.

Rebellions Against Philip: Pacatian & Jotapian (AD 248-9)

In 248, the legions on the Danube declared their commander Pacatian emperor. It is thought he tried to make an agreement with Philip, but the rebel emperor was killed. Pacatian (AD 248-9) did strike a few coins at Viminacium, but they are extremely rare (Fig.19.). In the East, Philip's brother Priscus had become extremely unpopular for the oppressive regime he oversaw. As a result, another rebel emperor was declared in 248-9, Jotapian (Fig.20.). His revolt did not last long and he was killed by his own soldiers, but not before he had struck a series of rare coins at a mint somewhere in Syria or Cappadocia (eastern Turkey).

In 249, Philip made Quintus Decius Valerinus commander of the Roman armies on the Rhine; this proved a fatal mistake because after Decius had defeated the Goths, he was urged to rebel against Philip. At a battle in Macedonia, Decius defeated and killed Philip I. Philip II was

also killed in Rome. This left Decius in charge; he took the name of the great emperor Trajan, titling himself Trajan Decius.

Coinage of Philip & His Family

The silver "radiate" continued to be the main denomination – of the 153 coins of Philip I, Philip II and Otacilia Severa on the database, over 120 are radiates (Figs.10-12 & 15.). The rest are *sestertii* and *asses* which still arrive in a significant, if declining, number (Figs.13 & 17-18.). The most notable coins of his reign were those struck to celebrate Rome's 1000th Anniversary (Figs.11 & 16.).

Trajan Decius (AD 249-51)

Trajan Decius' (Figs.21-3.) short reign was mostly spent campaigning against the Goths on the Danube. There were also two rebellions that had to be suppressed. Decius is best known as a persecutor of the Christians. He decreed that all citizens should make pagan sacrifices for the emperor. A number of Christians, including the Bishop of Rome, lost their lives for refusing. Decius finally died with his son, Herennius Etruscus (Fig.25.), when his army was ambushed by

Fig.16. Gold *aureus* of Otacilia Severa, minted in Rome, AD 248. This coin was struck to celebrate the games held for Rome's 1000th Anniversary. RIC IV, pt 3, no. 116. © British Museum (21mm)

Fig.17. Copper-alloy *as* of Otacilia Severa, minted in Rome, AD 244-9. The recorded coins of this type have a left-facing bust therefore this appears to be a new variety. RIC IV, pt 3, c.f. 203d. Found in Hertfordshire, BH-410A78. © Portable Antiquities Scheme (23mm)

Fig.18. Copper-alloy "frontier forgery" (*limesfalsum*) with the obverse of Otacilia Severa and the reverse of Nero. This coin was probably cast in the Rhineland sometime in the late AD 240s or 250s. Found in Surrey, SUR-EC7923. © Portable Antiquities Scheme (22mm)

Fig.19. Silver "radiate" of Pacatian (AD 248), probably struck at Viminacium. This coin was found in a hoard in Derbyshire in 1988; this is one of four coins of Pacatian in the British Museum. RIC IV, pt 3, 4. © British Museum (23mm)

Fig.20. Base silver "radiate" of Jotapian (AD 248), minted in Antioch. This is the only coin of Jotapian in the British Museum. RIC IV, pt 3, 2cvar. © British Museum (23mm)

Fig.21. Silver "radiate" of Trajan Decius (AD 249-51), minted in Rome. The reverse shows Victory. RIC IV, pt 3, no. 29c. Found in Oxfordshire, HAMP422. © Portable Antiquities Scheme (22.5mm)

Fig.22. Silver "radiate" of Trajan Decius (AD 249-51), minted in Rome. The reverse honours the "spirit" of the Roman army in Illyria (Balkans). RIC IV, pt 3, no. 18. Found in Sussex, SUSS-63E8D1. © Portable Antiquities Scheme (21.5mm)

Fig.23. Copper-alloy double *sestertius* of Trajan Decius (AD 249-51) minted in Rome. This large denomination was only struck in his reign. The coin appears official, although the pronounced line border is unusual. RIC IV, pt 3, no. 126a. Found in Oxfordshire, SUR-A56AE5. © Portable Antiquities Scheme (38mm)

Fig.24. Gold *aureus* of Herennia Etruscilla (AD 249-51), minted in Rome. The reverse shows Modesty. RIC IV, pt 3, no. 58a. © British Museum (20mm)

Fig.25. Silver "radiate" of Herennius Etruscus as Caesar (AD 250-1) under Trajan Decius, minted in Rome. The reverse shows sacrificial implements. RIC IV, pt 3, no. 143. Found in Warwickshire, WMID-BEFBD6. © Portable Antiquities Scheme (22.5mm)

Fig.26. Silver "radiate" of Hostilian as Caesar (AD 251) under Trajan Decius, minted in Rome. The reverse shows the young emperor holding a standard and spear. RIC IV, pt 3, no. 182. Found in Northamptonshire, NARC-02EC07. © Portable Antiquities Scheme (18mm)

Fig.27. Silver "radiate" of Hostilian as Caesar (AD 251) under Trajan Decius, minted in Rome. The reverse shows Mars, the god of war, advancing right. RIC IV, pt 3, c.f. no. 176a. Found in Sussex, SUSS-213574. © Portable Antiquities Scheme (23mm)

Fig.28. Silver "radiate" of Trebonianus Gallus (AD 251-3), minted at Rome. The reverse shows Pietas raising both hands. RIC IV, pt 3, no. 41. Found in Bedfordshire, BH-B388A1. © Portable Antiquities Scheme (20mm)

the Goths. His other son, Hostilian (Figs.26-27.), was in Rome and survived to be joint-emperor with Trebonianus Gallus (AD 251-3).

Coinage of Trajan Decius & Family

Decius struck in all metals for all of his family. The "radiate" now becomes almost the only denomination on the PAS database, there being 27 for Decius (Figs.21-22.) and 19 for Herennia Etruscilla, Herennius Etruscus, and Hositilian (Figs.25-27.).

Gold is scarce and I show an *aureus* of Herennia Etruscilla in the British Museum collection (Fig.24.). A major, but very short-lived, innovation in Decius' reign was the striking of a double *sestertius*, a massive coin which one assumes was used to make up for a shortage of silver. One is recorded on the database which, although slightly unusual in appearance, appears to be official (Fig.23.).

Trebonianus Gallus (AD 251-3)

Trebonianus was one of Decius' senior aides in the Danube War (Figs.28-29.). When he succeeded, he adopted Hostilian (Decius' surviving son) and made him co-emperor. Trebonianus' son Volusian was made Caesar (Figs.30-31.). Trebonianus made a somewhat unfavourable peace with the Goths, but when he arrived in

Rome he found that plague had broken out, claiming Hostilian as one of its victims. In the East, things were no better: the Persian king Shapur I invaded Roman territory in AD 252, ultimately capturing Antioch (Fig.9.).

On the Danube, the Goths tore up their treaty with Rome and invaded again. The governor of Upper Moesia, Aemilius Aemilianus, defeated the barbarians; the result was that his men declared him emperor. Aemilian then marched on Rome at great speed; Trebonianus and Volusian were swiftly murdered by their own men.

Aemilian (AD 253), Silbannacus (AD 253?) & Uranius Antoninus (AD 253-4)

Although he was a fair ruler and was liked by the senate, Aemilian failed to gain full support of the army (Fig.32.). One of Trebonianus' generals, Publius Licinius Valerianus, marched from the Danube to Italy to confront Aemilian. Aemilian marched to meet Valerian, but was killed by his own men near Spoleto. Aemilian only ruled for 88 days. It is thought that he left Silbannacus in charge at Rome – only two coins are known of this ruler who could have only been on the throne for a few days before he was dispatched by Valerian's forces (Fig.33.). Also, at around this time, there was an emperor called Uranius

Fig.29. Silver "radiate" of Trebonianus Gallus (AD 251-3), minted in Antioch (Syria). The reverse shows Equity with her scales. RIC IV, pt 3, no. 80. Found in Berkshire, HAMP-2D3043. © Portable Antiquities Scheme (20.5mm)

Fig.30. Silver "radiate" of Volusian as Augustus (AD 253), minted in Rome. The reverse shows the emperor or a soldier. RIC IV, pt 3, no. 186. Found in Lincolnshire, LIN-4F7B72. © Portable Antiquities Scheme (22mm)

Fig.31. Silver "radiate" of Volusian as Augustus (AD 253), minted in Rome. The reverse shows Pietas raising both hands. RIC IV, pt 3, no. 182. Found in Bedfordshire, BH-096642. © Portable Antiquities Scheme (21mm)

Fig.32. Silver "radiate" of Aemilian (AD 253), minted in Rome. The reverse shows Victory. RIC IV, pt 3, no. 11. Found in Gloucestershire, GLO-6374A7. © Portable Antiquities Scheme (21mm)

Fig.33. Silver "radiate" of Silbannacus (c.AD 253?). This is one of only two coins of Silbannacus known. The other is in a private collection in France. RIC IV, pt 3, 1. © British Museum (22mm)

Fig.34. Silver "radiate" of Cornelia Supera (AD 253), minted in Rome. The reverse shows Vesta, goddess of the hearth. BM Reg. B10367. © British Museum (21mm)

Antoninus who ruled from Emesa, but little is known about his career (Fig.35.).

Coinage of Trebonianus, Aemilian, Silbannacus & Uranius Antoninus

All of the coins for Trebonianus Gallus and Volusian on the PAS database are "radiates". There appears to have been a cessation of the import of base-metal coins in significant numbers. There are two regular "radiates" of Aemilian, and one contemporary copy, on the database (Fig.32.).

Some extremely rare coins are known for Cornelia Supera who is thought to have been Aemilian's wife (Fig.34.); none are recorded with the PAS. Silbannacus only struck in Rome (Fig.33.); it would be wonderful if another specimen was recorded through the PAS! Rome remained the major mint, although some coins from Antioch still arrived in Britain (Fig.29.). Uranius Antoninus struck mostly gold coins at Emesa (Fig.35.); as one might expect, none have so far been recorded with the PAS.

Summary

Between 238 and 253, the silver "radiate" becomes the dominant denomination, instead of the *denarius*. However, the silver content did begin to drop further. From Gordian III to Trajan Decius there was between 40% and 50% silver in the radiate; it dropped to around 35% under Trebonianus and Aemilian – Fig.30. shows how these coins often look bronze when found. In coming chapters you will see how the silver content drops even further.

Under Gordian III and Philip there is still a small, but significant, amount of base-metal coinage arriving in Britain. However, the PAS database suggests that this dries up significantly from the reign of Trajan Decius. It is known that on the Rhine frontier many base-metal copies – *limesfalsa* or "frontier forgeries" – were produced, probably to make up for a shortage of supply. Such coins are being recorded in increasing numbers on the PAS database (Fig.18.). The following table of coins recorded with the PAS gives an idea of relative rarity for rulers of this period.

Fig.35. Gold *aureus* of Uranius Antoninus (AD 253-4), probably struck in Emesa, Syria. The reverse shows that Uranius has been declared Consul. RIC IV, pt 3, no. 7. © British Museum (21mm)

Gordian III	244
Philip I	79
Otacilia Severa	43
Philip II	31
Trajan Decius	27
Herennia Etruscilla	8
Herennius Etruscus	7
Hostilian	4
Trebonianus Gallus	26
Volusian	22
Aemilian	6

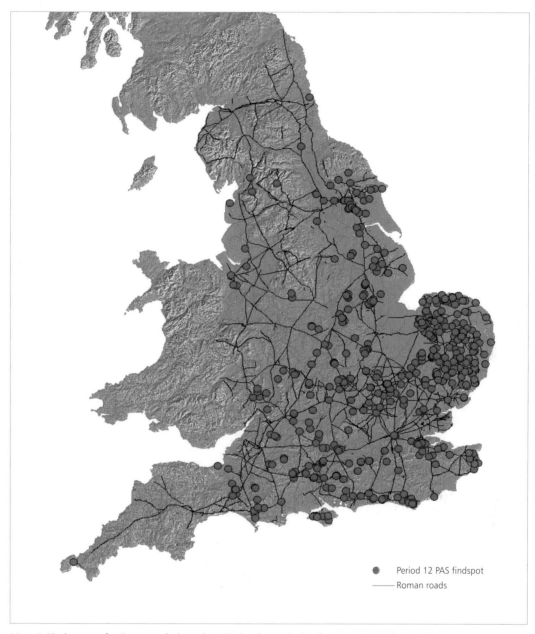

Map 1. Find spots of coins recorded on the PAS database, dating between AD 238 and 260. (© Philippa Walton)

Chapter XIX

Coinage of The Central Empire from Valerian to Quintillus

(AD 253-270)

Map 1. The Gallic and Central Empires as they existed AD c.260-74. (© Richard Kelleher)

An Empire Divided

The period from the accession of Valerian in AD 253 to the death of Quintillus in AD 270 was tumultuous. There were no fewer than 20 rulers and the Empire was split for much of the time. Between 253 and 260, Valerian and his family ruled the entire Empire, but in 260 his son, Gallienus, could not hang on to the entire dominion, but ruled only over the territory of Italy, the East and Africa – we call this the "Central Empire".

In the north-western part of the Empire (Gaul, Spain, Germany and Britain), Postumus (AD 260-8) was the first breakaway ruler of what we now call the "Gallic Empire"; this empire finally came to an end in AD 274.

The coinage of the Gallic emperors will be covered in the next chapter. This chapter will cover the coinage of the Central Empire, dealing mainly with the coinages of Valerian and his family (253-60), Gallienus' sole reign (260-8), Claudius II Gothicus (268-70) and Quintillus (AD 270).

Fig.2. Base silver radiate of Valerian I (AD 253-60), struck at an Eastern Mint. The reverse shows Valerian and Gallienus sacrificing. Cunetio 848. Found in Buckinghamshire, BUC-2C5E48. © Portable Antiquities Scheme (22mm)

Fig.3. Gold *aureus* of Valerian I (AD 253-60), struck at Rome. It declares Valerian as "Restorer of the World". This coin is very light at 2.24 gm. RIC V, pt 1, 50. © British Museum (17mm)

Fig.1. Base silver radiate of Valerian I (AD 253-60), struck at Rome. The two Gs in the reverse inscription, VICTORIA AVGG, signifies that Gallienus is joint emperor with Valerian. Cunetio no. 447. Found in Lincolnshire, LIN-888EF7. © Portable Antiquities Scheme (20mm)

Fig.4. Base silver radiate of Gallienus, joint reign (AD 253-60), minted in Gaul, 258-9. The reverse celebrates Gallienus' victories over the Germans. Cunetio 718. Found in Hertfordshire, BH-99F396. © Portable Antiquities Scheme (24mm)

Fig.5. Base silver radiate (pierced) of Gallienus, joint reign (AD 253-60), minted in Gaul, 258-9. The reverse celebrates Gallienus' victories over the Germans. Cunetio 724. Found in Sussex, SUSS-577014 (22mm)

Valerian AD 253-60

After the death of Aemilian (see previous chapter) in 253, Valerian arrived in Rome where he was hailed emperor by the senate and people. His 40 year old son Gallienus was immediately made joint-emperor with responsibility for the western provinces, while Valerian went to the East to bring order after the latest Persian invasion under Shapur (Fig.1). Valerian based himself in Antioch from where he defeated his rival Uranius Antoninus who had been declared emperor at Emesa (see previous chapter) (Fig.2.). Valerian apparently brought stability to the east, winning a victory in 257. He even declared himself RESTIVT ORIENTIS ("Restorer of the East") and RESTITVTOR ORBIS ("Restorer of the World") on his coins (Fig.3.). In the west, Gallienus had victories over the Germans on the Danube and on the Rhine which were also celebrated on his coins – he was titled GERMANICVS MAXIMVS (Figs.4-5.). In 259 he had to deal with an invasion of Juthungi across the Danube who had to be ejected from Italy.

Disaster in the East AD 260

The Persians under Shapur invaded again in 260. Ravaged by plague, Valerian's army took refuge at Edessa. Valerian and a small party went to negotiate with Shapur, but they were all taken prisoner (Fig.6). Valerian became a "foot-stool" for Shapur when mounting his horse; after Valerian's death in captivity, his skin was reputedly removed and tanned for exhibition in a Persian temple; one story claims that the emperor was stuffed!

Coinage of Valerian & His Family AD 253-60

A variety of mints begin to strike coins in Valerian's reign. Rome continues to issue the bulk of the coinage (Figs.1 & 11.), but from around 256 coins start to be struck in Gaul, possibly at Trier (Figs.4-5 & 7-10.). From 259, Milan appears to start striking coins, while Viminacium in Moesia Superior struck from around 254-6. In the east, a number of coins were struck at Antioch, but it is not known where the bulk of the eastern coins were minted, probably at another city in Syria (Fig.3). From now onwards, we are be confronted by an increasing number of mints issuing coins across the Roman Empire. This would ensure a ready supply of money for increasingly demanding soldiers. As a rule of thumb, coins from the mint of Gaul are the most

Fig.6. Sasanian rock carving showing the king Shapur I taking the surrender of Philip I (standing; AD 244-9) and Valerian I (kneeling; AD 253-60). Naqsh-e Rustam, Iran. © Sam Moorhead

common found in Britain in Valerian's reign (Figs.4-5 & 7-10.).

The dominant denomination remained the silver radiate, but its silver content dropped from 35% (for Aemilian) to just over 20% at the start of the reign. By 260, it had fallen under 20%.

The weight of gold coins is increasingly erratic and it does seem that there was less gold in circulation (Fig.3.). Base metal coins (*sestertii* and *asses*) continue to be struck, especially at Rome, but Valerian's is the last reign in which they really figure as a significant part of the currency in the Central Empire (Fig.11.) – the only base metal coins of Valerian on the PAS database are from Wales. With the debasement of silver coins, more needed to be produced to satisfy demand: this meant that less copper was available for base metal coinages. Furthermore, as silver coins were debased, their value decreased, making fractional base metal coins redundant. The old Augustan monetary system, which I outlined in Chapter VIII, was now collapsing.

Valerian struck a significant issue of coins for his wife Mariniana (Fig.12.); as they are all commemorative, we assume that she had died before he became emperor. Many coins were struck for Gallienus and his wife Salonina – coins of these two rulers struck in the reign of Valerian are listed under the heading "Gallienus joint reign" (Figs.4 & 5.) and "Salonina joint reign" (Fig.7.) to distinguish them from coins struck after AD 260 when Gallienus was "sole ruler" of the Central

Fig.7. Base silver radiate of Salonina, joint reign (AD 253-60), struck in Gaul. The reverse shows Ceres, the goddess of grain, standing in a temple. Cunetio 731. Found in Lancashire, LVPL335. © Portable Antiquities Scheme (20mm)

Fig.8. Base silver radiate of Valerian II (c.AD 256-8), minted in Gaul. The reverse shows the infant Jupiter riding the Amalthaean Goat. Found in Berkshire, SUR-B5BE18. © Portable Antiquities Scheme (21mm)

Empire. Gallienus' eldest son, Valerian II, was Caesar from around 256 until his death in around 258; coins were struck for him during his life (Fig.8.) and a commemorative series was issued after his death (Fig.9.). Following his death, Gallienus' second son Saloninus was made Caesar and coins were struck for him until his death at the hands of Postumus in Cologne in AD 260 (Fig.10.).

Fig.10. Base silver radiate of Saloninus (AD 258-60), minted in Gaul. The reverse shows sacrificial implements, a common reverse type for junior emperors. Found in Northamptonshire, NARC-A29A90. © Portable Antiquities Scheme (20mm)

Fig.11. Copper-alloy *sestertius* of Valerian I (AD 253-60) struck at Rome in 254. The reverse shows "concord" between the army and emperor. RIC V, pt 1, 155. © British Museum (28mm)

Fig.9. Base silver radiate, struck in Gaul to commemorate Valerian II (c.AD 256-8). The reverse shows an eagle, the bird commonly associated with the spirit of the dead emperor. Cunetio 741. Found in Hampshire, HAMP972. © Portable Antiquities Scheme (21mm)

Fig.12. Base silver radiate struck at Rome to commemorate Mariniana, the wife of Valerian (who probably died before he came to the throne), c.AD 253-60. The reverse shows a peacock, the bird commonly associated with the spirit of a dead empress. Cunetio 646. Found in Sussex, SUSS-B1BF70. © Portable Antiquities Scheme (22mm)

Fig.13. Base silver radiate of Macrianus (AD 260-1), struck at an Eastern mint. The reverse shows "Eternal Rome". RIC V, pt 2, 11. © British Museum (21mm)

Eastern Usurpers – Macrianus & Quietus AD 260-1

After the defeat of Valerian in 260, the Roman army rallied under Ballista, the praetorian prefect, and T. Fulvius Macrianus. Macrianus' sons, another Macrianus and Quietus were then made joint emperors. Macrianus marched west to challenge Gallienus, but was defeated in the Balkans by Gallienus' general Aureolus. Quietus, meanwhile, stayed in the East, but was besieged in Emesa and then killed by Odenathus, king of Palmyra.

Macrianus and Quietus struck coins at two mints in the east, but neither can be identified with certainty (Figs.13 & 14.). Their coins are rare in Britain: out of the 54,951 coins in the Cunetio hoard, there are eight of Macrianus and two of Quietus. There are no coins of these rulers on the PAS database, and only a few coins of these emperors have been found in British hoards.

Usurper in Pannonia – Regalian c.AD 260

It is thought that after the death of Valerian, the governor of Upper Pannonia (northern Balkans and Hungary), P. Caius Regalianus tried

Fig.14. Base silver radiate of Quietus (AD 260-1), struck at an Eastern mint. The reverse shows Sol, the sun god. © British Museum (21mm)

Fig.15. Base silver radiate of Regalian (c.AD 260), probably struck at Carnuntum. The reverse shows Sol, the sun god. This is the only coin of Regalian in the British Museum. RIC V, pt 2, 7. © British Museum (19mm)

to seize power. He was murdered by his own soldiers, but not before a few crude radiates were struck, probably at Carnuntum, for Regalian and his wife Dryantilla (Figs.15 & 16.). These coins are excessively rare and none ever appear to have been found in Britain.

Fig.16. Base silver radiate of Dryantilla, wife or Regalian (c.AD 260), probably struck at Carnuntum. The reverse shows Equity standing with her scales. This is the only coin of Dryantilla in the British Museum. RIC V, pt 2, 1. © British Museum (19mm)

Fig.17. Gold *aureus* of Gallienus, sole reign (AD 260-8) struck at Rome. The reverse proclaims the loyalty of the army. RIC V, pt 1, 33. © British Museum (21mm)

Fig.18. Copper-alloy radiate of Gallienus, sole reign (AD 260-8), struck in the sixth workshop in the mint at Rome. The reverse shows a goat, honouring the god Jupiter. Cunetio 1375. Found in the River Thames, LON-F35B21. © Portable Antiquities Scheme (20mm)

Fig.19. Copper-alloy radiate of Gallienus, sole reign (AD 260-8), struck in the twelfth workshop in the mint at Rome. The reverse shows a gazelle, honouring the goddess Diana. Cunetio 1408. Found in Lincolnshire, LIN-E82CB6. © Portable Antiquities Scheme (20mm)

Fig.20. Base silver radiate of Gallienus, sole reign (AD 260-8), minted in Milan. The reverse shows a centaur, the emblem of Legio II Parthica, one of 17 legions honoured on the coinage of Gallienus. Cunetio 1452. Found in Somerset, SOM-A60804. © Portable Antiquities Scheme (22mm)

"Sole Reign" of Gallienus & Salonina AD 260-8

Although the usurpers Macrianus and Regalianus had been dealt with by Gallienus, the situation in Gaul was precarious. The Alemanni advanced across Gaul and reached Tarragona in Spain. Saloninus, based at Cologne, was powerless (Fig.10.). However, the governor of Lower Germany, M. Cassianius Postumus, had some successes against the barbarians and then besieged Saloninus in Cologne. The young emperor was handed over and killed; Postumus now had control of the "Gallic Empire". Gallienus made one unsuccessful attempt to regain the territory in 265; Postumus declared that he had no interest in taking the Central Empire. I will cover the coinage of the Gallic Empire in the next chapter.

More Trouble in the East AD 260-7

After Shapur had been ejected by Ballista in 260, and Odenathus of Palmyra had killed Quietus in 261, Gallienus gave Odenathus the titles "Ruler of the Romans" and "Governor or the East". In 266, Odenathus invaded Persia and defeated the Sasanians at their capital,

Ctesiphon in Iraq. In 267, Odenathus defeated Gothic invaders in northern Turkey, but was murdered soon afterwards. Gallienus tried to defeat Palmyra but failed; it was now that the famous Queen Zenobia became ruler of Palmyra with her son Vaballathus. I will deal with their coins in Chapter XXI.

End of Gallienus AD 268

In 268, the Goths invaded across the Danube in massive numbers, but were defeated by Gallienus at Naissus. His general, Aureolus, who was at Milan, then defected to Postumus. Gallienus defeated Aureolus' army and besieged the general in Milan. However, Gallienus was to fall victim to a plot hatched by his own staff. Although Gallienus is given a bad press by historians, the reality is that he struggled manfully to keep the Empire together.

Coinage of Gallienus' "Sole Reign" AD 260-8

Gallienus was to strike coins at Rome, Milan, Siscia (in Croatia) and three mints in the East. Gold coins remain variable in weight (Fig.17.). The radiates are debased further,

Fig.21. Base silver radiate of Salonina, sole reign (AD 260-8), struck in the second workshop at Milan. The reverse shows the Roman goddess of the hearth, Vesta. Found in Leicestershire, LEIC-8EC134. © Portable Antiquities Scheme (21mm)

Fig.22. Base silver radiate of Salonina, sole reign (AD 260-8), struck in second workshop at Milan. The reverse proclaims (untruthfully) the peace of the times. Cunetio 1765. Found in Somerset, SOM-E81C37. © Portable Antiquities Scheme (20mm)

Fig.23. Copper-alloy radiate of Salonina, sole reign (AD 260-8), struck in the fourth workshop of the mint of Rome. The reverse celebrates the empress' fertility. Cunetio 1318. Found in Hampshire, HAMP-C1F594. © Portable Antiquities Scheme (17mm)

Fig.24. Copper-alloy medallion of Gallienus (AD 253-60), probably struck in Rome. This is one of only three base metal medallions on the PAS Database. The reverse shows Salus feeding a snake. BMC Medallions no.10. Found in North Yorkshire, SWYOR-9A9EF5. © Portable Antiquities Scheme (24mm)

Fig.25. Copper-alloy radiate of Claudius II (AD 268-70), struck in the first workshop at Milan. The reverse shows Spes ("Hope"). Cunetio 2240. Found in Hampshire, SUR-815394. © Portable Antiquities Scheme (19mm)

having as little as 6% silver by the end of the reign (Figs.18-23.). Base metal coins (*sestertii* and *asses*) become much rarer and are only really struck at Rome. It is in Gallienus' sole reign that the debased radiate becomes effectively the only coin in common circulation. Because the coins were so debased, they had to be struck in enormous numbers. Coins of Rome are the most common in Britain.

Several issues were struck by up to 12 workshops (*officinae*) at the mint – each workshop had its own mark (e.g. A for workshop one, B for workshop two, up to XI for workshop 11 and XII for workshop 12) (Figs.18 & 19 & 23). Probably the most popular coins from Rome are the animal reverse types struck in Issue 5 (Figs. 18 & 19.).

Coins of Milan were struck in three workshops; these coins tend to be of better quality than the Rome pieces, but are scarcer (Figs.20-22.). In AD 262, Siscia was opened with two workshops; a small number of Siscia coins have been found in Britain. Coins from Eastern mints are generally scarcer. Although the majority of the coins were struck for Gallienus, a large number was struck for his empress Salonina (Figs.21-3.). One unexpected find in Britain is of a medallion of Gallienus, probably presented to a soldier or official in the Province (Fig.24.).

Claudius II (AD 268-70) & Quintillus (AD 270)

Claudius had been a successful general in the armies of Valerian and Gallienus. After the death of Gallienus, Claudius marched on Milan and killed Aureolus. He then quickly marched against the Alemanni and defeated them at Lake Garda. The following year he defeated the Goths and took the title "Gothicus Maximus". However, in 270, a plague spread across the Balkans, not only killing many Goths, but also Claudius. His brother, Quintillus, was declared emperor at Aquileia in northern Italy, but only survived a couple of months at the most. He committed suicide when it was clear that the Danube legions were supporting another claimant to the throne, Aurelian.

Claudius and Quintillus continued to strike highly debased radiates, normally even smaller than those of Gallienus. Once again, the products of Milan (Figs.25 & 26 & 28.) were superior in quality to those of Rome (Figs.27 & 29-30.). Coins of Claudius are amongst the most common found in Britain.

Fig.26. Copper-alloy radiate of Claudius II (AD 268-70), struck in the second workshop at Milan. The reverse shows Victory. Cunetio 2243. Found in Leicestershire, LEIC-DD5428. © Portable Antiquities Scheme (21mm)

Fig.27. Copper-alloy radiate of Claudius II (AD 268-70), struck in Rome. The reverse shows the Genius of the Roman army. Cunetio 2150. Found in Hampshire, HAMP-6C4B01. © Portable Antiquities Scheme (19mm)

Fig.28. Copper-alloy radiate of Quintillus (AD 270), struck in the first workshop at Milan. This is one of only three examples of Milan coins for Quintillus from England on the PAS Database. Normanby 1222. Found in Dorset, DOR-2CBA14. © Portable Antiquities Scheme (19mm)

Fig.29. Copper-alloy radiate of Quintillus (AD 270), struck in the third workshop at Rome. Quintillus' curly hair distinguishes him from his brother Claudius. Cunetio 2324. Found in Dorset, DOR-FD24F0. © Portable Antiquities Scheme (19mm)

Fig.30. Copper-alloy radiate of Quintillus (AD 270), struck in the tenth workshop at Rome. The reverse shows Mars. Normanby 1190. Found in Hampshire, HAMP-992D48. © Portable Antiquities Scheme (20mm)

Divus Claudius

Claudius was a very popular emperor and was deified after his death. Many coins were struck in his honour, apparently by Aurelian (AD 270-5). Most of them show Claudius with the inscription DIVO CLAVDIO ("To the Divine Claudius") while the reverse has the inscription CONSECRATIO around an altar or an eagle (Figs.31 & 32.). The official coins of this series are quite scarce in Britain, but barbarous copies of them are very common.

Summary Totals

Overall, radiate coins of the years 253-60 are much scarcer than those for 260-70. This is because the silver content dropped from over 20% in the early 250s to under 3% in 270. Therefore, many more coins had to be struck to make-up for the declining amount of silver in each coin. We have some enormous hoards from this period, notably the Cunetio hoard of 54,951 coins (Fig 33) and the Normanby hoard of 47,912 coins. These two hoards have proven vital for our understanding of the coinages and are now used as standard references – you will see that I cite them in the coin captions. There are no gold coins from this period on the database, and no

Fig.31. Copper-alloy "barbarous radiate" copying a commemorative coin of Claudius II (AD 268-70), struck c.AD 270-285. The reverse shows an altar. These copies are very common; much more so than the official issues. Cunetio 2875. Found in Flintshire, LVPL-0FA336. © Portable Antiquities Scheme (17mm)

Valerian I	123
Mariniana	5
Valerian II	39
Saloninus	11
Gallienus (both reigns)	1939
Salonina (both reigns)	223
Claudius II	2601
Quintillus	106

sestertii or *asses* from England on the database. The table above shows rulers represented on the PAS database.

Coins of this period are found right across Britain – see Map 2.

Fig.32. Copper-alloy "barbarous radiate" copying a commemorative coin of Claudius II (AD 268-70), struck c.AD 270-285. The reverse shows an eagle. Cunetio 2877. Found in Hampshire, HAMP-BD71D7. © Portable Antiquities Scheme (15mm)

Fig.33. Radiate coins of Salonina in the Cunetio Hoard, Britain's largest hoard, which contained 54,951 coins. The last coin in the hoard dates to AD 275.

Map 2. Finds of radiate coins struck AD 260-75. (© Philippa Walton)

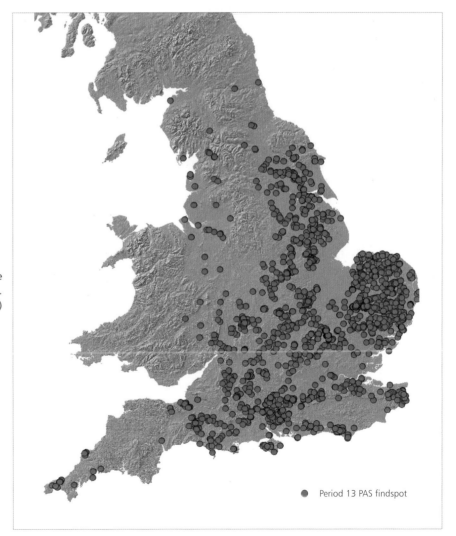

● Period 13 PAS findspot

Chapter XX

Coinage of The Gallic Empire from Postumus to The Tetrici

(AD 260-274)

Map 1. The Gallic Empire. (© Richard Kelleher)

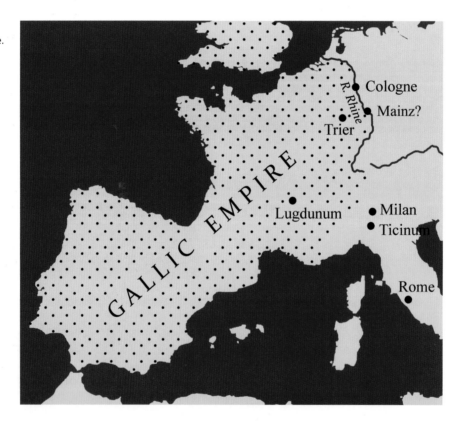

Turmoil in AD 260

In the last chapter I wrote about the emperors of the Central Empire from Valerian (253-60) to Quintillus (270). In AD 260, after the defeat and capture of Valerian by the Sasanians in the East, the Roman Empire effectively split into three parts. In the East, the semi-independent city of Palmyra took effective control of much of the Eastern Empire – I will cover Palmyra in the next chapter. In the West, there were some devastating barbarian invasions across the River Rhine – Frankish warriors swept into Gaul and even reached Spain; the Alamanni also invaded, reaching Gaul via Switzerland.

Postumus (AD 260-9) & Foundation of the Gallic Empire

On the German frontier, the seasoned general, and possibly Governor of Lower Germany, Postumus, rebelled. He probably had disagreements with other officials, acting for the junior emperor Saloninus who was at Cologne,

Fig.1. Base silver radiate of Postumus (AD 260-9), "principal" mint of Gaul (probably Trier). This coin was struck quite early in Postumus' reign. Cunetio 2381. Found in Lincolnshire, WMID-C62702. © Portable Antiquities Scheme (23mm)

Fig.2. Base silver radiate of Postumus (AD 260-9), "principal" mint of Gaul (probably Trier). The reverse shows the emperor and refers to "fortunate times". Found in Hampshire, HAMP814. © Portable Antiquities Scheme (20mm)

Fig.3. Copper-alloy *sestertius* of Postumus (AD 260-9), "principal" mint in Gaul (probably Trier), AD 260. The reverse shows the emperor standing. RIC V, pt 2, no. 107, Found in Surrey, SUR-218620. © Portable Antiquities Scheme (33mm)

Fig.4. Copper-alloy *sestertius* of Postumus (AD 260-9), "principal" mint in Gaul (probably Trier). The reverse shows two Victories attaching a shield to a tree above two captives. RIC V, pt 2, 168. Found in Suffolk, SF-0C1BB0. © Portable Antiquities Scheme (30mm)

Fig.5. Copper-alloy *dupondius* of Postumus (AD 260-9), "principal" mint in Gaul (probably Trier). The reverse shows a galley. Found in Sussex, SUSS-098736. © Portable Antiquities Scheme (22.5mm)

on how to deal with the barbarians. Saloninus was executed, and Postumus took control of the provinces of Germany, Gaul, Spain and Britain – the so-called "Gallic Empire". What is interesting is that Postumus never showed any desire to advance southwards to attempt to take control of the entire Empire; he was satisfied with defending the north-western part of the Empire and promoting stability in Gaul and surrounding territories.

It was not until 265 that Gallienus tried to remove Postumus from the throne. Gallienus, and his master of cavalry Aureolus, marched north from Italy. However, Aureolus failed to capture the fleeing Postumus and then Gallienus was wounded during a siege, forcing his army to retreat in failure. Postumus continued to rule his Gallic Empire for another four years.

Coinage of Postumus

Postumus appears to have struck most of his coins at a "principal" mint in Trier, his capital in Germany (Figs.1-5.). This mint continued to strike all of his coinage until a branch mint was set up at Cologne in AD 268 (Fig.6.). Another group of coins, in the name of Postumus, were struck by Aureolus at Milan in 268 (see Figs.7 & 8.).

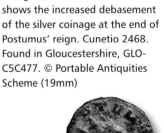

Fig.6. Base silver radiate of Postumus (AD 260-9), struck at Cologne, AD 268-9. This coin shows the increased debasement of the silver coinage at the end of Postumus' reign. Cunetio 2468. Found in Gloucestershire, GLO-C5C477. © Portable Antiquities Scheme (19mm)

Fig.7. Base silver radiate of Postumus (AD 260-9), struck at Milan in AD 268 by Aureolus. The coins of Milan are distinctive because they have a shorter obverse legend. Cunetio 2481. Found in Dorset, DOR-F1E4C6. © Portable Antiquities Scheme (20mm)

Postumus maintained his "radiates" at a higher silver content (over 15%) than the coins of Gallienus, until he was forced to debase the coinage in AD 268 (to 7-8% silver). This is why radiates of Postumus generally appear more silvery in appearance than their contemporaries struck in Gallienus' sole reign (see previous chapter). Because Postumus struck a better quality silver coinage, he was also able to issue a substantial number of *sestertii*, *dupondii* and *asses* in the earlier part of his reign. These base metal coins are found in Britain in small but significant numbers (Figs.3-5.). On the PAS database (www.finds.org.uk), there are 696 radiates, 46 *sestertii* and 5 *dupondii* and *asses*. Gold coins from the Gallic Empire are rare and none have been recorded on the PAS database; I show a British Museum specimen (Fig.9.).

Revolts of Aureolus & Laelian (AD 268-9) & the Death of Postumus

However, in AD 268, Aureolus rebelled against Gallienus at Milan; it appears that Aureolus was expecting assistance from Postumus because coins in Postumus' name were struck at Milan by Aureolus – these coins are scarce and there are about 30 on the PAS database (Figs.7 & 8.). However, Postumus did not move across the Alps. Aureolus was killed by Gallienus' successor Claudius II (see previous chapter). In 269, a Spaniard called Laelianus, rebelled against Postumus at Mainz and took Cologne. Postumus responded by marching on Mainz from his capital

at Trier – Laelian was defeated, but Postumus died at the hands of his own soldiers because he refused his men permission to sack Mainz.

Laelian's coinage was only struck at one mint, probably at Cologne or Mainz. A study has shown that there were only about 49 obverse dies and 54 reverse dies cut. His coins are particularly rare with only eight on the PAS database (Figs.10 & 11.).

Marius (AD 269)

It seems that Marius, a soldier of humble birth in Postumus' army at Mainz, was a hasty appointment by the army. He allowed the sack of the city and then returned to Trier. His long-term position was precarious because Victorinus, one of Postumus' most trusted comrades, was still at large. After only 12 weeks, Marius was murdered at Trier and succeeded by Victorinus.

Marius struck coins at two mints, probably Trier (Fig.12.) and Cologne (Fig.13.). This arrangement seems to have held until the last years of the Gallic Empire, but it should be said that scholars do disagree over the location of the two mints, and some think that there was actually only one. Because of this, we call the mints Gaul Mint I and Gaul Mint II on the PAS database. Marius' coins are very scarce, there only being 15 on the PAS database (Figs.12 & 13.).

Fig.8. Base silver radiate of Postumus (AD 260-9), struck at Milan in AD 268 by Aureolus. This coin shows the distinctive portrait of Postumus at Milan. Cunetio 2481. Found in Hampshire, HAMP-169920. © Portable Antiquities Scheme (18mm)

Fig.9. Gold *aureus* of Postumus (AD 260-9), struck at his "principal" mint in Gaul (probably Trier). The obverse shows Postumus and Hercules, the reverse Mars and Victory. RIC V, pt 2, 262. © British Museum (18mm)

Fig.10. Copper-alloy radiate of Laelian (AD 269), probably mint of Cologne. The reverse shows Victory. Cunetio 2501. Found in Worcestershire, WAW-05D402. © Portable Antiquities Scheme (21.5mm)

Fig.11. Copper-alloy radiate of Laelian (AD 269), probably mint of Cologne. The reverse shows Victory. From the Breamore Hoard, Cunetio 2500. © British Museum (21mm)

Fig.12. Copper-alloy radiate of Marius (AD 269), Mint I (probably mint of Trier). The reverse shows "concord" between the emperor and army. Found in Hampshire, BUC-8E60A4. © Portable Antiquities Scheme (18mm)

Victorinus (AD 269-71)

Unlike Marius, Victorinus appears to have come from a wealthy Gallic family. He was a very successful soldier under Postumus and was the logical successor when Postumus was assassinated. Victorinus seemed to have no problems with the German barbarians (the Franks and Alamanni), but he lost south-western Gaul and Spain to the Central Empire ruler, Claudius II (268-70 – see previous chapter). Victorinus was able to suppress a major revolt in south-eastern Gaul, sacking the city of Autun, which he celebrated with a triumph. Victorinus seems to have one major weakness, however, which was his tendency to womanise with soldiers' wives; when he tried it on with the wife of Attitianus, a senior officer, he was assassinated.

Victorinus continued to strike coins at the two Gallic mints, probably Trier (Figs.14-16.) and Cologne (Figs.17 & 18.). However, the silver content dropped to 3% or lower. His coins are very common, especially those showing Pax (Fig.14.) and Sol, the sun god (Fig.15.). There are 1179 of his coins on the PAS database. His coins look similar to his successor, Tetricus I, but Victorinus often has a distinctive Roman nose (see Figs.14 & 17.).

Domitian II (AD 271)

In 1901, a coin of Domitian II was found in France near Nantes. No Gallic emperor of this name is recorded, but there was an officer serving under Aureolus at Milan (see above) who went over to the Gallic cause in AD 268. Could this have been the same man who later seems to have become emperor briefly in AD 271? Doubt was cast on the authenticity of the coin, but in 2003 my colleague Richard Abdy discovered another example of exactly the same coin in the Chalgrove hoard (Fig.19.). The great rarity of the coins

Fig.13. Copper-alloy radiate of Marius (AD 269), Mint II (probably mint of Cologne). The reverse shows Victory. Cunetio 2508. Found in Dorset, DOR-6422B3. © Portable Antiquities Scheme (18.5m)

Fig.14. Copper-alloy radiate of Victorinus (AD 269-71), Mint I (probably mint of Trier). The reverse shows Pax (Peace). Cunetio 2534. Found in Hampshire, SUR-8C30C0. © Portable Antiquities Scheme (17mm)

Fig.15. Copper-alloy radiate of Victorinus (AD 269-71), Mint I (probably mint of Trier). The reverse shows Sol (sun god). Cunetio 2534. Found in Cambridgeshire, LANCUM-462CF2. © Portable Antiquities Scheme (18mm)

Fig.16. Copper-alloy radiate of Victorinus (AD 269-71), Mint I (probably mint of Trier). The reverse refers to the bravery (virtus) of the emperor. Cunetio 2553. Found in Lincolnshire, DENO-42F917. © Portable Antiquities Scheme (18mm)

Fig.17. Copper-alloy radiate of Victorinus (AD 269-71), Mint II (probably mint of Cologne). The reverse shows Salus feeding a snake in her arms. Found in Nottinghamshire, DENO-1D6753. © Portable Antiquities Scheme (19.5mm)

Fig.18. Copper-alloy radiate of Victorinus (AD 269-71), Mint II (probably mint of Cologne). The reverse shows Pietas. Cunetio 2572. Found in Hertfordshire, BH-73BA18. © Portable Antiquities Scheme (18mm)

Fig.19. Copper-alloy radiate of Domitian II, struck in Gaul c.AD 271. The reverse shows Domitian's good relationship with the army. RIC V, pt 2, no. 1. © British Museum (20mm)

does suggest that Domitian II's reign was very short and we can only surmise that he unsuccessfully attempted to take control of the Gallic Empire after the death of Victorinus. I eagerly await the first coin of Domitian II to appear on the PAS database!

The Tetrici (AD 271-4)

Whatever the role of Domitian, it seems that the person who really took power after Victorinus' death was his mother Victoria. She apparently ruled briefly and then bribed the troops to support her nominee, Tetricus I. He was of senatorial rank and had been Governor of the rich province of Aquitania in south-west Gaul. Early in his reign Tetricus had to campaign against the Germans and after successes held a triumph in Trier. Probably in 273, he raised his son, Tetricus II, to the rank of Caesar (junior emperor) and it seems that his realm was peaceful and prosperous when the Central Empire ruler, Aurelian (270-5) decided to march north. After a military stand-off, and possibly a bloody battle, Tetricus agreed to submit to Aurelian. Tetricus and his son appeared in Aurelian's triumph at Rome. Tetricus ended his career as an official, *corrector*, in southern Italy; he and his son were

the last of the Gallic emperors and the only ones to die peacefully.

Until the last part of his reign, there appear to have been two mints, probably Trier (Figs.20-3.) and Cologne (Fig.24.). Towards the end of the reign they might have merged at Trier. Tetricus I's coins are extremely common, there being 2416 on the PAS database.

The need for more coins might be explained by the fact that the silver content fell to about 1%. Tetricus II became emperor around 273 and his coins are also common with 1,054 on the PAS database (Figs.25-7.). There were over 16,000 of their coins in the Normanby hoard, and we have at least 12,500 in the recently discovered Frome hoard. The most common individual type shows Pax – this to the most common single issue of any Roman ruler to be found in Britain (Fig.21.).

Roger Bland reckons that up to 1 million coins a day might have been struck in the reign of Tetricus. Amongst the coins on the PAS database is an extremely rare coin from early in Tetricus I's reign showing the emperor on horseback; this coin is normally only known in gold and the British Museum did not have a specimen (Fig.20.). The finder, Tim Camm, has very kindly donated this coin to the British Museum.

Fig.20. Copper-alloy radiate of Tetricus I (AD 271-4), probably of Mint I (probably Trier). The reverse is an "Adventus" type with the emperor on horseback. This very rare coin has been generously donated to the British Museum by Tim Camm. RIC V, pt 2, c.f. no. 51. Found in Lincolnshire, LIN-2F4F73. © Portable Antiquities Scheme (16mm)

Fig.21. Copper-alloy radiate of Tetricus I (AD 271-4), Mint I (probably Trier). This coin of Tetricus I with PAX AVG is the most common single type ever struck in the Roman Empire. Normanby 1473. Found in Sussex, SUSS-A6EC32. © Portable Antiquities Scheme (17.5mm)

Fig.22. Copper-alloy radiate of Tetricus I (AD 271-4), Mint I (probably Trier). The reverse proclaims Victory the "companion" of the emperor. Normanby 1472. Found in Hampshire, HAMP-1AA117. © Portable Antiquities Scheme (18mm)

Fig.23. Copper-alloy radiate of Tetricus I (AD 271-4), Mint I (probably Trier). This is a rare coin with a Spes ("Hope") reverse used for the coinage of Tetricus II (see Fig.25.). c.f. Normanby 1497. Found in Somerset, SOM-FF48E3. © Portable Antiquities Scheme (18mm)

Fig.24. Copper-alloy radiate of Tetricus I (AD 271-4), Mint II (probably Cologne). The reverse shows Laetitia ("joyfulness"). Normanbyb 1515. Found in Dorset, DOR-E65660. © Portable Antiquities Scheme (17.5mm)

Although radiates of Tetricus are extremely common, his gold remains extremely rare and there are no *aurei* on the PAS database; again I show a British Museum coin (Fig.28.).

Gallic Empire Coins in Britain

Coins of the Gallic Empire are extremely common in Britain. Not only are they found on sites across the Province (Map 2), there are over 600 hoards which contain them. The PAS data provides an insight into the relative rarity of the coins, making it clear that Laelian and Marius only ruled for a very short period. Furthermore, the PAS data shows that as the silver content of the coins decreased, more coins were probably struck and subsequently lost. Totals for Gallic Empire rulers on the PAS Database (www.finds.org.uk)

Postumus	775
Laelian	8
Marius	15
Victorinus	1801
Domitian	0
Tetricus I	2416
Tetricus II	1054

Fig.27. Copper-alloy radiate of Tetricus II (c.AD 273-4), Mint II (probably Cologne). The reverse shows sacrificial implements, commonly found on coins of Caesars (junior emperors). Normanby 1543. Found in Hampshire, HAMP-547B06. © Portable Antiquities Scheme (17mm)

Fig.28. Gold *aureus* of Tetricus I (AD 271-4), struck in Mint II (probably Cologne). The reverse shows Victory. RIC V, pt 2, 30. © British Museum (18mm)

Fig.25. Copper-alloy radiate of Tetricus II (c.AD 273-4), Mint I (probably Trier). The reverse shows Spes ("Hope"). Normanby 1533. Found in Greater London, SUR-B9B5B1. © Portable Antiquities Scheme (19mm)

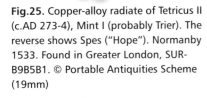

Fig.26. Copper-alloy radiate of Tetricus II (c.AD 273-4), Mint I (probably Trier). The reverse has the Comes type more commonly found for Tetricus I (see Fig.22.). Normanby 1528. Found in Hampshire, HAMP-210BB7. © Portable Antiquities Scheme (18mm)

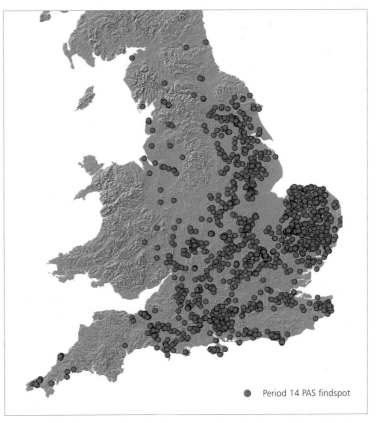

Period 14 PAS findspot

Map 2. Coins from AD 260-275 recorded with the PAS. (© Philippa Walton)

Chapter XXI
From Aurelian to Diocletian's Pre-Reform Coinage
(AD 270-296)

Fig.1. Copper-alloy radiate of Aurelian (AD 270-5), struck at Rome, c.AD 270-1. This is a pre-reform coin, following the style of coins of Claudius II. RIC V, pt 1, no. 29. Found in Wiltshire, WILT-492A03. © Portable Antiquities Scheme (21mm)

Fig.2. Base-silver radiate of Aurelian (AD 270-5), struck at Rome. The reverse proclaims "concord" between Aurelian and the army. RIC V, pt 1, 59. Found on the Isle of Wight, IOW-F320D1. © Portable Antiquities Scheme (20mm)

Fig.3. Base-silver radiate of Aurelian (AD 270-5), struck at Serdica. The reverse shows Sol, the sun god. The XXI in the exergue means 20 parts copper to 1 part silver (about 5% silver). RIC V, pt 1, no. 279. Found in Leicestershire, LEIC-F4D9B7. © Portable Antiquities Scheme (23mm)

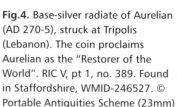

Fig.4. Base-silver radiate of Aurelian (AD 270-5), struck at Tripolis (Lebanon). The coin proclaims Aurelian as the "Restorer of the World". RIC V, pt 1, no. 389. Found in Staffordshire, WMID-246527. © Portable Antiquities Scheme (23mm)

In this chapter I will be discussing the radiate coinages from the reign of Aurelian (270-5) to the coinage reforms of Diocletian's in 294-6. I will deal with Diocletian's post-reform coinage in two chapters' time (XXIII).

Aurelian (AD 270-5) & the Walls of Rome

Aurelian (Figs.1-4.) was a brilliant cavalry commander who had been involved in the demise of Gallienus (260-8; see Chapter XIX). However, he remained loyal to Claudius II (268-70; Chapter XIX) and only made a move for the throne

after Claudius died of plague. We have seen how Quintillus committed suicide after a very short reign (AD 270; Chapter XIX) leaving Aurelian in charge of the Central Empire. Aurelian had to repel two invasions of barbarians from the north in 271, but the threat to Italy meant that Aurelian decided to build new fortification walls around Rome. You can still see these Walls of Aurelian to this day (Fig.5.).

Defeat of Palmyra & the Gallic Empire

In AD 260, the leader of the Syrian city Palmyra, Odenathus, drove the Sasanian Persians

Fig.5. The Walls at Rome, first begun by Aurelian (270-5) and completed by Probus (276-82). Later modifications were made in the early 5th century and in the medieval period. © David Stuttard

Fig.6. Base-silver radiate of Aurelian and Vabalathus, struck at Antioch, AD 270-1. The obverse shows Aurelian, the reverse Vabalathus of Palmyra. RIC V, pt 1, 308. Found in Lincolnshire, LIN-4C31F4. © Portable Antiquities Scheme (23mm)

Fig.7. Base silver radiate of Zenobia, struck at Antioch or Emesa, AD 272. This very rare coin was struck during her war with Aurelian. RIC V, pt 2, 2. © British Museum (20mm)

back over the River Euphrates, saving the Eastern Roman Empire. Gallienus gave Odenathus the titles "Ruler of the Romans" and "Governor of the East" placing Palmyra at the centre of Eastern Empire.

Palmyra was a great caravan city in the desert of eastern Syria that became very rich through its role in trade along the Silk Route, which went all the way to China. Odenathus inflicted a further defeat on the Persians in 266, and then helped the Romans by defeating the Goths in Turkey. However, he was assassinated in 267, to be succeeded by his queen, Zenobia, and son, Vabalathus.

In 270, Zenobia decided to follow her own ambitions – she invaded and took control of parts of Turkey and Egypt, where she struck coins at Alexandria. Aurelian did give Vabalathus the same titles as Odenathus and Vabalathus struck coins at Antioch with his and Aurelian's portraits (Fig.6.).

However, when Vabalathus declared himself Augustus, Aurelian marched east and defeated Zenobia and Vabalathus in 272. During this war, Zenobia struck a small number of radiates (Fig.7.). After a further revolt in 273, Aurelian ransacked Palmyra and the city never recovered.

Aurelian now had control of the East. This enabled Aurelian to turn his attention to the West where, in AD 274, he defeated Tetricus I and II and brought the breakaway Gallic Empire to an end (see Chapter XX).

It is thought that Zenobia and Tetricus I both appeared in Aurelian's triumph in Rome.

Back in Rome, Aurelian built a new temple to Sol Invictus (the Invincible Sun God), a deity who figures prominently on his coins (Fig.3.).

Revolt at the Mint & the Coinage Reforms of Aurelian

When Aurelian came to the throne, the currency had declined to a lamentable state. The radiates of Claudius and Quintillus were very low quality, as were the pieces of the Tetrici in Gaul. The silver content fell to as low as 1% and Aurelian's earliest coins were of poor quality (Fig.1.). Furthermore, it seems that corruption was rife in the mint at Rome and when Aurelian tried to remedy the situation the Controller of the Mint, Felicissimus, led a rebellion of mint workers who barricaded themselves in on the Caelian Hill. When they were finally overcome, there were 7,000 dead Roman soldiers. The mint was closed until later in the reign.

Aurelian's reforms happened over time, but by 274 there was a new silver-washed radiate coin with 5% silver (Fig.3.). This better quality coin was to be the standard denomination until the reforms of Diocletian in AD 294-6. Many of the coins were marked XXI denoting that there were 20 parts copper to one part silver (i.e. c.5% silver); in the east, the Greek letters KA also represents 20 to 1.

Aurelian struck coins at an extensive network of mints across the empire: Lyon, Milan, Ticinum (Pavia), Rome (Figs.1 & 2.), Siscia (Sisak in Croatia), Serdica (Sofiya, Bulgaria; Fig.3.), Cyzicus (Turkey), Antioch, and Tripolis (Lebanon, Fig.4.). In Britain, pre-reform coins of Aurelian are rare (Fig.1.), but post-reform coins are more common (Figs.2-4.).

In 275, Aurelian had just defeated a barbarian army and was on his way East when he was assassinated. Although the details are unclear, it seems that his empress, Severina, ruled for a short while before another emperor was found. This means that she might be the only empress ever to rule, and strike coins, in her own name (Fig.8.). Her coins are scarce in Britain, there only being 10 on the PAS database (www.finds.org.uk).

Tacitus & Florian (AD 275-6)

Traditionally it was thought that Tacitus (Figs.9-10; 25.) was from a senatorial background in Italy. However, it seems that the sources are unreliable and it is now believed that Tacitus was another general chosen by the army to be emperor. He did not last long and was murdered after a reign of only six months. His successor, Florian (Fig.11.), who had been prefect of the Praetorian Guard, only lasted 88 days, succumbing to Probus who had been declared emperor in the East. There are 99 coins of Tacitus on the PAS database, but only seven of Florian whose coins are very rare.

Probus (AD 276-82)

Probus (Figs.12-14.) was another rigorous military emperor, dealing with numerous barbarian invasions on the Rhine and Danube frontiers during the first three years of his reign. However, in 280 he had to spend much time dealing with a revolt of Bonosus and Proculus in Gaul and Germany; there was even a revolt by a British governor.

In the East, a certain Saturninus declared himself emperor, but was killed by his own men. After holding a triumph and extravagant games at Rome in 281, Probus headed east to fight the Persians. However, this led to the rise of a contender to the throne, Carus, the prefect of the Praetorian Guard. In a short period of time the army switched its allegiance to Carus and Probus was killed near Sirmium (Croatia). Probus' coinage was extensive, being struck at mints across the Empire. There are many interesting varieties of his bust, making his coins popular with collectors. In the period from AD 270-286 his coins are the most common, there being 142 on the database.

Carus & His Family (AD 282-5)

Carus was declared emperor at Sirmium and made his sons Carinus and Numerian junior emperors (Caesars). He travelled to Rome where he put Carinus in charge of the western provinces and promoted him to be joint-Augustus. Carus and Numerian then marched east and managed to capture the Persian capital at Ctesiphon. However, soon afterwards, Carus was killed by a "bolt of lightning", or, more likely, assassinated (Fig.15.). This left Numerian to make peace and retreat (Fig.16.). On his way back through Turkey he was assassinated and the soldiers declared Diocletian, a leading general, to become the next emperor.

Meanwhile, in the west, Carinus had won victories over the barbarians and even campaigned in Britain, taking the title Britannicus Maximus in 284 (Fig.17.). However, he was then faced with a

Fig.8. Base-silver *denarius* of Severina, struck at Rome, AD 274-5. *Denarii* were only struck at Rome, and in small numbers, in this perioAd. RIC V, pt 1, 6. Found in Cambridgeshire, CAM-6CCE74. © Portable Antiquities Scheme (19mm)

Fig.9. Base-silver radiate of Tacitus (AD 275-6), struck in Gaul. The reverse shows Mars. RIC V, pt 1, 30. Found in Somerset, SOM-456497. © Portable Antiquities Scheme (24mm

Fig.10. Base-silver radiate of Tacitus (AD 275-6), struck in Rome. The reverse shows Providentia. RIC V, pt 1, 92. Found in Oxfordshire, BERK-2D7077. © Portable Antiquities Scheme (21mm

Fig.11. Base-silver radiate of Florian (AD 276), struck in the fourth workshop at Lyon. This is one of 10 coins of Florian so far identified in the Frome Hoard, Somerset. RIC V, pt 1, 2. © Portable Antiquities Scheme (22mm)

Fig.12. Base-silver radiate of Probus (AD 276-82), struck in the first workshop at Lyon. The reverse shows Felicitas. RIC V, pt 2, no. 51. Found in Lincolnshire, LIN-D4FBC3. © Portable Antiquities Scheme (22mm)

Fig.13. Base-silver radiate of Probus (AD 276-82), struck at Siscia. This rare coin shows the wolf with Romulus and Remus. RIC V, pt 2, 701. Found in Gloucestershire, GLO-B05425. © Portable Antiquities Scheme (19mm)

Fig.14. Base-silver radiate of Probus (AD 276-82, struck at Antioch. The reverse shows the emperor and Jupiter. RIC V, pt 2, 920. Found in Greater London, SUR-BC0DE7. © Portable Antiquities Scheme (23mm)

Fig.15. Base-silver radiate commemorating Carus (AD 282-3), struck in the second workshop at Lyon. The reverse shows an eagle, associated with the spirit of the dead emperor. RIC V, pt 2, 29. Found in Leicestershire, DENO-3B3AF6. © Portable Antiquities Scheme (21mm)

Fig.16. Base-silver radiate of Numerian as Caesar (AD 282-3), struck at Rome. This is one of only two coins of Numerian on the PAS Database. RIC V, pt 2, no. 362. Found in Leicestershire, LEIC-980733. © Portable Antiquities Scheme (21mm)

Fig.17. Gold *aureus* of Carinus (AD 282-5), struck at Siscia. This is only the second example of this type known. RIC V, pt 2, 312. Found in Nottinghamshire, DENO-3B3AF6. © Portable Antiquities Scheme (19mm)

Fig.18. Gold *aureus* of Magnia Urbica (wife of Carinus, AD 283-5), struck at Rome. The reverse shows Venus. RIC V, pt 2, 340. © British Museum (20mm)

Fig.19. Base-silver radiate of Magnia Urbica (wife of Carinus, AD 283-5), struck at Rome. The reverse shows Venus. RIC V, pt 2, 343. © British Museum (21mm)

Fig.21. Gold *aureus* of Julian of Pannonia (AD 284-5), struck in Siscia. The reverse shows Liberty. RIC V, pt 2, 1. © British Museum (19mm)

Fig.22. Base-silver radiate of Diocletian (AD 284-305), struck at Lyon, AD 285. The reverse shows Jupiter holding a thunderbolt. RIC V, pt 2, 41. Found in Somerset, SOM-703934. © Portable Antiquities Scheme (22mm)

Fig.20. Base-silver commemorative radiate of Nigrinian (grandson of Carus), struck in Rome, AD 284-5. RIC V, pt 2, Carinus 472. © British Museum (22mm)

usurper in Italy, Julian (Fig.21.). Carinus defeated Julian at Verona and then turned to face Diocletian who was coming from the east. We are told that many of Carinus' officers turned against him because he had seduced their wives; we are even told that he had nine wives of his own, although only Magnia Urbica is known (Figs.18 & 19.). Whatever the truth, Carinus succumbed to Diocletian and died with his wife, and probably his son Nigrinian (Fig.20.).

All coins of Carus are scarce in Britain, only 37 coins being recorded for the entire dynasty with the PAS. However, there is an outstanding gold *aureus* of Carinus from Nottinghamshire (Fig.17.). As a rule, gold coins of this period are very rare.

Diocletian & the Tetrarchy (AD 284-305)

After the assassination of Carinus in 285, Diocletian became sole emperor of the Roman world (Figs.22 & 23.). However, there were challenges from Aelianus and Amandus in Gaul. Diocletian sent Maximian to quell the revolts and the following year made him joint emperor (Fig.24.). In 293, two junior emperors were appointed, Constantius I and Galerius. In Chapter XXIII I will discuss the reign of Diocletian more. However, what is important here is that he continued to issue radiate coins until AD 294-6

when he completely reformed the coinage, introducing the *nummus* (see chapter XXIII). Radiate coins for Diocletian and Maximian are more common than those for the dynasty of Carus. There are only two pre-reform radiates for Constantius I on the database, and one for Galerius.

Barbarous Radiates – A Response to the New Radiates

With the demise of the Gallic Empire in AD 274, the supply of low value small change to Britain ceased overnight. The better quality post-reform coins of Aurelian and his successors were never as common in Britain – there is a much higher proportion of post-reform coins from hoards than from sites (Fig.25.). It does seem that the Britons had a serious need for, and like of, small denomination coins: between c.AD 275 and c.AD 285, millions of "barbarous radiates" were made in Britain (Fig.26.).

These coins played a very important role in the economic boom that was beginning in Britain's countryside at this time, rather like the token coinages that played a vital role in Britain's "Industrial Revolution". There are at least 4,167 "barbarous radiates" on the PAS database, showing how much more common they were than official coins.

Fig.23. Base-silver radiate of Diocletian (AD 284-305), struck at Lyon, AD 290-1. The reverse shows Jupiter and eagle. RIC V, pt 2, 28. Found in Leicestershire, LEIC-F37BB6. © Portable Antiquities Scheme (22mm)

Fig.24. Base-silver radiate of Maximian (AD 286-310), struck at Lyon, AD 290-4. The reverse shows Salus. RIC V, pt 2, 422. Found in Hampshire, HAMP-D9ED61. © Portable Antiquities Scheme (22mm)

Fig.25. A selection of base-silver post-reform radiates of Tacitus (AD 275-6) from the Alton Barnes hoard (Wiltshire), found in 2005 and now on display in the Wiltshire Heritage Museum, Devizes. © British Museum.

Fig.27. Copper-alloy "barbarous radiate" probably copying a Gallic emperor, c.AD 275-85. Found in Hertfordshire, BH-7357E5. © Portable Antiquities Scheme (16mm)

Fig.26. A selection of "barbarous radiates" from the Alton Barnes hoard (Wiltshire). These coins date from c.AD 275 to c.AD 285. © British Museum

Summary of Emperor Numbers

Aurelian 126
Severina 10
Tacitus 99
Florian...7
Probus...226
Carus...14
Numerian..3
Carinus..18
Magnia Urbica...1
Nigrinian...1
Julian of Pannonia 0
Diocletian (pre-reform) 37
Maximian (pre-reform)..................................40
Constantius I (pre-reform) 2
Galerius (pre-reform) 1
Barbarous Radiates....................at least 4,167

Distribution of Coins

The Map shows that coins of this period are common in South-Eastern Britain, but they are rarer in the West Midlands and North. This is a pattern we will see in 4th century chapters and seems to show how the Province is dividing with regards coin use.

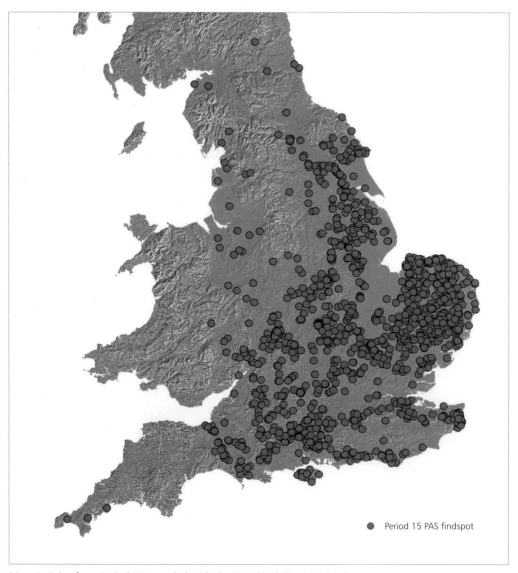

● Period 15 PAS findspot

Map 1. Coins from Period 15 recorded with the PAS. (© Philippa Walton)

Chapter XXII
Coinage of The Britannic Empire: Carausius and Allectus
(AD 286-296)

Fig.2. Richborough "Saxon Shore Fort" in Kent, probably built in the decade before Carausius came to power. © Sam Moorhead

I n AD 286, Diocletian (see Chapters XXI and XXIII) appointed Maximian as his co-emperor. Maximian was given charge of the western provinces where there was still unrest after the civil wars and where the barbarians were still a serious threat. Maximian had to deal with renegade people, called *bacaudae*, within the Empire, and with seaborne raiders such as the Saxons and Franks who came from the Germanic lands beyond the Rhine. One of Maximian's most successful generals was called Marcus Aurelius Mausaeus Carausius (Fig.1.), a man from

Fig.1. Gold *aureus* of Carausius (AD 286-93), struck at Rouen. This crudely designed coin was struck hastily at the start of Carausius' reign – it is the fourth example of this type known. RIC V, pt 2, no. 624. It was found in Derbyshire in 2007 and was acquired by Derby Museum and Art Gallery. DENO-64DAE1; 2007 T709. © Portable Antiquities Scheme (20mm)

Fig.4. Copper-alloy radiate of Carausius (AD 286-93), struck at Rouen. This crudely struck coin is typical of coins from Rouen. RIC V, pt 2, c f 666 & 684. Found in Surrey, SUR-372B61. © Portable Antiquities Scheme (22mm)

Fig.5. Silver *denarius* of Carausius (AD 286-93), struck at London (RSR). This coin probably celebrates the arrival of Carausius in London. RIC V, pt 2, 536var. Frome Hoard. © Portable Antiquities Scheme (19mm)

Fig.3. Silver *denarius* of Carausius (AD 286-93), struck at London (RSR). The reverse shows a galley, surely an emblem of Carausius' powerbase. RIC V, pt 2, no. 560. Found in Warwickshire, WAW-9E1EA6. © Portable Antiquities Scheme (20mm)

Fig.6. Copper-alloy medallion of Carausius (AD 286-93), struck at London. The letters in the exergue of this coin refer to a line of poetry by Virgil. RIC – © British Museum (35mm)

Fig.7. Silver *denarius* of Carausius (AD 286-93), struck at London (RSR). The reverse shows Britannia greeting Carausius with the inscription EXPECTATE VENI ("Welcome, O long awaited one"). RIC V, pt 2, 554. Found in Hertfordshire, BH-059652. © Portable Antiquities Scheme (19.5mm)

Menapia (the region of modern northern France, Belgium and Holland).

Carausius had some form of control of the northern fleet which had bases in Gaul (i.e. Boulogne) and Britain (i.e. Richborough – Fig.2.) and was responsible for defending Roman property from the Saxons. We are told by the ancient author Eumenius that Carausius abused his power: he waited until the Saxons had raided before intercepting them and reclaiming their loot – then he kept the booty, rather than returning it to its rightful owners. It is highly possible that this is a slur on Carausius, an accusation by his enemies (Maximian and Diocletian) to justify their war against him. Whatever the truth, we do know that in AD 286 Carausius fled from Maximian and created his own empire in Northern Gaul and Britain. The backbone of his new realm was the fleet that patrolled the North Sea and English Channel (Fig.3.).

Carausius' Accession (AD 286) & the Mint at Rouen

Coin evidence suggests that Carausius was proclaimed emperor at Rouen on the northern coast of France. Numismatists have identified Rouen as Carausius' first mint where hastily struck coins were issued. There are now nine gold coins known of this general type from Rouen – the latest example to be found was discovered in Derbyshire in 2007 (Fig.1.). These pieces were probably struck as payment to Carausius' core supporters; it was traditional for emperors to give money to the army upon their accession. The portrait is crude and is not a likeness of Carausius; it is more reminiscent of Maximian. In addition to these gold coins, there was a small, but not insignificant, issue of bronze radiates from Rouen. These are crude coins and on initial inspection look like "barbarous radiates" – these are the kinds of coins I find discarded in "grot pots", another good reason for letting the PAS see your poorly preserved Roman coins! Coins of Rouen are rare in Britain – four gold pieces have been found here, and there are only four Rouen radiates on the database, one from Hampshire (Fig.4.) and one from East Yorkshire.

The "Golden Age" Begins in Britannia

Carausius appears to have moved swiftly to Britannia where London became his capital. On an early silver *denarius* from the recent Frome Hoard, the emperor is shown "arriving" (*adventus* in Latin), probably in London (Fig.5). It was reckoned a while ago that coins marked RSR (e.g. Fig.5.) were struck in London, but it

Fig.8. Silver *denarius* of Carausius (AD 286-93), struck at London (RSR). The reverse shows Britannia greeting Carausius as on Fig.7. RIC V, pt 2, 555. Frome Hoard. © Portable Antiquities Scheme (19mm)

Fig.9. Silver *denarius* of Carausius (AD 286-93), struck at London (RSR). The reverse appears to show the emperor and Britannia clasping hands over an altar; this is the first coin with this type and the inscription EXPECTATE VENI ("Welcome, O long awaited one"). RIC – Found in Staffordshire, WMID-02BDE6. © Portable Antiquities Scheme (19mm)

Fig.10. Silver *denarius* of Carausius (AD 286-93), struck at London (RSR). The reverse shows the wolf and twins. The spelling of the inscription is a new variety. RIC V, pt 2, 615var. Found in Wiltshire, SUR-2F5234. © Portable Antiquities Scheme (19mm)

Fig.11. Silver *denarius* of Carausius (AD 286-93), struck at London (RSR). The reverse shows the wolf suckling Romulus and Remus. RIC V, pt.2, 572. Frome Hoard. © Portable Antiquities Scheme (19mm)

Fig.12. Gold *aureus* of Carausius (AD 286-93), struck at London. This unique coin proclaims Carausius' bravery (Virtus). RIC – It was found in Derbyshire in 2007 and was acquired by the British Museum. DENO-651C91; 2007 T709. © Portable Antiquities Scheme (20mm)

is only recently that Guy de la Bedoyère has explained what the letters mean. The RSR letters are associated with the letters INCPDA on a unique medallion of Carausius from London (Fig.6.) – they spell out the first letters for two lines in the Latin poet Virgil's Eclogues: *Redeunt saturnia regnia, Iam nova progenies caelo demittitur alto* ("The Golden Age returns, now a new generation comes down from heaven above"). This dovetails perfectly with a quite common *denarius* that shows Britannia greeting the new emperor, with the inscription *Expectate Veni* ("Welcome, O long awaited one"), another quotation from Virgil (Figs.7-9.). Not only did Carausius quote classical authors (the only emperor ever to do so), but he also made it clear that he regarded himself as a truly Roman emperor – the wolf suckling Romulus and Remus appeared on many of his coins (Figs.10-11.).

Carausius' Silver Coinage

Carausius struck an exceptional silver coinage of good quality *denarii* – such coins were not being issued by the Central Empire rulers at this time. It is possible that these silver coins were struck because there was a shortage of gold for

Fig.13. Silver *denarius* of Carausius (AD 286-93), struck at London (RSR). The reverse proclaims the "concord" between the emperor and his army. RIC V, pt 2, 548. Frome Hoard. © Portable Antiquities Scheme (19mm)

striking the high denomination *aureus* – only 26 gold coins are known for Carausius (Figs.1 & 12.), which might suggest that Maximian and Diocletian were active in restricting the flow of gold to Gaul and Britain. It is quite possible that the silver coins (replacing the more normal gold ones) were intended as donatives for his senior officers and soldiers – one coin does state his "concord with the army" (Fig.13.). The silver coins show many different designs, although it seems that only small numbers were struck of each different type. This means that there is a large variety of

Fig.14. Silver *denarius* of Carausius (AD 286-93), struck at London (RSR). This VICTORIA AVG reverse type is unpublished. RIC – Found in Norfolk, NMS-784AF4. © Portable Antiquities Scheme (20mm)

Fig.15. Silver *denarius* of Carausius (AD 286-93), struck at London (RSR). This coin, showing the sun god Sol, provides a more complete description of the coin than the example in RIC. RIC V, pt 2, 611var. Found in East Sussex, SUR-890187. © Portable Antiquities Scheme (19mm)

Fig.16. Copper-alloy radiate of Carausius (AD 286-93), struck at London (RSR). The reverse shows Moneta which might allude to the setting up of the new mint in London. RIC V, pt 2, c.f. 610. Found in Greater London, SUR-B45FD1. © Portable Antiquities Scheme (18mm)

Fig.17. Copper-alloy radiate of Carausius (AD 286-93), struck in London. This is the only example known of a coin of its type with the F O//RSR mintmark. It was acquired by the British Museum. RIC Found in Somerset, SOM-DF0782. © Portable Antiquities Scheme (23mm)

Fig.18. Copper-alloy radiate of Carausius (AD 286-93), mint uncertain. This is an early "unmarked" coin. Many unmarked coins were struck at the start of the reign before mintmarks were applied. RIC V, pt 2, c.f. 1015. Found in Lincolnshire, LVPL-737905. © Portable Antiquities Scheme (22mm)

pieces and that there are many rare variants – the PAS database has 25 *denarii* from England, of which nine are new varieties (Figs.14 & 15.) This is a good example of where PAS data has made a major impact on our knowledge of a particular Roman coinage.

Carausius' Mint at London

We have seen above that Rouen was probably Carausius' first, and only short-lived, mint. We have also seen that the early RSR coins were struck at London (Figs.3 & 7.). RSR appears on coins of gold, silver and bronze. The RSR radiates are quite rare – one type with Moneta on the reverse probably alludes to the recent opening of the mint at London (Figs.16 & 17.). Most of the earliest radiates from London do not bear a mintmark and are quite crude in design (Fig.18.). It seems that Carausius had to rush out a massive issue of low value coins to satisfy demand in the Province. This was all the more urgent as it appears that supplies from the Continent were being blocked. However, within a few years, London coins began to be marked with L (Londinium) (Fig.19.) or ML (Moneta Londiniensis) (Fig.20.); some even follow the Continental practice by having MLXXI which proclaims the coins

Fig.19. Silver *denarius* of Carausius (AD 286-93), struck at London. The L for London is visible in the exergue (under the figure on the reverse). RIC V, pt. 2, c.f. 9. Found in Leicestershire, LEIC-8C2497. © Portable Antiquities Scheme (19mm)

Fig.20. Copper-alloy radiate of Carausius (AD 286-93), struck at London. The reverse shows a bull which honours Legio VII, and the ML mintmark for London. RIC V, pt 2, c.f. 75. Found in Lincolnshire, WMID-158F02. © Portable Antiquities Scheme (20mm)

are of 5% silver (Fig.20.). The coins at London have letters in the reverse field which enable us to order Carausius' issues – e.g. F O, B E, S P and S C (Figs.17, 21 & 31.).

Fig.22. Copper-alloy radiate of Carausius (AD 286-93), struck at C Mint. The reverse shows Providentia and a C in the exergue. RIC V, pt 2, 355. Found in Somerset, SOMDOR-552258. © Portable Antiquities Scheme (24mm)

Fig.23. Copper-alloy radiate with much surviving silver wash, struck by Carausius (AD 286-93) at C Mint. The mintmark MC is a new variety. RIC V, pt 2, 368var. Found in Essex, ESS-EEBD65. © Portable Antiquities Scheme (23mm)

Fig.21. Copper-alloy radiate of Carausius (AD 286-93), struck at London. The reverse shows Pax with the mintmark B E//MLXXI. RIC V, pt 2, 101. Found in Hampshire, HAMP3187. © Portable Antiquities Scheme (24.5mm)

Fig.24. Copper-alloy radiate of Allectus (AD 293-6) with CL mintmark. This is traditionally assigned to C Mint, but some would like CL to mean Classis (fleet). RIC V, pt 2, 105. © British Museum.

Fig.25. Silver *denarius* of Carausius (AD 286-93), struck at London. The reverse shows the common reverse type of Pax. RIC V, pt 2, no. 719. Found in Lincolnshire, LVPL-E23B32. © Portable Antiquities Scheme (21mm)

Fig.26. Copper-alloy radiate of Carausius (AD 286-93), struck at the C Mint. This coin, with the mintmark in front of Spes is an unrecorded variety. RIC V, pt 2, cf. 411ff. Found in Gloucestershire, NMGW-615228. © Portable Antiquities Scheme (23mm)

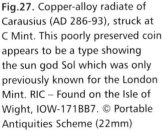

Fig.27. Copper-alloy radiate of Carausius (AD 286-93), struck at C Mint. This poorly preserved coin appears to be a type showing the sun god Sol which was only previously known for the London Mint. RIC – Found on the Isle of Wight, IOW-171BB7. © Portable Antiquities Scheme (22mm)

The Mystery of "C" Mint

In addition to London, there was another mint which marked its coins with a C (or a G). Edward Besly, in his recent discussion of the Rogiet Hoard, has shown that this was almost certainly a separate mint from London. Many contenders for "C" mint have been suggested – Camulodunum (Colchester), Clausentum (Bitterne, near Southampton), Corinium (Cirencester) or even Colonia (for York) (Figs.22 & 23.). Some coins are marked CL which is why Clausentum was a popular choice (Fig.24.); however, it has even been suggested that CL might stand for Classis, suggesting that this was a mint operated by Carausius' fleet (classis in Latin). If the C is actually a G, then Glevum (Gloucester) is a contender. So far, attempts to identify the mint by the distribution of C Mint coin finds has failed. Philippa Walton has shown that C Mint coin find-spots (as recorded with the PAS) do not create a discernible pattern. This is undoubtedly a debate that will run and run. C mint struck no gold to the best of our knowledge and very little silver. The bulk of its output consisted of radiates which shared the XXI marks and the S C and S P field marks with the London issues (Figs.22 & 23.).

Carausius' Types

The most common design used by Carausius had the inscription PAX AVG with a standing figure of Pax (Peace) holding a branch and sceptre – at a guess, well over 50% of his coins have this design (Fig.25.). However, his other coins

Fig.28. Copper-alloy radiate of Carausius (AD 286-93), struck at C Mint. This is a new variety of an issue that shows a griffin. RIC V, pt 2, 193var. Found in Hampshire, HAMP-369611. © Portable Antiquities Scheme (20.5mm)

Fig.29. Copper-alloy radiate of Carausius (AD 286-93), struck at London. This coin honours Legio II Augusta, showing the legion's mascot, the Capricorn. RIC V, pt 2, c.f. 57-58. Found in Lincolnshire, SWYOR-7E97B4. © Portable Antiquities Scheme (19mm)

Fig.31. Copper-alloy radiate of Diocletian, struck by Carausius (AD 286-93) at London. The mintmark S P//MLXXI is not recorded in RIC. RIC V, pt 2, 5var. Found in Greater London, SUR-E74522. © Portable Antiquities Scheme (23mm)

Fig.32. Copper-alloy radiate of Diocletian, struck by Carausius (AD 286-93) at London. This coin is not published in RIC, but there are three examples from the recent Elveden hoard. RIV V, pt 2, c.f. 9. Found in Worcestershire (24.5mm)

Fig.30. Copper-alloy radiate of Carausius (AD 286-93), struck at C Mint. The obverse shows, from left to right, Carausius, Diocletian and Maximian. RIC V, pt 2, 1. © British Museum (23mm)

show an enormous variety of types. Since the RIC volume was published in 1933, many new types have been found. A significant number of new coins have been recorded with the PAS, which is proving to be an invaluable source of new information about the emperor's coinage (Figs.26-28.). Possibly the most interesting are coins struck in honour or various legions, showing their mascots, a number of which have been recorded with the PAS (Figs.20 & 29.).

Carausius & His Brothers

In AD 289, Maximian tried to retake Britain from Carausius, but failed. It seems that Carausius even retained his Continental possessions, such as Boulogne. It is now that Carausius began to strike a fascinating series of coins which honour the emperors Diocletian and Maximian. One rare design shows the busts of all three emperors on the obverse with the inscription *Carausisus et fraters sui* ("Carausius and his brothers") (Fig.30.). Two series of coins were also struck by Carausius in the name of Diocletian and Maximian – these coins are rare and the PAS has recorded some new varieties (Figs.31-33.). Finally, a large number of Carausius' own coins have the reverse inscription ending in AVGGG

instead of AVG, alluding to the three emperors (e.g. PAX AVGGG) (Fig.34.). The irony is that all of this effort on Carausius' part apparently failed – he was never acknowledged as a co-emperor by Diocletian and Maximian.

The Frome Hoard

Some of the silver *denarii* from the recently discovered Frome Hoard are illustrated here (Figs.5, 8, 11 & 13.). However, there are also over 840 other radiates of Carausius in the hoard, making it the largest group of Carausian coins ever found. There is even a possible *quinarius* radiate (or half *denarius*) in the hoard. When conserved, these coins will provide an enormous amount of new information about Carausius' coinage.

Allectus Assassinates Carausius

Carausius managed to rule for around seven years. Through a powerful fleet and army, he managed to keep the Central Empire rulers at bay. However, it was not his enemies on the Continent who removed him, but his own finance minister Allectus; and Allectus had no intention of giving in to Diocletian and Maximian either.

Fig.34. Copper-alloy radiate of Carausius (AD 286-93), struck at C Mint. This coin has an unrecorded mintmark. The three Gs in AVGGG refers to Carausius, Diocletian and Maximian. RIC Found in East Yorkshire, YORYM-247132. © Portable Antiquities Scheme (22mm)

Fig.35. Gold *aureus* of Allectus (AD 293-6), struck at London. The reverse shows Mars. RIV V, pt 2, no. 13. © British Museum (19mm)

Fig.33. Copper-alloy radiate of Maximian (AD 286-310), struck by Carausius (AD 286-93) at C Mint. The reverse type with Providentia is a new variety. RIC V, pt 2, 49var. Found in Lincolnshire, WMID-14D3C2. © Portable Antiquities Scheme (22mm)

Fig.36. Copper-alloy radiate of Allectus (AD 293-6), struck at London. This reverse shows the "arrival" (ADVENTVS) of the emperor on horseback, presumably in London. This reverse is not recorded at London. RIC – Found in Lincolnshire, LIN-20F942. © Portable Antiquities Scheme (20mm)

Fig.37. Copper-alloy radiate of Allectus (AD 293-6), struck at London. The mintmark S P// ML continues from the issues of Carausius. RIC V, pt 2, no. 18. Found in Hampshire, HAMP-9B14C4. © Portable Antiquities Scheme (20.5mm)

Allectus' Coinage

Allectus only struck gold at London (Fig.35.), but did not really strike any *denarii*. This does support the belief that Carausius' silver coinage was struck early is his reign. Allectus continued to strike radiates at London and C Mint, following the same system of mint-marking. However, there is less variety of reverse types, the most common types being Pax, Providentia and Laetitia (Figs.36-39.).

Early in his reign, Allectus introduced a new coin, marked with QL or QC in the exergue. This almost certainly stands for "Quinarius of London" or "Quinarius of C Mint" (Figs.40-42.). We can assume that this smaller coin was valued at half of a radiate. It is possible that Allectus issued this new coin in order to replace the small base pre-AD 274 Gallic and Central Empire radiates that were still in circulation. Because Allectus ruled for only three years (or fewer), we will never know how successful this reform was. The reverse of the Q Radiates showed a variety of ships, mostly galleys – it can be argued that this was Allectus displaying his naval powerbase that underpinned his rule. Because all of Allectus' coins are mint-marked, it is easier to analyse the output of the two mints – it is interesting to note that London

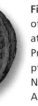

Fig.38. Copper-alloy radiate of Allectus (AD 293-6), struck at C Mint. The reverse shows Providentia ("foresight"). RIC V, pt 2, 105. Found in Lincolnshire, NLM-1F9363. © Portable Antiquities Scheme (23mm)

Fig.39. Copper-alloy radiate of Allectus (AD 293-6), struck at C Mint. The reverse shows Laetitia ("joyfulness"). RIC V, pt 2, 79. Found in Gloucestershire, GLO-C55A10. © Portable Antiquities Scheme (21mm)

outstrips C Mint by 355 to 289. Overall, the quality of Allectus' coins was better than those of Carausius, the flans being rounder and the designs being more consistent. This really shows that by

Fig.41. Copper-alloy Q-radiate of Allectus (AD 293-6), struck at C Mint. The VIRTVS AVG inscription was used at both mints. RIC V, pt 2, no. 128. Found in Essex, ESS-BCAB23. © Portable Antiquities Scheme (20mm)

Fig.42. Copper-alloy Q-radiate of Allectus (AD 293-6), struck at C Mint. The LAETITIA AVG inscription was only used on this type at C Mint. RIC V, pt 2, no. 124. Found in Somerset, SOM-F69C60. © Portable Antiquities Scheme (19mm)

Fig.40. Copper-alloy Q-radiate of Allectus (AD 293-6), struck at London. Only the VIRTVS AVG inscription was used for this type at London. RIC, V, pt 2, no 55. Found in Hampshire, HAMP-DAB272. © Portable Antiquities Scheme (20mm)

Fig.43. The Elveden Hoard of 627 radiates being excavated in 2005. © Portable Antiquities Scheme

the end of Carausius' reign, the mint-workers at both mints had developed high skills.

Rogiet & Elveden Hoards

We have learnt a great deal about the coinage of Allectus from two recently discovered hoards. The first, the Rogiet hoard, was found in South Wales. It contained 3,813 coins, of which 757 were Q-Radiates. This enabled Edward Besly at Cardiff Museum to show that the London and C Mint were indeed separate institutions with different die-engravers. The second hoard was found at Elveden in Suffolk. In contains the largest number of Allectus radiates from any find in Britain – 347 pieces. These coins are also in excellent condition and are now an important part of the British Museum collection. (Figs.43-5.)

Barbarous Copies

Although the majority of barbarous radiates were struck in the period 275-285, a significant number of barbarous copies are known for Carausius (Fig.46.). These appear to come from early in his reign before his mints had started to produce sufficient numbers of coins to satisfy demand. However, there are times when it is quite difficult to distinguish official coins from copies – it is quite possible that some copies were in fact poorly executed coins made by inexperienced engravers.

End of the Britannic Empire

In 293, Constantius I (293-306) was made junior emperor (Caesar) under Maximian in the Western Empire. It was his task to reclaim

Fig.44. The Elveden Hoard pot reconstructed. © Portable Antiquities Scheme

Fig.45. Copper-alloy radiate of Allectus (AD 293-6), struck at London. This is one of 347 coins of Allectus from the hoard. RIC V, pt 2, 49var. © British Museum (23mm)

Fig.46. Copper-alloy "barbarous radiate" copying a coin of Carausius (AD 286-93). The reverse shows a crude rendition of a PAX AVG type. Found in Leicestershire, LEIC-D51406. © Portable Antiquities Scheme (20mm)

Fig.47. Gold medallion of Constantius I (AD 293-306), struck at Trier. This electrotype copy shows Constantius riding into London with his fleet, being welcomed by a kneeling London. © British Museum (41mm)

Britain for the central Roman Empire. Fairly swiftly, Constantius deprived Allectus of his bases in northern Gaul, notably Boulogne. In 296, or possibly earlier, an invasion of Britain was led by Constantius' praetorian prefect, Asclepiodotus. We are told that Allectus fled, but was captured and killed. A gold medallion found at Arras in France shows Constantius I riding into London while his fleet sails up the Thames. London kneels in supplication (Fig.47.). With this event, Britain was brought back into the Roman Empire. However, the mint at London was to continue in use for several decades as we shall see.

Numbers of Coins

There are 2,025 coins of Carausius on the PAS Database. Of these, two are gold *aurei* and 25 silver *denarii*. There are four coins from Rouen, 417 from London and 129 from "C" Mint. There are 1,087 coins of Allectus, of which at least 352 are Q-radiates. A total of 355 coins are from London and 289 from "C" Mint.

Where are the Coins Found?

Map 1 (overleaf) shows that coins of both emperors are found from East Yorkshire to Somerset; there are few coins from the West Midlands and the North.

A Personal Note About Coins Struck in Britain

Detectorists who have met me know that my main priority is to get all Roman coins found in Britain recorded. The new data that you have provided in the last few years has been incredibly important and has changed a number of our views about Roman coinage in Britain, and even the history of Roman Britain. Most of the Roman coins recorded are of primary importance for the archaeological and general economic information that they provide. However, there are certain coins found in Britain which are of particular importance to us – these are coins which are struck in Britain which have an especial importance. This obviously covers most Iron Age/Celtic coins, many contemporary copies and, in this case, coins of Carausius and Allectus. A number of detectorists have donated rare examples of such coins to local museums and the British Museum, and we are very grateful. When funds are available (and they are incredibly tight, as you might imagine) we have been able to buy the odd coin. However, there are many coins of

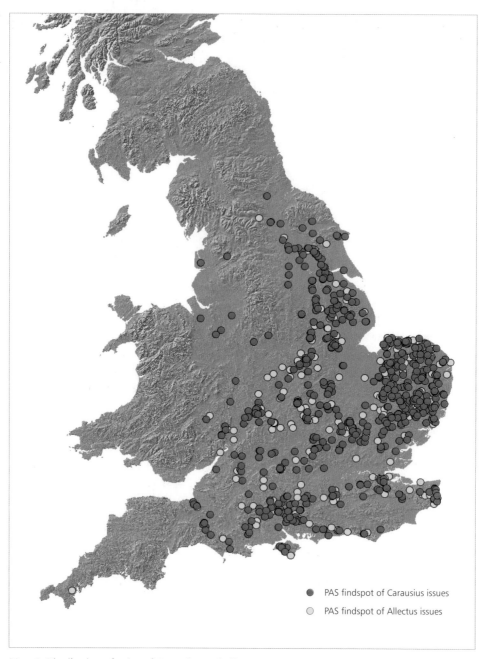

Map 1. Distribution of coins of Carausius and Allectus, recorded with the Portable Antiquities Scheme. (© Philippa Walton)

Carausius and Allectus on the PAS Database that are new varieties and which are not present in the national collection at the British Museum. If you are ever considering parting with your rare coins of Carausius or Allectus, please do think of contacting me at the British Museum. Finally, I am writing the new edition of *Roman Imperial Coinage* for Carausius and Allectus – the original edition was published in 1933 and there are many new types and varieties which will be included in the new edition. I would like to thank all of you who have recorded coins of Carausius and Allectus with the PAS – all of them will help with my research into our "British emperors", and I intend to credit all finders in the volume.

Chapter XXIII
Coinage of The Tetrarchy and The Early Constantinian Period
(AD 294-317)

Fig.1. Statue of the four Tetrarchs – Diocletian, Maximian, Constantius I and Galerius – on the corner of St. Mark's Basilica, Venice. © Sam Moorhead

In chapter XXI, I ended in AD 294 during the reign of Diocletian (284-305). Diocletian made Maximian his co-Augustus in AD 286 and Constantius I and Galerius were made Caesars (junior emperors) in AD 293. This system with four emperors was called the Tetrarchy (Fig.1.). Until 294, the standard coin was the radiate, but in 294 Diocletian started to reform the coinage in a major way. This chapter will cover this new coinage down to AD 317, thus including the first part of Constantine the Great's reign.

Coinage Reform of Diocletian

It is now generally accepted that Diocletian began his monetary reforms in AD 294. By the

Fig.3. Silver *argenteus* of Diocletian (AD 284-305), struck at Carthage, AD 300. The reverse indicates the weight standard of the coin, at 96 to the pound. RIC VI, 424. © British Museum (16mm)

Fig.4. Silver *argenteus* of Diocletian (AD 284-305), probably a contemporary copy of a coin struck at Trier in c.295-7. RIC VI, c.f. 109a. Found in Wiltshire, WILT-CA45F1. © Portable Antiquities Scheme (17mm)

Fig.2. Gold *aureus* of Maximian (AD 286-305), struck at Rome, AD 294-5. The reverse shows Diocletian and Maximian on horseback. RIC VI, 3. © British Museum (19mm)

Fig.5. Copper-alloy *nummus* of Diocletian (AD 284-305), struck at Lyons, AD 301-3. The reverse of GENIO POPVLI ROMANI with Genius standing is the most common type on *nummi* of this period. The B on the reverse tells us it was struck in the second workshop at Lyon. RIC VI, 108. Found in Dorset, DOR-830633. © Portable Antiquities Scheme (27mm)

Fig.6. Copper-alloy "post-reform radiate" of Constantius I as Augustus (AD 293-305), struck at Rome in AD 297-8. These coins are very rare in Britain. RIC VI, 87a. © British Museum (20mm)

time the reform was complete in 296, there were a number of coins in use:-

Gold *aureus* (60 to the pound) (Fig.2.)
Silver *argenteus* (96 to the pound) (Figs.3 & 4.)
Copper *nummus* (with about 3-4% silver; 32 to the pound) (Fig.5.)
Copper post-reform radiate (about 110 coins to the pound) (Fig.6.)
Copper "laureate" coin (about 220 coins, or more, to the pound) (Fig.7.)

To this, we can add older radiate coins still in circulation. It is probable that the silver-washed radiates issued after the reforms of Aurelian (see Chapter XXI) were tariffed at a higher value than the earlier base radiates of Gallienus, Claudius II and the Gallic Empire (see Chapters XIX and XX).

There is much debate about the relative values of the coins, but one interpretation is:-

1 gold *aureus* = 12 silver *argentei* = 48 base *nummi*
1 *argenteus* = 4 base *nummi*
1 *nummus* = c.6 bronze post-reform radiates

Gold Aureus & Silver Argenteus

Diocletian standardised the weight of the *aureus* at 60 to the pound (5.2-5.5gm) (Fig.2.); for much of the 3rd century, its weight had fluctuated enormously. Gold coins of this period are rarely found in Britain and only three are recorded on the database (Figs.8, 39 & 40.). In addition, possibly taking the lead from Carausius (see chapter XXII), Diocletian introduced a new silver coin, the *argenteus*, struck at 96 to the pound (normally around 3.0-3.3gm) (Fig.3.). These coins were struck in increasingly small numbers and are also rarely found in the Britain (Fig.4.).

Silver-Washed Bronze Nummus

Diocletian introduced a new, large bronze coin which contained around 5% silver – we call it the *nummus* (Latin for a low denomination coin), although it has (incorrectly) been called the *follis* in the past (Fig.5.). This coin weighs about 8.5-11gm and is around 28mm in diameter. It contained around 3.4 to 4.3% silver. The coins were given a distinctive silver-wash, but this is often not present on coins found today. There are two major reasons for this: firstly, in ancient

Fig.7. Copper-alloy fraction of a *nummus* of Maximian (AD 286-310), struck at Ticinum, AD 294-5. Fractions were only struck in small numbers and are very rare in Britain. RIC VI, 27. © British Museum (16mm)

Fig.8. Gold *aureus* of Maximinus II (AD 305-11), minted in Aquileia (AD 305-8). This is the only Tetrarchic period *aureus* on the database. RIC VI, 50b. Found in Berkshire, BERK-E53380 (19 mm)

Fig.9. Copper alloy *nummus* of Maximian (AD 286-310), struck at Trier, AD 303-5. This coin has the common reverse type showing the Genius of Rome. Found in Somerset, SOMDOR-C829C2. © Portable Antiquities Scheme (27mm)

Fig.10. Copper-alloy *nummus* of Constantius I as Caesar (AD 293-305), struck at Lyon, AD 303-5. RIC VI, 178a. Found in Hampshire, HAMP-61B5D7. © Portable Antiquities Scheme (30mm)

Fig.11. Copper-alloy *nummus* of Constantius I as Caesar (AD 293-305), struck at Rome, AD 302-3. The reverse shows Moneta, the personification of minting and money. RIC VI, 104a. Found in the West Midlands, WAW-41AA65. © Portable Antiquities Scheme (29mm)

times people illegally removed the silver through a process called "sweating"; secondly, the silvering often corrodes away as the coin lies in the ground. This *nummus* is the only commonly found Tetrarchic coin in Britain. However, it is still scarcely found among site-finds, more commonly being found in hoards. This is probably because of its enhanced value in relationship to the radiates already in circulation. As a general rule of thumb, I reckon that these *nummi* only normally turn up in larger assemblages of over 100 coins.

The most common reverse type on the *nummus* in the Tetrarchic period was GENIO POPVLI ROMANI – "To the genius/spirit of the Roman People". This coin, with Genius standing, holding a patera (dish used for sacrifices) and a cornucopiae, was struck by mints across the entire Roman Empire (Figs.5, 9 & 10.)

There were also some other types, notably coins commemorating the new coinage by showing Moneta (Figs.11 & 12.) and others celebrating Carthage, the city through which much of Rome's grain travelled on its way north from the African wheat fields (Fig.13.).

Fractions, Post-Reform Radiates & Laureates

In addition to the silver-washed *nummus*, Diocletian introduced two smaller coins (fractions). One was made of bronze and weighed around 3gm. It bore a radiate head and we know it as a "post-reform radiate" (Fig.6.). Its relationship to the *nummus* is not clear but it is suggested that it was one-sixth of a *nummus*. These coins were only struck in any great number at Rome and Carthage and it does not seem that they circulated widely. In addition, an even smaller copper coin of 1.3gm was struck, bearing a laureate head. This coins is sometimes reckoned to have been one-twelfth of a *nummus*, but it was struck in very small numbers and was not issued for circulation in Britain (Fig.7.).

Diocletian's Mints

Although a large number of mints had been in operation in the second half of the 3rd century, Diocletian's reforms rationalised their marks. During this period, up to 16 mints were operating, nearly all being clearly identified by marks which abbreviated their names. From West to

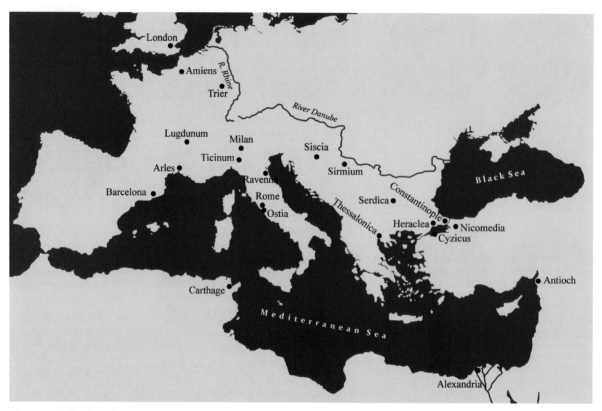

Map 1. Distribution of Roman Mints used in the late 3rd-5th centuries AD. (© Richard Kelleher)

East, Diocletian's mints were:-

London .... LN
               (i.e. Fig.33.)
Trier (Treveri, Germany).................................TR
               (i.e. Fig.9.)
Lugdunum (Lyons, France)..................... L or LG
               (i.e. Fig.10.)
Ticinum (Pavia, Italy)...T
               (i.e. Fig.12.)
Aquileia (Italy)...AQ
               (i.e. Fig.8.)
Rome.. R
               (i.e. Fig.21.)
Ostia (Port of Rome)...................................... OST
               (i.e. Fig.14.)
Carthage (Tunisia) .... KP or K
               (i.e. Fig.13.)
Siscia (Sisak, Croatia) .... SIS
               (i.e. Fig.25.)
Serdica (Bulgaria)...SD
Thessalonica (Greece)...................................... TS
Heraclea (Turkey) ....H or HT
Nicomedia (Turkey) ....N
Cyzicus (Turkey) .... K or KV
               (i.e. Fig.16.)
Antioch (Turkey)..ANT
Alexandria (Egypt) .... ALE

In addition, the recording of *officinae* (workshops) within a mint became much more prevalent. From now on, most mints tell us which workshop struck the coins, using Roman numerals, Roman letters or Greek letters (Figs.5 & 14.)

Price Edict & Monetary Reform of AD 301

Diocletian (Fig.3.) was still faced with rising prices in the late 3rd century. In an attempt to suppress rising prices, he issued an edict that gave the maximum price allowed to be charged. This proclamation was advertised on inscriptions across the Roman Empire, the best preserved example coming from the city of Aphrodisias in Turkey. Included in the reform were the prices for British beer and woollen overcoats. However, this did not stop inflation and the size and weights of coins continued to decline in the 4th century.

Persecutions

In 303, Diocletian and his colleagues began to persecute Christians who were not prepared to worship the emperor. The most enthusiastic persecutor was Galerius (Fig.16.) who led a reign of terror in the East. Persecutions continued until his death in 311, and ceased completely after the Edict of Toleration was proclaimed by

Fig.12. Copper-alloy *nummus* of Galerius as Caesar (AD 293-305), struck at Ticinum, AD 300-303. Coins of Galerius are often attributed to Maximian because he took the senior emperor's name. RIC VI, 46b. Found in Wiltshire, WILT-1BFDA6. © Portable Antiquities Scheme (26mm)

Fig.13. Copper-alloy *nummus* of Galerius as Caesar (AD 293-305), struck at Carthage, AD 299-303. The reverse shows the personification of Carthage holding fruits. RIC VI, 32b. Found in Somerset, SOMDOR-D8DA23. © Portable Antiquities Scheme (30mm)

Fig.14. Copper-alloy *nummus* of Licinius I (AD 308-24), struck at Ostia, AD 312-3. The mintmark MOSTQ stands for "Moneta Ostia Workshop Four". RIC VI, 84b. Found in Hampshire, HAMP-08CF76. © Portable Antiquities Scheme (21.5mm)

Fig.15. Copper-alloy *nummus* of Diocletian (AD 284-305), struck after his abdication at Trier, AD 305. The reverse refers to the emperors Diocletian and Maximian having rest (*quies*). RIC VI, 80. Found in Leicestershire, LEIC-1DA214. © Portable Antiquities Scheme (28mm)

Constantine (Fig.29.) and Licinius (Fig.14.) in Milan in 313.

Diocletian's Retirement in AD 305

In 305, Diocletian announced that he and Maximian, the senior emperors, would retire, and coins were struck in celebration (Fig.15.). It meant that Constantius I and Galerius (Fig.16.) would replace them as Augusti and that two new junior emperors would be appointed: Severus in the West (Figs.17 & 18.) and Maximinus II in the East (Figs.8 & 37.). Diocletian lived out his days at a fortified palace at Split on the Croatian coast; his favourite pastime was growing cabbages. However, in the West, Maximian was not so keen to step into the shadows and twice came out of retirement before he finally died in AD 310 (Figs.19 & 36.); his son Maxentius declared himself emperor in 306 in Italy (Figs.20 & 21.), in response to events in Britain to which I now turn.

Death of Constantius I & the Elevation of Constantine I, AD 306

We have already seen how Constantius I had reclaimed Britain from Allectus in AD 296 (see Chapter XXII and Fig.22.). In 306, Constantius returned to Britain to deal with the northern frontier where the Picts had been troublesome.

Fig.16. Copper-alloy *nummus* of Galerius as Augustus (AD 305-11), struck at Cyzicus, c.AD 311. RIC VI, 65. Found in Merseyside, LVPL-26AE34. © Portable Antiquities Scheme (27mm)

Fig.17. Copper-alloy *nummus* of Severus as Caesar (AD 305-6), struck at Lyon. RIC VI, 199a. Found in Somerset, SOMDOR-582246. © Portable Antiquities Scheme (29mm)

However, he died at York in the same year and was commemorated on the coinage (Fig.23.). This event was to change the course of history because the army, breaking the rules laid down by Diocletian about the succession, declared Constantius' son, Constantine, as their emperor.

Fig.18. Copper-alloy *nummus* of Severus as Caesar (AD 305-6), struck at Trier. RIC VI, 651. Found in Cambridgeshire, CAM-1C8BD2. © Portable Antiquities Scheme (27mm)

Fig.19. Copper-alloy *nummus* of Maximian (AD 286-310), struck at Trier, AD 307-8. This coin was issued after Maximian had come out of retirement for the first time. RIC VI, 768. Found in Wiltshire, WILT-A16507. © Portable Antiquities Scheme (25mm)

Fig.21. Copper-alloy *nummus* of Maxentius (AD 306-312), struck at Rome, AD 310-12. The reverse shows Roma in a temple. Found in Nottinghamshire, DENO-DFFCD4. © Portable Antiquities Scheme (28mm)

Fig.22. Gold medallion of Constantius I as Caesar (AD 293-305), struck at Trier. The reverse shows Constantius raising Britannia, commemorating the defeat of Allectus and recapture of Britain in AD 296. RIC VI, 33. © British Museum (34mm)

Fig.20. Copper-alloy *nummus* of Maxentius (AD 306-12), struck at Ticinum, AD 307-8. Coins of Maxentius are scarce in Britain. Found in Gloucestershire, NMGW-14AA02. © Portable Antiquities Scheme (27mm)

Constantine managed to gain grudging acceptance from the other emperors and gradually established himself as ruler north of the Alps, with his capital at Trier (Fig.24.).

Imperial Jockeying, AD 306-312

In the East, Galerius remained the senior emperor until his death in 311, even striking coins for his wife, Galeria Valeria (Fig.25.). His deputy Maximinus survived until 313 (Fig.37.). However, in the West, Maximian did not want to retire, and his son Maxentius took control of Italy and Rome in 306 (Figs.19-21.). In 307, the senior emperor in the West, Severus, died, and was replaced in 308 by Licinius I (Fig.14.); Maximian finally died in 310. However, by this time, Constantine I was also an Augustus (senior emperor) with high ambition. Until 312, Constantine, Licinius, Maximinus and Maxentius ruled in an uneasy alliance, but it was clear that there were too many emperors for stable rule to last.

Battle of the Milvian Bridge, AD 312

In 312, Constantine finally advanced south to challenge Maxentius. Just before the battle of the Milvian Bridge, outside Rome, Constantine had a vision of the Christian "chi-rho" symbol' and the

Latin *Hoc signo victor eris* ("In this sign you will conquer") (Fig.26.). He instructed his soldiers to paint the symbol on their shields and they went on to win the battle.

Maxentius' dead body ended up in the River Tiber (Fig.27.), and Constantine was to be the first emperor to adopt Christianity. He quickly made a treaty with Licinius I (Fig.14.) who was to take control of the East after he defeated Maximinus II (Fig.37.) in AD 313.

Coinage from AD 306-317

The gold *aureus* was replaced by the gold *solidus* (72 coins to the pound) in 309-10 by Constantine at the mint of Trier (Fig.28.). The *solidus* became the standard gold coin of the Roman and Byzantine world for several centuries. Silver coins of any sort became very rare and were not to be struck in any quantity until the second half of the 4th century. The silver-washed bronze *nummus* continued to be struck in large numbers, but the size and weight of the coin gradually declined until, in 317, the coin that had weighed over 8.5gm only weighed around 3gm (Fig.29.). This shows the full effect of the reforms.

The reverse types of the *nummi* tended to be quite standard. Because of the reduced size of

Fig.24. Copper-alloy *nummus* of Constantine I (AD 306-337), struck at Trier, AD 310-13. The reverse shows Sol, the sun god. Found in Lincolnshire, LIN-D51323. © Portable Antiquities Scheme (18mm)

Fig.25. Copper-alloy *nummus* of Galeria Valeria, wife of Galerius (AD 305-11), struck at Siscia, AD 309-11. RIC VI, 211. Found in Herefordshire, WMID-32E0F4. © Portable Antiquities Scheme (24mm)

Fig.23. Copper-alloy *nummus*, struck in commemoration of Constantius I (AD 305-6), struck at London, AD 307-10. Constantius died at York. Found in Hampshire, HAMP-3184. © Portable Antiquities Scheme (25mm)

Fig.26. Copper-alloy *nummus* of the short-lived emperor Vetranio (AD 350-1), struck at Siscia. The reverse bears the inscription HOC SIGNO VICTOR ERIS, harking back to Constantine's victory at the Battle of the Milvian Bridge. RIC VIII, 287. © British Museum (22mm)

Fig.28. Gold *solidus* of Constantine I (AD 306-37), struck at Trier, AD 310-3. The *solidus* was to become the major gold denomination of the Roman Empire. RIC VI, 812. © British Museum (20mm)

Fig.27. Carved stone relief from the Arch of Constantine in Rome showing Constantine's men hurling Maxentius' soldiers into the River Tiber during the Battle of the Milvian Bridge in AD 312. © David Stuttard

163

Fig.29. Copper-alloy *nummus* of Constantine I (AD 306-37), struck at London, AD 313-4. This coin shows that by 314 the diameter of *nummi* had fallen from around 28 to 21mm. RIC VII, 10. Found in Warwickshire, WAW-9ECA86. © Portable Antiquities Scheme (21mm)

Fig.30. Copper-alloy *nummus* of Licinius I (AD 308-24), struck at London, AD 310-2. GENIO POP ROM is the common reverse for Licinius. RIC VI, 209c. Found in Surrey, SUR-211B17. © Portable Antiquities Scheme (22.5mm)

Fig.31. Copper-alloy half-*nummus* of Constantine I (AD 306-37), struck at Trier, AD 310-11. The reverse shows Mars. RIC VI, 897. Found in Somerset, SOM-4159B8. © Portable Antiquities Scheme (19mm)

Fig.32. Copper-alloy *nummus* of Constantine I (AD 306-37), struck at Trier, AD 310-313. The reverse shows Mars, the god of war. RIC VI, 862. Found in Lincolnshire, LANCUM-CE8434. © Portable Antiquities Scheme (23mm)

the coins, the GENIO POPVLI ROMANI reverse became GENIO POP ROM. This type was to be the most common used on the coins of Licinius (Fig.30.). Constantine's favoured reverse shows the sun god, Sol, with the inscription SOLI INVICTO COMITI ("To my companion, the invincible Sun God") (Figs.24, 29 & 38.). These are by far the most common coins found in Britain between 310 and 317.

Other types include coins honouring the army and Mars (Figs.31-33.). Trier did strike a small number of half-*nummi* in 310-11, a few being recorded on the database (Fig.31.).

London Mint

After the demise of Allectus in AD 296 (see Chapter XXII), the London mint continued to operate under Diocletian and his colleagues. No gold or silver was struck, but large issues of *nummi* were struck. Some of these coins do not actually bear a mint mark but can be attributed to London on the basis of their style (Fig.34.).

London struck coins for several emperors, although the most common coins are of Constantine I (Figs.30 & 34-8.). There was indeed a wide range of coins struck and several new varieties have been recorded with the PAS (Fig.35.). This is another area where detector data recorded with the Portable Antiquities Scheme (www.finds.org.uk) is making an important contribution

to our understanding of the coinage of Roman Britain. The London mint was to close in 326, as I will discuss in the next chapter.

Did Constantine Visit Britain?

I believe that Constantine held a soft-spot for Britain. He would surely have been indebted to the Province which supported his illegal claim to the throne in 306. It is quite possible that he gave tax-breaks and grants to the Britons, and it just might be that the PAS has indirectly recorded such activity. In 2007, a gold *festaureus* of Licinius I, struck at Trier between 313 and 315, was found in Wiltshire; a year later, another example of the same issue was found in Northamptonshire (Figs.39 & 40.).

There are only three other specimens of this coin recorded in *Roman Imperial Coinage* volume VII and they are all in British museums, suggesting that they might well have been found in Britain as well. It has been argued by some scholars that Constantine came to Britain around 314 – he even took the title Britannicus Maximus around this time. Can we argue that these gold coins were brought over to Britain at this time by Constantine and distributed on a tour of the Province? It is tempting to believe it!

In 317, Constantine and Licinius were to come to a major agreement whereby their sons, Crispus, Constantine II and Licinius II were made

Fig.33. Copper-alloy *nummus* of Constantine I (AD 306-37), struck at London, AD 310-12. This rare coin has been kindly donated to the British Museum by Tom Redmayne. Found in Lincolnshire, LIN-5AF4C4. © Portable Antiquities Scheme (22mm)

Fig.34. Copper-alloy *nummus* of Diocletian (AD 284-305), struck at London, c.AD 300-3. These coins were not marked with a mint mark. RIC VI, 6a. Found in Dorset, DOR-A78234. © Portable Antiquities Scheme (27.5mm)

Fig.35. Copper-alloy *nummus* of Constantine I (AD 306-37), struck at London, AD 310-2. This coin is not published in RIC and is not in the British Museum collection. Found in Berkshire, PUBLIC-FD5232. © Portable Antiquities Scheme (23mm)

Fig.36. Copper-alloy *nummus* of Maximian (AD 286-310), struck at London, AD 307. This coin was struck after Maximian came out of retirement. RIC VI, 85. Found in Dorset, DOR-A2AD53. © Portable Antiquities Scheme (26.5mm)

Fig.37. Copper alloy *nummus* of Maximinus II (AD 309-13), struck at London, AD 310-2. RIC VI 209b. Found in Lincolnshire, DENO-9707C6. © Portable Antiquities Scheme (24mm)

Fig.38. Copper-alloy *nummus* of Constantine I (AD 306-37), struck at London, c.AD 310. SOLI INVICTO COMITI is the most common reverse type for Constantine in this period. RIC VI, 121a. Found in Lincolnshire, LIN-BCAA62. © Portable Antiquities Scheme (22mm)

Fig.39. Gold *festaureus* (one and a half *solidi*) of Licinius I (AD 308-24), struck at Trier, AD 313-5. This unusual denomination was most likely produced for ceremonial purposes. RIC VII, 5. Found in Wiltshire, WILT-D86FB6. © Portable Antiquities Scheme (21mm)

Fig.40. Gold *festaureus* (one and a half *solidi*) of Licinius I (AD 308-24), struck at Trier, AD 313-5. This is from the same issue as no. 39 above. RIC VII, 5. Found in Northants, NARC-A1A418. © Portable Antiquities Scheme (22mm)

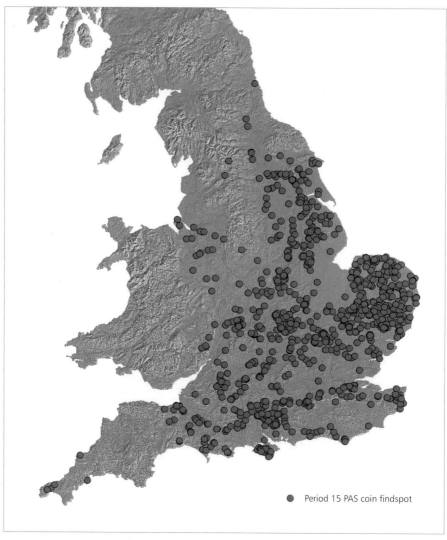

Map 2: Distribution of Period 15 (AD 294/6-317) coins recorded with the Portable Antiquities Scheme. (© Philippa Walton)

junior emperors (Caesars). Because coins began to be struck for them as well, 317 is an appropriate place to stop this chapter. I will cover the period AD 317 to 348 in the next chapter.

Coins of the Tetrarchy & Early Constantinian Period in Britain

These coins all fall into Reece Period 15 (AD 294/6-317). As a general rule, as the coins decrease in size, more were struck and/or lost. We can break down the number of coins by ruler as shown in table 1.

It is interesting to note that after 306 the coins of Constantine are much more common than those of other emperors: Galerius, Severus, Maximinus II and Licinius I. Coins of this period are found across England, as shown by Map 2.

Diocletian (284-305)	233
Maximian (286-310)	223
Constantius I (293-306)	202
Galerius (293-311)	99
Galeria Valeria	2
Severus (305-7)	13
Constantine I (306-337)	*1,235
Licinius I (308-24)	*c.174
Maxentius (306-12)	21
Romulus (died 309)	0
Maximinus II	110

*These totals are for coins struck before 317.

Table 1. Number of coins by ruler.

Chapter XXIV
Coinage of The House of Constantine
(AD 317-330)

Licinius & Constantine (AD 313-7)

The last chapter covered the Tetrarchy and traced the rise to power of Constantine (Fig.1.) until, in AD 313, only he and Licinius I (Fig.2.) were emperors (Chapter XXIII). Their alliance was cemented when Licinius married Constantine's half-sister, Constantia, but the two men never ruled in harmony. In 316, there was a dispute over the appointment of junior emperors and Constantine advanced into the Balkans; Licinius declared one of his generals, Valens, his co-emperor. Constantine defeated Valens at Hadrianople and had his adversary executed. In the meantime a few coins had been struck for Valens at Cyzicus and Alexandria, but they are incredibly rare. Finally, however, a treaty was signed between Constantine and Licinius at Serdica in 317. It resulted in Licinius' son, Licinius II (Fig.3.), being made Caesar, along with Constantine's sons, Crispus (Fig.4.) and Constantine II (Fig.5.).

Constantine Supreme (AD 324)

Relations between Licinius and Constantine did not improve, especially as Licinius was suspicious of Constantine's support of Christianity.

Fig.1. Copper-alloy *nummus* of Constantine I (AD 306-37), struck at Siscia, AD 319. RIC VII, 61. Found in Shropshire, HESH-D4BA36. © Portable Antiquities Scheme (20mm)

Fig.2. Base-silver *nummus* or *argenteus* of Licinius I (AD 308-24), struck at Trier, AD 318-9. The reverse proclaims that Jupiter is the protector of Licinius. RIC VII, 211. Found in Wiltshire, WILT-369E64. © Portable Antiquities Scheme (17mm)

Fig.4. Copper-alloy *nummus* of Crispus (AD 317-26), struck at Trier, AD 320-1. The reverse is the rarer variety with a trophy instead of a standard. RIC VII, 284. Found in Lincolnshire, NLM-D6FE42.© Portable Antiquities Scheme (20.5mm)

Fig.3. Copper-alloy *nummus* of Licinius II (AD 317-324), struck at Antioch, AD 317-20. The emperor holds a globe and *mappa* (cloth thrown down to start a chariot race). RIC VII, 45. Found in Hertfordshire, BH-562597. © Portable Antiquities Scheme (19mm)

Fig.5. Copper-alloy *nummus* of Constantine II as Caesar (AD 317-37), struck at Siscia, AD 321-4. RIC VII, 173. Found in Leicestershire, LEIC-02D871. © Portable Antiquities Scheme (18.5mm)

Licinius turned on some bishops and churches, so in 324 Constantine marched east. Licinius fled across the Bosphorus to Asia Minor (Turkey), but made the commander of his personal guard, Martinian, co-emperor (Fig.6.).

After being defeated in battle, both men surrendered to Constantine at Nicomedia in 324 – both were executed, along with Licinius II in 325. Constantine was now the sole senior emperor (Augustus) and he promoted another son, Constantius II (Fig.7.) to the rank of Caesar. It was now also that Constantine started to build the site of his new capital, Constantinople, on the site of the ancient city of Byzantium on the Bosphorus (I will cover this city in the next chapter).

This was to be a Christian city, as shown by one of its earliest issues of coins (Fig.8.). Constantine is also shown at this time on several coins with his head gazing heavenwards in an attitude of prayer (Fig.9.).

Demise of Crispus & Fausta (AD 326)

Crispus (Fig.4.) was the son of Constantine by his first wife, Minervina. He had played an important part in the defeat of Licinius and was given control of the Western Empire, which he ruled from Trier. However, it is said that Constantine's second wife, Fausta (Fig.10.), tried to seduce Crispus; he refused her advances and

she accused him of adultery. The result was that Constantine had Crispus executed; however, Helena, Constantine's mother (Fig.11.), managed to persuade Constantine that Fausta was guilty. It is quite possible that Fausta wanted Crispus out of the way to further the cause of her sons, Constantine II, Constantius II, and later, Constans. Whatever the truth, Fausta died of suffocation in her bath as the heat was stoked up.

Gold & Silver Coinage (AD 317-330)

The gold *solidus* was the standard gold coin, being struck mainly where the emperors were in residence. These coins are very rarely found in Britain with only one example on the database, a coin of Helena (Fig.11.). In addition, a number of medallions were also struck (Fig.9.). Silver is even rarer with very few issues at all, there being a few *miliarenses* and *siliquae* (Fig.12.). At the start of the period, there were some base-silver coins which some call base *argentei*, but which are often listed alongside even baser *nummi* (Fig.2.).

Bronze Coinage

The bronze coinage of the period consisted of *nummi* with a small proportion of silver. From 318 to 324 this was as much as 4%, but fell back to 2% from 324 to 330. This shows how inflation was increasingly becoming a problem. In the next

Fig.6. Copper-alloy *nummus* of Martinian (AD 324), struck at Nicomedia. No coins of this emperor are recorded with the PAS. RIC VII, 45. © British Museum (20mm)

Fig.7. Copper-alloy *nummus* of Constantius II as Caesar (AD 324-37), struck at Trier, 324-5. RIC VII, 456. Found in Surrey, SUR-44D592. © Portable Antiquities Scheme (17mm)

Fig.9. Gold medallion of Constantine I (AD 306-37), struck at Nicomedia, AD 326-7. This coin shows Constantine looking heavenwards in an attitude of prayer. RIC VII, 206. © British Museum (25mm)

Fig.8. Copper-alloy *nummus* of Constantine I (AD 306-37), struck at Constantinople, AD 327. The reverse of this very rare coin shows the imperial Christian standard, the labarum, piercing a snake (probably representing evil). RIC VII, 19. © British Museum (19mm)

Fig.10. Copper-alloy *nummus* of Fausta (died AD 326), struck at Nicomedia, c.AD 326. This coin has a mintmark which was apparently only used after Fausta's death. RIC VII. Found in Hampshire, HAMP-381386. © Portable Antiquities Scheme (19mm)

chapter we will see how bad it became in the coming decades. In the 4th century, we numismatists tend to categorise *nummi* by their reverse types rather than by emperor. This is because there were often many emperors who shared the same reverse types – in the previous chapter you would have seen coins of the GENIO POPVLI ROMANI type struck for all the Tetrarchs and SOLI INVICTO COMITI coins struck for Constantine, Licinius I and Maximinus. In the period 317-330, the most common reverse types in the western mints are as shown in Table 1.

This does give an indication of relative rarity, showing that the BEATA TRANQVILLITAS and camp gate issues are the most common.

Fig.11. Gold *solidus* of Helena (mother of Constantine I), struck at Ticinum, AD 324-5. Helena is famous for discovering the True Cross at Jerusalem. RIC VII, 183. Found in Buckinghamshire, BUC-6DB111. © Portable Antiquities Scheme (21mm)

Fig.12. Silver *miliarensis* of Crispus (AD 317-26), struck at Nicomedia, AD 324-5. This coin shows Constantine and his three sons: Crispus, Constantine II and Constantius II. Found in a hoard near Portsmouth in the 19th century. © British Museum (23mm)

Fig.13. Copper-alloy *nummus* of Crispus Caesar (AD 317-26), struck at Ticinum, AD 318-9. This appears to be an unpublished variety for Ticinum, showing Crispus helmeted. RIC – Found in Hertfordshire, BH-FBB2F6. © Portable Antiquities Scheme (16mm)

Reverse Inscription & Type	Date of Issue	Number on PAS Database	Figs
VICTORIAE LAETAE PRINC PERP Two Victories holding wreath	318-320	647	1, 13 & 34
VIRTVS EXERCIT Two captives seated under standard or trophy	320-1	198	4, 14 & 35
BEATA TRANQVILLITAS or similar Globe on altar, inscribed VOTIS XX	321-4	1620	15, 36, 37
SARMATIA DEVICTA Victory with trophy and enemy	323-4	286	16, 17 & 39
D N CONSTANTINI MAX AVG, CAESARVM NOSTRORVM and others Vota inscription in wreath types	320-5	591	5, 18, 19, 20, 21 & 38
PROVIDENTIAE AVGG or CAESS; VIRTVS AVGG or CAESS: Camp-Gate types	326-30	975	7 & 23-25
SALVS and SPES REI PVBLICE For Fausta	324-6	92	10, 26 & 42
SECVRITAS REI PVBLICE For Helena	324-8	90	27

Table 1. Common reverse types.

There was also a rare issue of coins which had no inscription on the obverse, but the emperor's name on the reverse – there are very few of these coins on the PAS Database (Figs.28 & 9.). A few other scarce types are recorded, for example an early piece of Crispus showing the young emperor on the reverse (Fig.30.) In the east, the major type was IOVI CONSERVATORI (Jupiter the Protector) – Licinius was eager to proclaim his favourite god, Jupiter. (Figs.3, 6, 31 & 32). There is also one example of a rare issue from Thessalonica that shows Sol and solar rays (Fig.33.)

It is also interesting to show the approximate number of coins for each ruler on the PAS Database from this period, 317-330:

Licinius I (308-24)	60
Licinius II (317-324)	49
Constantine I (306-337)	1,792
Crispus (317-326)	1,054
Constantine II (317-337)	728
Constantius II (324-337)	127
Fausta (coins struck 324-6)	95
Helena (coins struck 324-8)	96

Because most of the coins come from western and Italian mints (London, Trier, Arles, Lyons and Ticinum/Pavia), it is probably no surprise that there are relatively few coins of Licinius I and II found in Britain. Although western mints did strike coins for these eastern rulers, they did so in much smaller numbers, probably reflecting the awkward relations between east and west. Furthermore, probably because he was prominent in the western provinces and ruled from the city of Trier which had the main mint in the west, Crispus is very well represented. Indeed, he is better represented than his half-brother Constantine II who was made Caesar at the same time as Crispus – this obviously reflects the assumed seniority of Crispus and gives credence to the supposition that Fausta saw him as a threat to her sons' advancement. It is also interesting that there are the same number of coins for Fausta and Helena, even though Helena's issues continued for two years more after Fausta's death.

Although most coins do come from western mints, a small but significant number come from the Balkan mints at Siscia and Thessalonica, and a few travel all the way from the east (Figs.3, 5, 23, 31, 32 & 33.).

Fig.14. Copper-alloy *nummus* of Constantine I (AD 306-37), struck at Lyon, AD 321. The reverse shows two captives under a standard and proclaims the "bravery of the army". RIC VII, 113. Found in Nottinghamshire, LVPL-DABFC3. © Portable Antiquities Scheme (19.5mm)

Fig.15. Copper-alloy *nummus* of Constantine I (AD 306-37), struck at Trier, AD 322-3. RIC VII, 368. Found in Hampshire, SUR-BD7FF8. © Portable Antiquities Scheme (19.5mm)

Fig.16. Copper-alloy *nummus* of Constantine I (AD 306-37), struck at Lyons, AD 323. The reverse celebrates the defeat of the Sarmatians across the Danube. RIC VII, 214. Found in Leicestershire, LEIC-373598. © Portable Antiquities Scheme (20mm)

Fig.17. Copper-alloy *nummus* of Crispus Caesar (AD 317-26), struck at Trier, AD 323-4. This coin is not recorded for Crispus with the mintmark PTR. RIC VII, 429var. Found in Hampshire, HAMP-23E0B2. © Portable Antiquities Scheme (18mm)

Fig.18. Copper-alloy *nummus* of Constantine I (AD 306-37), struck at Ticinum (Pavia), AD 320-1. RIC VII, 140. Found in Somerset, SOM-955A72. © Portable Antiquities Scheme (19mm)

Fig.20. Copper-alloy *nummus* of Constantine I (AD 306-37), struck at Aquileia, AD 322. This coin is over-struck, probably on a coin of Constantine II as Caesar. RIC VII, 104. Found in Worcestershire, WAW-27802A4. © Portable Antiquities Scheme (19mm)

Fig.21. Copper-alloy *nummus* of Constantine II as Caesar (AD 317-37), struck at Lyons, AD 323. RIC VII, 217. Found in Somerset, SOMDOR-614C87. © Portable Antiquities Scheme (20mm)

Fig.19. Copper-alloy *nummus* of Licinius I (AD 308-24), probably struck at Arles, AD 321. RIC VII, c.f. 229. Found in Lincolnshire, DENO-6B6AC7. © Portable Antiquities Scheme (19mm)

Fig.22. Copper-alloy *nummus* of Licinius II (AD 317-24), struck at Arles, ad 320-1. RIC VII, c.f. 21. Found in Nottinghamshire, DENO-72A086. © Portable Antiquities Scheme (18mm)

Fig.23. Copper-alloy *nummus* of Constantine I (AD 306-37), struck at Cyzicus, AD 325-6. This coin is only recorded with a laureate head, as opposed to a diademed head. RIC VII, 34var. Found in Lincolnshire, LVPL-724062. © Portable Antiquities Scheme (18mm)

Fig.24. Copper-alloy *nummus* of Constantine I (AD 306-37), struck at Trier, AD 327-8. RIC VII, 504. Found in Hampshire, SUR-360600. © Portable Antiquities Scheme (20mm)

Fig.25. Copper-alloy *nummus* of Constantine I (AD 306-37), struck at Arles, AD 324-5. This coin is has four turrets on top of the camp gate, instead of the normal two. RIC VII, 264var. Found in Oxfordshire, BERK-5AA8A2. © Portable Antiquities Scheme (18mm)

Fig.27. Copper-alloy *nummus* of Helena (mother of Constantine), struck at Trier, AD 327-8. The reverse shows Securitas. RIC VII, 515. Found in Dorset, DOR-9925F1. © Portable Antiquities Scheme (19mm)

Fig.28. Copper-alloy *nummus* of Constantine I (AD 306-37), struck at Trier, AD 326. RIC VII, 485. Found in Sussex, SUSS-4A1BD5. © Portable Antiquities Scheme (17mm)

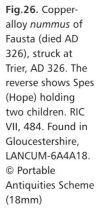

Fig.26. Copper-alloy *nummus* of Fausta (died AD 326), struck at Trier, AD 326. The reverse shows Spes (Hope) holding two children. RIC VII, 484. Found in Gloucestershire, LANCUM-6A4A18. © Portable Antiquities Scheme (18mm)

171

Mint of London

The mint at London continued to strike bronze coins in this period until its closure in AD 325. Its output is quite prolific and London mint coins of this period are commonly found in Britain. The VICTORIAE LAETAE PRINC PERP (Fig.34.) and VIRTVS EXERCIT (Fig.35.) issues follow the normal types used on the Continent. However, at the end of BEATA TRANQVILLITAS issue, London uses an abbreviated inscription, BEATA TRANQLITAS, and the style of the coins becomes a bit rough (Figs.36 & 7.). After issues of SARMATIA DEVICTA and Vota types (Figs.38 & 9.), the mint closes with an issue of camp gate coins and pieces for Fausta and Helena (Figs.40-2.). Why London was closed remains a mystery. Perhaps it was reckoned that Trier and other Continental mints would be able to supply Britain without the need for a mint at London.

There certainly does not appear to be an overt political reason. The mint at London was only to operate once again, in the 380s under Magnus Maximus (see Chapter XXVIII).

Coins of Interest

Amongst the thousands of coins from this period on the PAS Database are a number of new varieties. Two coins, of Crispus from Ticinum and Constantine from Cyzicus, have unrecorded obverse types (Figs.13 & 23.). Two more coins, of Crispus from Trier and Fausta from Nicomedia, have mintmark varieties (Figs.10 & 17.). Finally, a camp gate piece of Constantine from Arles has four instead of two turrets! (Fig.25.). All of this new information is increasing our knowledge of the coinage of the period, and in the case of the Fausta coin might make us rethink the dating of a particular issue (Fig.10.).

Fig.29. Copper-alloy *nummus* of Constantius II as Caesar (AD 324-37), struck at Trier, AD 326. This is from a small issue that only has the emperor's name on the reverse. RIC VII, 490. Found in Dorset, DOR-F217C7. © Portable Antiquities Scheme (15mm)

Fig.30. Copper-alloy *nummus* of Crispus Caesar (AD 317-26), struck at Arles, AD 317. This rare coin celebrates the accession of Crispus. RIC VII, 129. Found in Lincolnshire, DENO-40A086. © Portable Antiquities Scheme (21mm)

Fig.31. Copper-alloy *nummus* of Licinius I (AD 308-24), struck at Heraclea, AD 321-4. The reverse shows Jupiter, Licinius' favourite god. RIC VII, 52. Found in Lincolnshire, WMID-4E9E60. © Portable Antiquities Scheme (20mm)

Fig.32. Copper-alloy *nummus* of Constantine I (AD 306-37), struck at Heraclea, AD 321-4. This issue was struck under the authority of Licinius I. RIC VII, 51. Found in Kent, KENT-B49523. © Portable Antiquities Scheme (20mm)

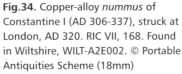

Fig.34. Copper-alloy *nummus* of Constantine I (AD 306-337), struck at London, AD 320. RIC VII, 168. Found in Wiltshire, WILT-A2E002. © Portable Antiquities Scheme (18mm)

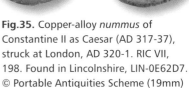

Fig.35. Copper-alloy *nummus* of Constantine II as Caesar (AD 317-37), struck at London, AD 320-1. RIC VII, 198. Found in Lincolnshire, LIN-0E62D7. © Portable Antiquities Scheme (19mm)

Fig.33. Copper-alloy *nummus* of Constantine I (AD 306-37), struck at Thessalonica, AD 319. This rare coin shows Sol standing above what might be solar rays. RIC VII, 67. Found in Sussex, SUSS-899073. © Portable Antiquities Scheme (18mm)

Fig.36. Copper-alloy *nummus* of Crispus Caesar (AD 317-26), struck at London, AD 321. NOBIL C on the obverse means "most noble Caesar". RIC VII, 211. Found in Sussex, SUSS-7E5DF2. © Portable Antiquities Scheme (19.5mm)

Fig.37. Copper-alloy *nummus* of Constantine II as Caesar (AD 317-37), struck at London, AD 323-4. The reverse inscription is abbreviated to BEATA TRANQLITAS. RIC VII, 257. Found in Buckinghamshire, SOM-97FC62. © Portable Antiquities Scheme (18.5mm)

Fig.38. Copper-alloy *nummus* of Crispus Caesar (AD 317-326), struck at London, AD 323-4. The reverse celebrates 10 years of reign, although Crispus had only been in power for six! RIC VII, 291. Found in Cambridgeshire, CAM-E30C00. © Portable Antiquities Scheme (19mm)

Fig.39. Copper-alloy *nummus* of Constantine I (AD 306-37), struck at London, AD 323-4. SARMATIA DEVICTA. RIC VII, 289. Found in Essex, ESS-7AFCC2. © Portable Antiquities Scheme (21mm)

Fig.40. Copper-alloy *nummus* of Crispus Caesar (AD 317-326), struck at London, AD 324-5. This coin is from the last issue struck at London before the mint closed in AD 325. RIC VII, 295. Found in Buckinghamshire, NARC-4207B4. © Portable Antiquities Scheme (20.5mm)

Fig.41. Copper-alloy *nummus* of Constantius II as Caesar (AD 324-37), struck at London, AD 324-5. This comes from the last issue of the London mint. RIC VII, 298. Found in Hertfordshire, BH-A81E82a. © Portable Antiquities Scheme (19.5mm)

Fig.42. Copper-alloy *nummus* of Fausta (died AD 326), struck at London, AD 324-5. SALVS REI PVBLICAE. RIC VII, 300. Found in Buckinghamshire, BUC-C50990. © Portable Antiquities Scheme (20.5mm)

Fig.43. The "Near Shrewsbury" Hoard of around 9,315 coins of this period, found in 2009. As I write, the coins are coming out of conservation in batches and being catalogued by Eleanor Ghey in the Department of Coins and Medals at The British Museum.

Site Finds & Hoards in Britain (AD 317-330)

Map 1 shows that detectorists have found coins of this period (317-330: Reece Period 16) across England. Hoards of this period are not particularly common, but a hoard of over 9,000 pieces from Shropshire has recently been conserved and catalogued (2009 T450) in the British Museum (Fig.43.).

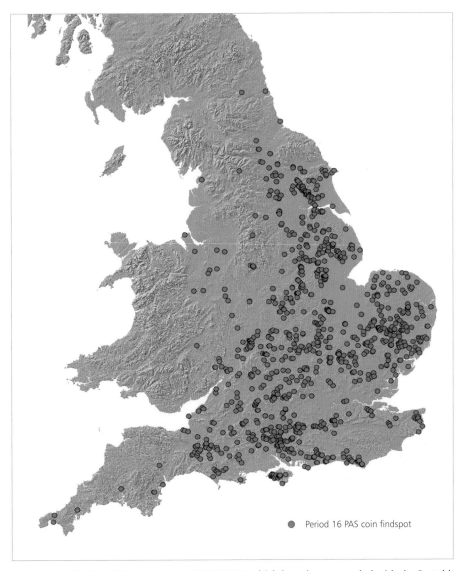

Map 1. Distribution of Roman coins, AD 317-330, which have been recorded with the Portable Antiquities Scheme. (© Philippa Walton)

Chapter XXV
Coinage of The Middle Years of The House of Constantine
(AD 330-348)

Fig.1. The skyline of Istanbul (ancient Constantinople) looking over the Bosphorus. © David Stuttard

In the previous two chapters, I covered the coinage of Constantine I (AD 306-337) up to AD 330. This chapter will cover the last seven years of Constantine's reign and will consider the coinage of his successors up until the great coinage reform of 348 (which I will discuss in the next chapter).

Constantinople

On 8 November, AD 324, Constantine founded the city of Constantinople, to be built on the site of the ancient city of Byzantium on the Bosphorus (Fig.1.). It was to be a Christian city; it had its own Senate; it even received grain from Egypt to provide for the population. It took six years to complete before it was dedicated in 330. Coins were struck at the city before 330 (Fig.2.), but a large issue of very small *nummi* was issued in celebration in 330.

These coins are common in the Mediterranean region, but much scarcer in Britain (Figs.3 & 4.). However, Constantine was to initiate a major

Fig.2. Copper-alloy *nummus* of Constantine I (AD 306-37), struck in Constantinople, AD 327. The reverse shows the Christian standard, the "labarum" piercing a snake. The anti-pagan symbolism of this very rare coin is clear. RIC VII, 19. © British Museum (18mm)

Fig.3. Copper-alloy *nummus* of the House of Constantine, struck at Constantinople, c.AD 330. This coin was struck to celebrate the foundation of Constantinople; it has a star on the reverse. RIC VIII, 22. Found in Hampshire, HAMP-33D253. © Portable Antiquities Scheme (13.5mm)

Fig.4. Copper-alloy *nummus* of the House of Constantine, struck at Constantinople, c.AD 330. This coin was also struck to celebrate Constantinople's foundation; its reverse shows a bridge over a river. RIC VII, 21. Found in Gloucestershire, LANCUM-395FE7. © Portable Antiquities Scheme (12mm)

Fig.5. Copper-alloy *nummus* of the House of Constantine – VRBS ROMA issue – struck at Trier, AD 332-3. The reverse shows the wolf suckling Romulus and Remus. RIC VII, 542. Found in East Yorkshire, YORYM-4AE023. © Portable Antiquities Scheme (18.5mm)

Fig.6. Copper-alloy *nummus* of the House of Constantine – VRBS ROMA issue – struck at Arles, AD 333. RIC VII, 373. Found in Cambridgeshire, CAM-4E5B56. © Portable Antiquities Scheme (17mm)

Fig.7. Copper-alloy *nummus* of the House of Constantine – CONSTANTINOPOLIS issue – mint of Lyon, AD 333-4. The reverse shows Victory standing on a prow. RIC VII, 266. Found in Dorset, DOR-65DB91. © Portable Antiquities Scheme (16mm)

Fig.8. Copper-alloy *nummus* of the House of Constantine – CONSTANTINOPOLIS issue – mint of Thessalonica (in Greece), AD 330-3. RIC VII, 187. Found in East Yorkshire, SWYOR-26FD93. © Portable Antiquities Scheme (17mm)

bronze coinage honouring his new capital and the old capital at Rome.

The helmeted personifications of the respective cities adorn the obverses of the coins with the inscriptions VRBS ROMA ("The City of Rome") (Figs.5 & 6.) and CONSTANTINOPO-LIS ("The City of Constantine") (Figs.7 & 8.). The Rome coin's reverse shows the famous scene of Romulus and Remus being suckled by the wolf; Constantinople's shows Victory standing on the prow of a ship (Figs.5-8.). These coins

were struck across the Empire, mostly between 330 and 335, although a few were issued down to the end of the decade. They are very common in Britain.

Constantine's Last Years

In 332, Constantine (Fig.9.) launched a war against the Goths on the Danube which resulted in a major victory and a treaty with the barbarians who now began to serve in the Roman army. He followed this up with a campaign against the

Fig.10. Copper-alloy *nummus* of Hanniballianus (AD 335-7), struck at Constantinople, AD 335-7. This rare coin shows the personification of the River Euphrates. RIC VII, 146. © British Museum (17mm)

Fig.11. Copper-alloy *nummus* struck in commemoration of Constantine I (AD 306-37) at Constantinople, AD 337-40. RIC VIII, cf. 37. Found in Wiltshire, WILT-8910E8. © Portable Antiquities Scheme (13mm)

Fig.9. Copper-alloy *nummus* of Constantine I (AD 306-37), struck at Arles, AD 332-3. The obverse shows Constantine wearing a rosette-diadem. RIC VII, 364. Found in Dorset, DOR-A93072. © Portable Antiquities Scheme (18mm)

Fig.12. Copper-alloy *nummus* struck in commemoration of Constantine I (AD 306-37) at Lyon, AD 337-40. This coin has a new mintmark variety, and we do not have a similar specimen in the British Museum. RIC VIII 3var. Found in East Yorkshire, YORYM-FF29E6. © Portable Antiquities Scheme (14mm)

Fig.13. Copper-alloy *nummus* of Delmatius (AD 335-7), struck at Constantinople, AD 336-7. This is one of only 16 coins of Delmatius on the PAS Database. RIC VII, 141. Found in Surrey, SUR-DFB4C1. © Portable Antiquities Scheme (16.5mm)

Sarmatians, regaining much of the province of Dacia (modern Romania) by 336. His next plan was to campaign against Persia (the Sasanians) and he made his nephew, Hanniballianus, "King of Armenia and neighbouring regions" (Fig.10.).

However, this campaign never occurred because on 22 May, 337, Constantine died. He was baptised on his death-bed and then buried in his own special mausoleum at the east end of the newly built Church of the Holy Apostles in Constantinople. Ironically, after he died, the Senate deified Constantine, not something that was appropriate for a Christian emperor (Figs.11 & 12.).

The Succession (AD 337-40)

In 335, Constantine raised his nephew Delmatius (Fig.13.) to be a junior emperor alongside his sons Constantine II (Fig.14.), Constantius II (Fig.15.), and Constans (Fig.16.). They each had a part of the Empire to rule (Constantine II the West; Constans Italy, Africa and the Upper Danube; Delmatius Greece and the Lower Danube; Constantius II the East) and it can be assumed that on his death in 337, Constantine intended there to be another Tetrarchy ("Rule of Four Emperors") with these emperors ruling alongside each other.

Fig.14. Copper-alloy *nummus* of Constantine II as Caesar (AD 317-37), struck at Lyons, AD 330-1. The reverse is the common GLORIA EXERCITVS, two soldiers and two standards, type. RIC VII, 244. Found in Shropshire, WMID-D5ECB3. © Portable Antiquities Scheme (16mm)

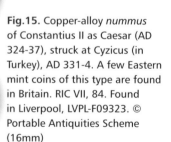

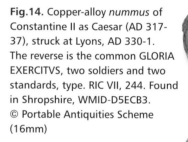

Fig.15. Copper-alloy *nummus* of Constantius II as Caesar (AD 324-37), struck at Cyzicus (in Turkey), AD 331-4. A few Eastern mint coins of this type are found in Britain. RIC VII, 84. Found in Liverpool, LVPL-F09323. © Portable Antiquities Scheme (16mm)

This did not happen. Delmatius and Hannibalianus (Fig.10.), were both quickly assassinated. The three sons of Constantine then ruled together for three years, striking coins in their

Fig.16. Copper-alloy *nummus* of Constans as Caesar (AD 333-37), struck at Trier, AD 333-4. Coins of Constans as Caesar are scarce. RIC VII, 552. Found in Leicestershire, LEIC-676453. © Portable Antiquities Scheme (18mm)

Fig.17. Copper-alloy *nummus* of Constantius II (AD 337-61), struck at Trier, c.AD 340-1. This is one of the last soldier and standard pieces to be issued. RIC VIII, 102. Found in Lincolnshire, LIN-8DBFB7. © Portable Antiquities Scheme (13mm)

Fig.18. Copper-alloy *nummus* of Constantius II (AD 337-61), struck at Trier, AD 337-40. The VIRTVS AVGG NN type is quite scarce. Found in Lincolnshire, SUR-CE48E0. © Portable Antiquities Scheme (14.5mm)

Fig.19. Copper-alloy *nummus* of Constans (AD 337-50), struck at Rome, AD 337-40. There is only one coin of this scarce SECVRITAS REIP type on the PAS database. RIC VIII, 11. © British Museum.

Fig.20. Copper-alloy *nummus* of Helena (mother of Constantine), struck at Trier, AD 337-40. The reverse shows Pax. RIC VIII, 78. Found in Leicestershire, LEIC-594965. © Portable Antiquities Scheme (16mm)

Fig.21. Copper-alloy *nummus* of Theodora (step-mother of Constantine), struck at Trier, AD 337-40. The reverse shows Pietas holding an infant. RIC VIII, 43. Found in Leicestershire, LEIC-834453. © Portable Antiquities Scheme (16mm)

Fig.22. Copper-alloy contorniate-medallion of Constans (337-50), struck at Rome, c.AD 343. The reverse shows Constans on a galley on the sea off Boulogne. RIC VIII, 338. This image taken from Alföldi, Die Kontorniaten, pl II, no. 12. (30mm)

invaded Italy only to be defeated and killed by his younger brother. This left Constans ruling the Western Empire and Constantius II the Eastern half. This was to remain the case until AD 350 when Constans was deposed by Magnentius (see next chapter).

Constans Visits Britain (AD 343)

We know that in the winter of 343, Constans was forced to come over to Britain from Boulogne. The purpose of the visit is not known, but it might have been to deal with unhappy Britons who had been supporters of Constantine II, or it might have been to deal with the Picts on the northern frontier; or even both. A medallion was struck to commemorate the crossing of the Channel and this might have been the inspiration for a coin struck as part of the coinage reforms of 348 (Fig.22.). (See next chapter for the coinage reforms.)

Gold & Silver Coinage (AD 330-348)

Gold coinage of the period mainly consisted of gold *solidi*. These are coins that are rarely found in Britain, the PAS having only one specimen (Fig.23.). Equally scarce are silver coins, but in the 340s silver *siliquae* and *miliarenses* do begin to be struck in increasing numbers and

own names (Figs.17-19.) and for Helena (mother of Constantine) and Theodora (step-mother of Constantine) (Figs.20-21.). In 340, unhappy with Constans' share of the Empire, Constantine II

Fig.23. Gold *solidus* of Constans (AD 337-50), struck at Trier, AD 342-3. The coin simultaneously celebrates Constans' victory over the Franks, in 342, and his 10 year jubilee (he was made Caesar in 333). RIC VIII, 124. Found in Suffolk, CAM-1E75C4. © Portable Antiquities Scheme (c.23mm)

Fig.24. Silver *miliarensis* of Constantine II (AD 337-40), struck at Thessalonica, c.AD 340. This fine coin might have been struck after Constantine's death, but before the news reached Thessalonica. RIC VIII, 46. Found in Hampshire, HAMP-2197A7. © Portable Antiquities Scheme (25mm)

Fig.25. Silver *miliarensis* of Constans (AD 337-50), struck at Siscia, AD 340-50. The British Museum does not have an example of this rare coin. RIC VIII, 161. Found in Essex, BH-8AC6D3. © Portable Antiquities Scheme (24.5mm)

Fig.26. Silver *siliqua* of Constantius II (AD 337-61), struck at Trier, AD 342-7. This rare coin is the only example of its type on the PAS database. RIC VIII, 162. Found in Essex, ESS-101EA7. © Portable Antiquities Scheme (20mm)

Fig.27. Silver *siliqua* of Constans (AD 337-50), struck at Trier, AD 347-8. The reverse proclaims the victorious emperors (Constans and Constantius II). RIC VIII, 176. Found in Cambridgeshire, CAM-4FAB91. © Portable Antiquities Scheme (20mm)

Fig.28. The Thornbury Hoard of 11,460 *nummi* (and a few radiates). Most of the coins come from the period AD 330-348. This hoard is now in Bristol Museum and Art Gallery. Photograph © British Museum

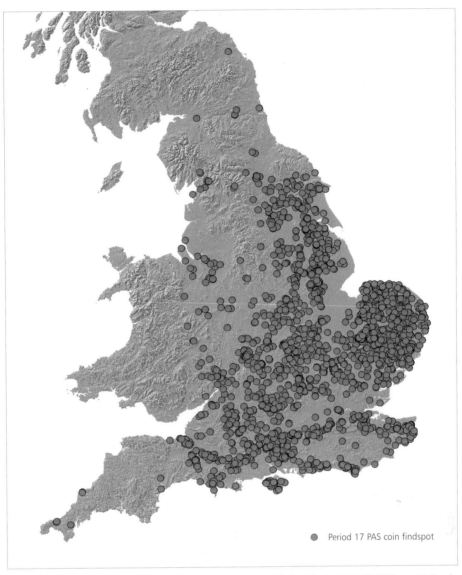

Map 1. Distribution of Period 17 (AD 330-48) coins recorded with the PAS. (© Philippa Walton)

are found in small numbers in Britain, the PAS records showing two *miliarenses* and 11 *siliquae* (Figs.24-7.).

Bronze Coinage (AD 330-348)

Bronze coins from this period are the most common from any period in Roman Britain. Work by Richard Reece and Philippa Walton show a marked peak in coin loss at this time, with over 25% of all Roman coins recorded with the PAS coming from this period. This is largely due to rampant inflation at the time. Depending on which ancient Roman papyrus of accounts from Egypt one uses, the 11,460 *nummi* from the Thornbury Hoard (found in 2004 and now on display in Bristol Museum and Art Gallery), equated to only one or two gold *solidi*, two or

four months' salary for a soldier, or payment for food for a soldier for one year or six months (Fig.28.).

Whichever way you look at it, you needed an enormous number of *nummi* to buy anything of significance. On the other hand, it does seem that Britain's agricultural economy was booming. In the reign of Constantine, we see the heyday of British villas, lavish country residences such as Bignor, Chedworth and Woodchester. It is quite likely that food was being exported in quantity to the Continent, especially to the Roman army on the Rhine. Therefore, the large quantity of *nummi* probably also represents this high level of farming activity in the province; certainly coins of Period 17 are the most widespread in Britain (see Map 1.).

Fig.29. Copper-alloy *nummus* of Constans (AD 337-50), struck at Trier, AD 347-8. This is a very common variety. Found in Somerset, SOM-454E63. © Portable Antiquities Scheme (15.5mm)

Fig.30. Copper-alloy *nummus* of Constantius II (AD 337-61), struck at Siscia (Croatia), AD 347-8. RIC VIII, 194. Found in Hampshire, SUR-8771C0. © Portable Antiquities Scheme (18mm)

Fig.31. Copper-alloy *nummus* of the Constans (AD 337-50), struck at an Eastern mint, AD 347-8. The reverse celebrates 20 years of rule and looks forward to 30. Found in Berkshire, SUR-FFA433. © Portable Antiquities Scheme (14mm)

Type	Date	No. on PAS Database	Figs.
POP ROMANVS bridge and star types	c. 330	38	3-4
GLORIA EXERCITVS – 2 soldiers & 2 standards	330-5	6,912	9, 14-16
GLORIA EXERCITVS – 2 soldiers & 1 standard	335-41	5,338	13 & 17
VRBS ROMA / Wolf and Twins	330-c.340	4,350	5-6
CONSTANTINOPOLIS / Victory on Prow	330-c.340	2,534	7-8
Helena / PAX PVBLICA	337-40	992	20
Theodora / PIETAS ROMANA	337-40	804	21
Constantine I commemoratives	337-40	93	11-12
VIRTVS AVGVSTI / AVGG NN / Emperor	337-40	38	18
SECVRITAS REI P / Securitas	337-40	5	19
VICTORIAE DD AVGGQ NN / 2 Victories	347-8	2,744	29-30
VOT XX MVLT XXX (Eastern Mint type)	347-8	10	31-32

Table 1. Types of *nummi*.

There are several types of *nummi* struck in this period. Table 1 only provides provisional totals which will change when further research is carried out. As the table shows, the most common types are the GLORIA EXERCITVS, VRBS ROMA and CONSTANTINOPOLIS issues. A significant number of coins were struck for Helena, Constantine's mother, and for Theodora, his step-mother. There are a reasonable number of commemorative coins for Constantine I, but the VIRTVS and SECVRITAS types are quite rare in Britain. The last issue of the VICTORIAE DD AVGGQ NN, two Victories type is also very common (Figs.29 & 30.); its eastern counterpart, the VOT XX MVLT XXX issue, is rarely found in Britain (Figs.31 & 32.).

Mints (AD 330-48)

The vast majority of coins come from the mint at Trier (in Germany), the imperial capital of the Western provinces (Figs.5, 16-18, 20-23, & 26-28.). The city boasted splendid baths, a very large amphitheatre, and a massive basilica which was built by Constantine; you can still see the original Roman bridge which spans the Moselle (Fig.34.). After Trier, a significant number of coins

Fig.32. Copper-alloy *nummus*, probably of the Constantius II (AD 337-61), struck at an Eastern mint, AD 347-8. Found in Oxfordshire, WMID-4D63A4. © Portable Antiquities Scheme (15mm)

Fig.34. The Aula Palatina, often called the Basilica of Constantine, at Trier. It is often dated to the reign of Constantine, but might have been built slightly earlier in the reign of his father, Constantius I (AD 293-305). © Richard Abdy

Fig.33. Contemporary copy of a copper-alloy *nummus* of the House of Constantine – GLORIA EXERCITVS, two soldiers and two standards type – struck c.AD 330-40 or later. Found in Lincolnshire, LIN-0CCAC6. © Portable Antiquities Scheme (13mm)

Fig.35. Contemporary copy of a copper-alloy *nummus* of the House of Constantine – CONSTANTINOPOLIS issue – struck c.AD 330-40 or later. Found in Bedfordshire, BH-ED46C2. © Portable Antiquities Scheme (13.5mm)

Fig.36. Copper-alloy contemporary copy of a *nummus* of the House of Constantine, struck c.AD 330-40 or later. It has the VRBS ROMA obverse with the Victory reverse of the CONSTANTINOPOLIS issue. Found in Suffolk, SF-835E03. © Portable Antiquities Scheme (13mm)

come from the Gallic mints of Lyons and Arles (Figs.6 & 7, 9, 12 & 14.), and a few coins find their way from Rome, Aquileia, Siscia and Eastern mints (Figs.2-4, 8, 10 & 11, 13, 15, 24 & 5, 30-2.).

Contemporary Copies

In addition to the vast number of official *nummi* flooding into Britain, there was a very large output of locally-produced imitations. It is probable that a large number were made at the same time as the official coins, although it is tempting to see a large output in the years 341-7 when few official coins were being struck. These contemporary copies are often quite good quality, although normally smaller than the official coins. They normally copy the originals quite closely (Figs.33 & 5.), but some do combine different types – for example, you might get a VRBS ROMA obverse with a CONSTANTINOPOLIS Victory reverse (Fig.36.). Sometimes these two types can be mixed with GLORIA EXERCITVS types.

By 348, the authorities probably realised that the very low value of the *nummus* was making it very hard to operate an effective monetary economy. This led to a major coinage reform which I will discuss in the next chapter.

Chapter XXVI

Coinage of The Last Years of The House of Constantine

(AD 348-364)

Coinage Reforms AD 348

In the last chapter (XXV) I covered how the small bronze *nummus* was reduced in size and was struck in enormous numbers, reflecting rampant inflation in the 330s and 340s. In response, in AD 348, the emperors Constantius II (337-61) and Constans (337-50) initiated a major reform of the bronze coinage. It resulted in the production of three different denominations, all bearing the FEL TEMP REPARATIO (Felicium Tempus Reparatio – "Happy days are here again") inscription.

1. The largest *nummus* (sometimes termed the AE2a or *maiorina*) of about 5.25 grams with up to 3% silver. The most common type of this coin in the West was the FEL TEMP REPARATIO "emperor on galley" type (Figs.1-3.). In the East, it was the FEL TEMP REPARATIO "fallen horseman" type (Fig.4.).

2. The slightly smaller *nummus* (sometimes termed the AE2b) of about 4.25grams with up to 1.5% silver. The most common type was the FEL TEMP REPARATIO "soldier leading small figure

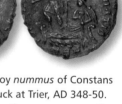

Fig.2. Copper-alloy *nummus* of Constans (AD 337-50), struck at Siscia, AD 348-50. This coin appears to have been struck in the fifth workshop, which is not recorded in RIC. RIC VIII, 199var. Found in Hampshire, HAMP-2076F1. © Portable Antiquities Scheme (21mm)

Fig.3. Copper-alloy *nummus* of Constans (AD 337-50), struck at Trier, AD 348-50. The reverse shows the emperor on galley, holding a Victory on globe. RIC VIII, 219. Found in Surrey, SUR-474A96. © Portable Antiquities Scheme (21mm)

Fig.1. Copper-alloy *nummus* of Constans (AD 337-50), struck at Rome, AD 348-50. The reverse shows the emperor on a galley, steered by Victory, holding a phoenix on globe and standard. RIC VIII, 109. Found in Nottinghamshire, DENO-2F8217. © Portable Antiquities Scheme (22mm)

Fig.4. Copper-alloy *nummus* of Constantius II (AD 337-61), struck at Arles, AD 348-50. RIC VIII, 120. Found in Nottinghamshire, DENO-CA0EC3. © Portable Antiquities Scheme (21mm)

Fig.5. Copper-alloy *nummus* of Constans (AD 337-50), struck at Rome, AD 348-50. The reverse shows a soldier leading a figure from a hut, a type used at Western mints. RIC VIII, 140. Found in Hampshire, HAMP-9A03A8. © Portable Antiquities Scheme (19.5mm)

from hut" type (Figs.5 & 6.). In the East, there was also the FEL TEMP REPARATIO "emperor and two captives" type (Fig.7.).

3. The smallest *nummus* (sometimes termed the AE3) had no significant silver content and weighed about 2.4 grams. The reverse bore the FEL TEMP REPARATIO "phoenix on globe or rocky mound" types (Figs.8 & 9.).

These coins coincided with the 1100th anniversary of Rome, hence the inclusion of the phoenix (representing rebirth) on several of the coins (Figs.1-2 & 8-9). This attempt to check inflation appears to have failed; from AD 353, the *nummi* returned to having a small module (see Fig.30.).

Demise of Constans (337-50) & Reign of Magnentius (350-3)

Constans became increasingly unpopular in the West until he was finally assassinated by his senior staff. It was the general Magnentius, who one source tells us had a British father, who became the next ruler in the West (Figs.12-20 & 23.). In Rome, Nepotian, a nephew of Constantine I, briefly seized power for a month but was murdered by Magnentius' followers (Fig.10.). Magnentius' powerbase was north of the Alps and in 351 he made his (probable) brother Decentius

his junior emperor (Caesar) (Figs.21-22 & 24.). Magnentius was quick to advance into Italy and then the Balkans. Here, the army of Illyria proclaimed Vetranio their emperor in 350, in opposition to Magnentius (Fig.11.). Meanwhile,

Fig.6. Copper-alloy *nummus* of Constans (AD 337-50), struck at Aquileia, AD 348-50. The reverse shows a soldier leading a figure from a hut, a type used at Western mints. RIC VIII, cf. 101/103. Found in Surrey, SUR-DBDD57. © Portable Antiquities Scheme (21mm)

Fig.7. Copper-alloy *nummus* of Constantius II (AD 337-61), struck at Nicomedia, AD 348-50. This type depicting the emperor and two captives is rarely found in Britain. RIC VIII, 67. © British Museum (20mm)

Fig.8. Copper-alloy *nummus* of Constans (AD 337-50), struck in Trier, AD 348-50. The phoenix on the globe reverse represents the rebirth of Rome on her 1100th anniversary. RIC VIII, 228. Found in Hampshire, BERK-FD0855. © Portable Antiquities Scheme (16.5mm)

Fig.9. Copper-alloy *nummus* of Constans (AD 337-50), struck at Trier, AD 348-50. The phoenix stands on a rocky mound. RIC VIII, 234. Found in Bedfordshire, BH-982FF5. © Portable Antiquities Scheme (17.3mm)

Fig.10. Copper-alloy *nummus* of Nepotian (AD 350), struck in Rome. Nepotian only ruled for a month and his coins are very rare. RIC VIII, 202. © British Museum (25mm)

Fig.11. Copper-alloy *nummus* of Vetranio (AD 350), struck in Siscia. The reverse refers to Constantine's Christian vision before the battle of the Milvian Bridge in AD 312. RIC VIII, 287. © British Museum (22mm)

Fig.12. Gold *solidus* of Magnentius (AD 350-3), struck in Aquileia, AD 350-1. RIC VIII, 124. © British Museum (21mm)

Fig.14. Copper-alloy *nummus* of Magnentius (AD 350-3), struck at Trier, AD 350-1. This type was briefly struck at the start of Magnentius' reign. RIC VIII, 260. Found in Lincolnshire, DENO-A91FA2. © Portable Antiquities Scheme (22mm)

Fig.15. Copper-alloy *nummus* of Magnentius (AD 350-3), struck at Lyons, AD 350-1. The emperor is riding down an enemy. RIC VIII, 115. Found in Hampshire, HAMP-E34771. © Portable Antiquities Scheme (23mm)

Fig.13. Silver medallion of Magnentius (AD 350-3), struck at Trier, AD 350-1. The reverse of this large piece proclaims the "security" of the state. RIC VIII, 255. © British Museum (34mm)

Fig.16. Copper-alloy *nummus* of Magnentius (AD 350-53), struck in Aquileia, AD 350-1. This is the only coin from Aquileia for Magnentius on the PAS database. RIC VIII, 160-2. Found in Hampshire, HAMP-BD9893. © Portable Antiquities Scheme (23.5mm)

Fig.17. Copper-alloy *nummus* of Magnentius (AD 350-3), struck at Trier, AD 350-1. RIC VIII, 266. Found in Somerset, SOM-932FA2. © Portable Antiquities Scheme (22mm)

Fig18. Copper-alloy *nummus* of Magnentius (AD 350-3), struck at Rome, AD 350. This rare type with the emperor kicking a captive was only struck at Rome. RIC VIII, 177. Found in Wiltshire, SOM-48ECF0. © Portable Antiquities Scheme (21.5mm)

Fig.19. Copper-alloy *nummus* of Magnentius (AD 350-3), struck at Amiens, AD 351-3. The mint at Amiens only operated for a few years, under Magnentius and briefly under Constantius II (AD 350-3). RIC VIII, 11/13. Found in Buckinginhamshire, BH-20EC67. © Portable Antiquities Scheme (21mm)

Fig.20. Copper-alloy *nummus* of Magnentius (AD 350-3), struck at Arles, AD 351-3. RIC VIII, 181. Found in Somerset, SOMDOR-BA7021. © Portable Antiquities Scheme (20mm)

Fig.21. Copper-alloy *nummus* of Decentius (AD 351-3), struck at Lyons, AD 351-3. Decentius is normally shown only wearing a cuirass, without drapery. RIC VIII, 137. Found in Berkshire, PUBLIC-78EB06. © Portable Antiquities Scheme (22mm)

Fig.22. Copper-alloy *nummus* of Decentius (AD 351-3), struck at Rome, AD 351-3. Coins of this type from Rome are rarely found in Britain. Found in North Yorkshire, SWYOR-4AB3A7. © Portable Antiquities Scheme (20mm)

in the East, Constantius II was preparing to advance westwards to counter Magnentius. Firstly, Constantius promoted his cousin Constantius Gallus to be his junior emperor (Caesar) (Figs.26 & 7.). Secondly, Constantius gained the abdication of Vetranio. Thirdly, Magnentius was defeated at the Battle of Mursa, in 352, which resulted in the rebel emperor fleeing back to Gaul. Fourthly, after another defeat near Lyons in 353, Magnentius committed suicide, as did his brother Decentius shortly afterwards.

Coinage of Magnentius

Magnentius struck gold and silver coins, but they are very rarely found in Britain (Figs.12 & 13.). However, he struck copious issues of bronze coins, *nummi* of large module. Most of his coins were struck in Gallic and German mints: Arles, Lyons and Trier were joined by a new mint at Amiens, which might have been Magnentius' birth-place (Figs.14-15, 17, 19, 20-1 & 23-4.). Coins from Aquileia and Rome are much scarcer (Figs.16 & 18.); Siscia only briefly struck for Magnentius and coins from this mint are rare.

Before the accession of Decentius in 351, Magnentius struck a number of types in his name only:

1. At the very start of his reign (AD 350) a few FEL TEMP REPARATIO "emperor on galley"

types were struck, continuing on from the issues of Constans and Constantius. These coins are scarce (Fig.14.).

2. A more common *nummus* of AD 350-1 was the GLORIA ROMANORVM "emperor riding down enemy" type (Figs.15 & 16.).

3. The most common *nummus* of the AD 350-1 period is the FELICITAS REI PVBLICE "emperor holding Victory and standard" type (Fig.17.).

4. There are some other scarcer types, notably the VICTORIA AVG LIB ROMANOR "emperor kicking captive" type of Rome, struck in 350 (Fig.18.).

After the accession of Decentius in AD 351, two very common issues were struck:

5. The VICTORIAE DD NN AVG ET CAE(S) "Two Victories and wreath" type was struck from AD 351-353 across the Western mints (Figs.19-22.).

6. The SALVS DD NN AVG ET CAES "large Chi-Rho (Christogram) between Alpha and Omega" type was struck in various sizes by the western mints (Figs. 23 & 24.).

It is interesting to note the similarity between the bust of Magnentius on the large Chi-Rho coins (Fig.23.) with the probable head of Christ on the Hinton St Mary mosaic (Fig.25.), which also has a large Chi-Rho behind. On the mosaic,

Fig.24. Copper-alloy *nummus* of Decentius (AD 351-3), struck at Lyons, AD 352-3. Large Chi-Rho coins of Decentius are much scarcer than those of Magnentius. RIC VIII, 171ff. Found in Leicestershire, LEIC-C117C7. © Portable Antiquities Scheme (22mm)

Fig.23. Copper-alloy *nummus* of Magnentius (AD 350-3), struck at Amiens, AD 352-3. This is the first coin to feature the Christian symbol, the Chi-Rho, exclusively. RIC VIII, cf. 39. Found in Wiltshire, HAMP-EA42B5. © Portable Antiquities Scheme (25mm)

Fig.25. The head of Christ at the centre of the Hinton St Mary (Dorset) mosaic in the British Museum, c.AD 350s. © British Museum

the Alpha and Omega ("the beginning and the end") are replaced by pomegranates, ancient symbols of everlasting life. Is it possible that the mosaicist used a coin of Magnentius as a model for this design?

Outlawing of Magnentius' Coins

After the deaths of Magnentius and Decentius in 353, Constantius II regained control of the West with his junior emperor Constantius Gallus (351-4) (Figs.26 & 27.). Amiens was soon closed as a mint and Constantius sent Paul the Chain to punish the supporters of Magnentius in Britain. Paul was ruthless, confiscating and ravaging the estates of Constantius' enemies, but also of people who had remained neutral. Even the

governor lost his life. This episode can be seen to be the turning point in the fortunes of Roman Britain, the province starting to decline from the 350s onwards. Coin assemblages at several sites in southern Britain do appear to end with pieces of Magnentius and the collapsed wall of a barn at Meonstoke Villa might be evidence for Paul the Chain's destructive activity (Fig.28.).

However, in addition, to erase the memory of Magnentius and Decentius, Constantius appears to have passed a monetary decree in 354 that outlawed their coins. The surviving text refers to the movement of coins between Gaul and Africa, but is explicit in forbidding the use of large module *nummi*. Because most of the coins of Magnentius and Decentius were large module coins,

Fig.26. Copper-alloy *nummus* of Constantius Gallus (AD 351-5), struck at Siscia. Note how the bust of Gallus is nearly always shown bare-headed. RIC VIII, 347. Found in Dorset, DOR-0FF0C0. © Portable Antiquities Scheme (22.6mm)

Fig.27. Copper-alloy *nummus* of Constantius Gallus (AD 351-4), probably struck at Lyons, AD 353-4. Coins of Gallus are scarce in Britain. RIC VIII, cf. 191. Found in Lincolnshire, LIN-01E660. © Portable Antiquities Scheme (17mm)

Fig.28. Facade of a barn from Meonstoke Villa (Hampshire) which was possibly destroyed around the time of Paul the Chain, c.AD 353-4. © British Museum

this would be a convenient way to remove them from circulation. There are a number of hoards which terminate with the coins of Magnentius and Decentius, notably ones found recently in Shropshire and Buckinghamshire, suggesting that people were forced to bury such coins as a result of this legislation (Fig.29.).

Constantius II & Julian (AD 355-61)

Constantius Gallus had been left in Antioch to govern the eastern provinces, but he became unpopular. Constantius subsequently had him executed in 354. In 355, Constantius appointed Julian (another nephew of Constantine the Great) to be his junior emperor (Caesar) (Figs.31, 33 & 36.). Julian was to be placed in charge of the western provinces where he spent much of his time fighting against the barbarians on the Rhine and Danube frontiers. It was under Julian that Britain became even more important as a source of food for the Rhineland. Julian increased the number of ships that brought grain from Britain to Germany from 200 to 600. It was probably Britain's importance as a source of grain that meant the authorities were keen to hold on to the province for as long as possible.

The reduced-module *nummus* of the FEL TEMP REPARATIO "fallen horseman" type continued to be struck for both emperors through to AD 360 (Figs.30 & 31.). That not enough of these coins were struck is shown by the enormous numbers of copies struck across Britain

Fig.29. A hoard of 1,456 *nummi* found near Milton Keynes; many of the coins are of Magnentius. It has been acquired by Aylesbury Museum, where it has been on display. © Aylesbury Museum

Fig.30. Copper-alloy *nummus* of Constantius II (AD 337-61), struck at Lyons, AD 363-60. RIC VIII, 190. Most of the "fallen horseman" types are of this smaller module. Found in Hampshire, SUR-E46263. © Portable Antiquities Scheme (18.5mm)

Fig.31. Copper-alloy *nummus* of Julian as Caesar (AD 355-60), struck at Sirmium. RIC VIII, cf. 69. Found in Leicestershire, LEIC-5FE6B7. © Portable Antiquities Scheme (19mm)

Fig.32. Copper-alloy *nummus* of Constantius II (AD 337-61), struck at Siscia, AD 355-61. SPES REI PVBLICE pieces are scarce in Britain, although very common around the Mediterranean. RIC VIII, cf. 390. Found on the Isle of Wight, IOW-3136E8. © Portable Antiquities Scheme (17.5mm)

Fig.33. Copper-alloy *nummus* of Julian as Caesar (AD 355-60), struck at Sirmium, AD 355-60. RIC VIII, 85. Found in Cornwall, CORN-6E4CB1. © Portable Antiquities Scheme (16mm)

(see below; Figs.46-51.). Possibly around 357/8-60, another even smaller *nummus* of the SPES REI PVBLICE "emperor standing with spear and globe" type was issued (Figs.32 & 33.). This coin is very common around the Mediterranean, but rare in Britain. Figs.32 & 33. come from Cornwall and the Isle of Wight, suggesting that these coins might have travelled by sea to Britain, directly from the Mediterranean.

Surge in Numbers of Silver Siliquae Under Constantius II & Julian

Although a small number of silver *siliquae* had been struck from the 340s (see previous chapter) it is around AD 357 that they began to be issued in large quantities. These coins were made with high quality silver and continued to be struck in copious numbers until AD 402. There are 109 *siliquae* for Constantius II on the PAS database, most of the coins coming from the mints of Arles and Lyons (Figs.34 & 35.). Coins for Julian as Caesar are scarcer (Fig.36.).

Julian as Augustus (AD 360-3)

Relationships between Constantius and Julian grew tense and in AD 360 Julian was declared Augustus in the West by his troops. In the East, there was nothing that Constantius could do about this. However, a year later, in 361, Constantius died, leaving Julian sole emperor. Julian is best known for his attempts to re-introduce paganism in the face of the rapid rise of Christianity under the House of Constantine. One of his coins, a large module *nummus*, depicts a bull which is certainly an emblem of paganism (Fig.37.). This coin barely circulated in Britain and there are no specimens recorded with the PAS. Furthermore, in emulation of pagan philosophers, Julian grew a beard (Figs.37 & 38.).

Julian continued to strike a large quantity of silver *siliquae*, there being around 269 on the PAS database. In fact, the PAS data shows that the *siliquae* of Constantius II and Julian are the most numerous in Britain, overturning the picture presented by hoards, most of which were buried in the late 4th and early 5th centuries – because the hoards are late, they suggest that there were more Theodosian coins arriving in Britain. Furthermore, many of the coins of Constantius II and Julian have not been clipped, showing that they were lost before clipping started in the late 4th or early 5th century (see Chapter XXVIII).

On the other hand, *nummi* of Julian are rarely found in Britain, there only being a handful on the database (Fig.40.). One assumes that

Fig.35. Silver *siliqua* of Constantius II (AD 337-61), struck at Lyon, AD 360-1. This issue shows Victory. RIC VIII, 214. Found on the Isle of Wight, IOW-B45BF0. © Portable Antiquities Scheme (17mm)

Fig.36. Silver *siliqua* of Julian as Caesar (AD 355-60), struck at Arles. RIC VIII, 264. Found in Wiltshire, WILT-F13024. © Portable Antiquities Scheme (18mm)

Fig.34. Silver *siliqua* of Constantius II (AD 337-61), struck at Arles, AD 355-61. This jubilee issue celebrates 30 years of reign, and looks forward to 40 years. RIC VIII, 261/291. Found in Dorset, DOR-80C357. © Portable Antiquities Scheme (17mm)

Fig.37. A large copper-alloy *nummus* of Julian (AD 360-3), struck at Cyzicus, AD 361-3. The reverse proclaims that the bull (representing paganism) is the "security" of the state. RIC VIII, 126. © British Museum (26mm)

Fig.38. Silver *siliqua* of Julian (AD 360-3), struck at Lyons, 360-1. RIC VIII, 215A. Found in Leicestershire, LEIC-3815A4. © Portable Antiquities Scheme (17.5mm)

contemporary copies were being made to make up for this shortage (see below and Figs.46-51.).

Death of Julian & Reign of Jovian (AD 363-4)

Julian marched west to invade the territory of the Sasanian Persians, an old enemy of Rome. On 26 June, 363, he was killed in battle, thus ending the House of Constantine. He was replaced by the commander of the Praetorian Guard, Jovian, who marched the army back to Roman territory. On his way to Constantinople, so the story goes, he was overcome by fumes from a brazier in his room on 16 February, 364. Coins of Jovian are scarce in Britain, but both *siliquae* (Figs.41 & 42.) and *nummi* (Figs.43 & 44.) are occasionally found. Because Jovian was declared emperor in the East, and was only on the throne for a few months, it might not be surprising that some of his coins found in Britain come from mints in Turkey and Syria (Figs.41 & 43.).

Contemporary Copies From the Period AD 348-64

There were an enormous number of contemporary copies made in the period. It is probably best to deal with them in one section, although the reasons for copying are not necessarily the same. It is simplest to discuss them in separate groups:

Group 1 – AD 348-53: large module copies

In this period there were many copies made of large module coins, notably the FEL TEMP REPARATIO "emperor on galley" types (Fig.45.). This was probably because these coins had the highest silver content and so were worth forging with a lower or non-existent silver content. It is interesting that the small module FEL TEMP REPARATIO "phoenix" types were not copied, probably because the official pieces contained no silver.

Group 2 – AD 353-64: small module copies

Because the small module FEL TEMP REPARATIO "fallen horseman" types (see Figs.30 & 31.), the SPES REI PVBLICE types (see Figs.32 & 33.), and the *nummi* of Julian (see Fig.49.) and Jovian (see Figs.43 & 44.) were not struck in sufficient numbers, an enormous number of copies were struck between c.353 and 364. The vast majority of these copies were of the FEL TEMP REPARATIO "fallen horseman" type, ranging in size from c.5mm-18mm (Figs.46 & 47.). In

Fig.39. Silver *siliqua* of Julian (AD 360-3), struck at Arles, 361-3. This coin shows Julian bearded. RIC VIII, 309. Found in Hampshire, HAMP-217D28. © Portable Antiquities Scheme (17.5mm)

Fig.40. Copper-alloy *nummus* of Julian (AD 360-3), struck at Arles, 361-3. This is a rare coin – *nummi* of Julian as Augustus are rarely found in Britain. RIC VIII, 324. Found in Warwickshire, WAW-F205C3. © Portable Antiquities Scheme (17mm)

Fig.41. Silver *siliqua* of Jovian (AD 363-4), struck at Antioch. RIC VIII, 227. Found in Dorset, DOR-013B65. © Portable Antiquities Scheme (18mm)

Fig.42. Silver *siliqua* of Jovian (AD 363-4), struck at Lyons. The only other coin of this type known is in the British Museum, from a hoard in Rutland. Found in Sussex, SUSS-F74487. © Portable Antiquities Scheme (16.5mm)

Fig.43. Copper-alloy *nummus* of Jovian (AD 363-4), struck at Heraclea. This is one of only 12 *nummi* of Jovian on the PAS database. RIC VIII, 108. Found in Kent, KENT-C27502. © Portable Antiquities Scheme (19mm)

addition, small module copies of coins of Magnentius were produced (Fig.48.). A number of these copies were over-struck on earlier, pre-AD 348 *nummi* emphasising that these earlier coins had been demonetised (Fig.49.). Many of these copies are small and crudely made, but it does seem that they played a role in Britain's economy when there was a shortage of official coinage.

Group 3 – AD 353-364 or later: "Cut-out" coins

There are an increasing number of small coins being recorded with the PAS which have been cut out of larger coins, mostly of Magnentius. Common among these are small coins cut from the large "Chi-Rho" *nummi* (Fig.50.). It even seems that copies were made of these cut out coins. In addition, some of the original coins with cut-out sections have been found. Is it possible that when Constantius II banned the large module coins in AD 354 people began to make small module pieces out of the outlawed coins? This seems quite plausible, although it is argued by some scholars that these coins were produced later in the century. There is certainly scope for much more study of these coins.

Group 4 – Siliqua copies

As in the earlier imperial period when people produced plated or base copies of silver *denarii*, so they also did with the *siliqua* (Fig.51.). Such copies were almost certainly made to deceive in order to make an illegal profit. These copies are more likely to be found as stray finds because they were normally rejected by hoarders.

Distribution of Coins AD 348-64 in Britain

Although there are fewer coins from the period AD 348-64 found in Britain than for the period AD 330-48, they are still found across the Province (see Map 1.). Coins of this period are very common at some temple sites.

Relative Rarity of Emperors

Although some of the coins listed in Table 1 are contemporary copies, the totals do provide a general impression of the rarity of coins of the different emperors in Britain, using the PAS Database. The coins for Constans and Constantius II are only the ones struck in this period, not earlier. Some totals are approximate – a number of entries are waiting for further editing.

Emperor	*siliquae*	*nummi*	Total
Constans	-	428	428
Constantius II	109	1892	2001
Magnentius	-	1808	1808
Decentius	-	144	144
Nepotian	-	-	-
Vetranio	-	-	-
Constantius Gallus	-	68	68
Julian	269	37	336
Jovian	15	12	27

Table 1. Rarity of coins of different emperors in Britain.

Fig.46. Copper-alloy contemporary copy of a *nummus* of Constantius II (AD 337-61), FEL TEMP REPARATIO "falling horseman" type of Trier, probably struck c.AD 353-64. Found in Nottinghamshire, DENO-E94216. © Portable Antiquities Scheme (13.5mm)

Fig.44. Copper-alloy *nummus* of Jovian (AD 363-4), possibly struck at Lyons. Coins of Jovian are scarce in Britain. RIC VIII, cf. 241. Found in Wiltshire, SUR-49CE67. © Portable Antiquities Scheme (17mm)

Fig.45. Copper-alloy contemporary copy of a *nummus* of Constans (AD 337-50). The original was probably struck at Lyons, AD 348-50. cf. RIC VIII Lyons 72. Found in Berkshire, PUBLIC-09EF84. © Portable Antiquities Scheme (21mm)

Fig.48. Copper-alloy contemporary copy of a *nummus* of Magnentius (AD 350-3), probably struck c.AD 353-64. The reverse is a copy of the VICTORIAE DD NN AVG ET CAE type with two Victories. Found in Oxfordshire, HAMP-55EE33. © Portable Antiquities Scheme (17mm)

Fig.49. Copper-alloy *nummus* of the House of Constantine – GLORIA EXERCITVS type – overstruck with a crude FEL TEMP REPARATIO "fallen horseman" type, c.AD 353-64. Found in Leicestershire, LEIC-0C0A85. © Portable Antiquities Scheme (17mm)

Fig.47. Copper-alloy contemporary copy of a *nummus* of Constantius II (AD 337-61), FEL TEMP REPARATIO "falling horseman" type of Trier, probably struck c.AD 353-64. Found in Hampshire, WILT-E5B795. © Portable Antiquities Scheme (14mm)

Fig.50. Cut-out coin from a large *nummus* of Magnentius (AD 352-3), SALVS DD NN AVG ET CAES "Chi-Rho" type. This coin might have been cut out in the 350s or later in the 4th century. Boon cf. 148. Found in Lincolnshire, LIN-3FC248. © Portable Antiquities Scheme (13mm)

Fig.51. Silver-plated contemporary copy of a *siliqua* of Julian (AD 360-3). The original coin was struck at Lyon. Type as RIC VIII, 234. Found in Suffolk, SF-C4ADD2 (15.5mm)

Map 1. Distribution of coins from the period AD 348-64 on the PAS Database. The plain red dots are *nummi*; the black on red dots are *siliquae*. (© Philippa Walton)

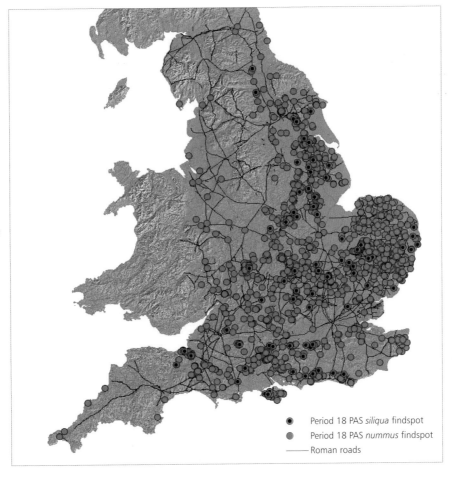

● Period 18 PAS *siliqua* findspot
● Period 18 PAS *nummus* findspot
—— Roman roads

193

Chapter XXVII
Coinage of The House of Valentinian
(AD 364-378)

Fig.1. Silver-gilt contemporary copy of a *solidus* of Valentinian I (AD 364-75), based on a coin of Trier struck AD 364-7. RIC IX, cf 1a. Found in Suffolk, SF-6955E6. © Portable Antiquities Scheme (22mm)

Fig.2. Gold *solidus* of Valens (AD 364-78), struck at Trier, AD 367-78. The OB in the mint-mark TROBS stands for *obryzum* or *obryziacum* which means that the gold has been tested for purity. RIC IX, 17e/39a. Found in Lincolnshire, LIN-71FB34. © Portable Antiquities Scheme (21mm)

Fig.3. Roman gold ingot from Crasna, Romania, naming the officials Flavianus and Lucianus. © British Museum (183mm)

Accession of Valentinian I (AD 364-75) & Valens (AD 364-78)

In the last chapter I ended with the death of Jovian in Turkey. He was succeeded by a military officer from Pannonia (Hungary), Valentinian I (AD 364-75) (Fig 6). Valentinian was to rule the Western Empire and Pannonia; he nominated his brother Valens (AD 364-78) to rule the Balkans and the Eastern Empire (Fig.1.). Valentinian was to spend most of his reign campaigning against German barbarians on the Rhine, before fighting the Quadi and Sarmatians in the Balkans. He died from a brain haemorrhage brought on by exasperation when trying to negotiate with uncooperative barbarians! Valentinian and Valens were both devout Christians, but they favoured their Pannonian followers more than the traditional Roman aristocracy. This did not endear them to many senior Roman officials.

Gold & Silver Coinage

We are told by Roman writers that there was a serious problem with the gold coinage. There were counterfeits, some apparently coming from official sources, and financial and mint officials were producing light and/or debased coins (Fig.1.). To

194

Fig.4. Silver *siliqua* of Valens (AD 364-78), struck at Trier, AD 367-78. RIC IX, 27e/45b. The PS in the mintmark TRPS• stands for *pusulatum* which means the coin is made of pure silver. Found in Wiltshire, WILT-105F45. © Portable Antiquities Scheme (17.5mm)

Fig.5. Late Roman silver ingot "from the workshop of Honorinus", found in London. © British Museum (height 102mm)

Fig.6. Silver *miliarensis* of Valentinian I (AD 364-75), struck at Trier, AD 367-75. The reverse proclaims the bravery of the army. RIC IX, 26a. Found in Yorkshire, YORYM-E7EA94. © Portable Antiquities Scheme (24mm)

Fig.7. Silver *miliarensis* of Valentinian I (AD 364-75), struck at Siscia, AD 367-75. RIC IX, 10a. Found on the Isle of Wight, IOW-2B37E6. © Portable Antiquities Scheme (20.5mm)

Fig.8. Silver *siliqua* of Valentinian I (AD 364-75), struck at Arles, AD 364-7. This coin was struck in the third workshop of the mint (OF III). RIC IX, 6a(5). Found in Oxfordshire, SUR-7E5BC6. © Portable Antiquities Scheme (17.5mm)

counter this, Valentinian and Valens introduced a new law that all gold that came into the treasury had to be refined and tested as pure. This is recorded by the presence of OB in the mint-mark of gold coins. It stood for *obryzum* or *obryziacum* which means tested or pure gold (Fig.2.).

Solidi were by far the most common gold coin and now had 99% gold. From this time onwards, gold was almost always minted at the court of the emperor (the *comitatus*) hence many coins are marked COMOB with letters in the field noting the mint city. We have a number of late Roman gold ingots surviving, sometimes stamped with the names of emperors or the names of officials (Fig.3.). These would have travelled with the emperor, ready for turning into coin. Gold coins

from this period are quite scarce, there being eight specimens (and a contemporary copy) on the PAS Database.

Silver coins were likewise subjected to the same rigorous quality control, the letter PS for *pusulatum* (pure silver) being added to the mint-mark (Fig.4.). Coins have a fineness of 93% to 98% silver. As with gold, silver ingots were also produced in large numbers and were probably also used as currency (Fig.5.). The largest silver coin was the *miliarensis*. These are scarce and normally found in hoards – there are only six recorded on the PAS Database (Figs.6 & 7.). They come from various mints and it is not unusual to have coins from Balkan mints such as Siscia (Fig.7.).

195

Fig.10. Silver *siliqua* of Valens (AD 364-78), struck at Rome, AD 364-7. This is one of only two coins known struck in the fourth workshop (RQ) for this issue. RIC IX, 10b. Found in Cambridgeshire, CAM-484352. © Portable Antiquities Scheme (18mm)

Fig.11. Lightly clipped silver *siliqua* of Valentinian I (AD 364-75), struck at Sirmium, AD 364. This is a rare issue from Sirmium, struck in AD 364. RIC IX, 2. Found in Bedfordshire, BH-99F6F7. © Portable Antiquities Scheme (15mm)

Fig.9. Clipped silver *siliqua* of Valens (AD 364-78), struck at Lyons, AD 364-7. This coin was probably in circulation for some time before being clipped. RIC IX, 6e. Found in North Yorkshire, BM-2F4125. © Portable Antiquities Scheme (17mm)

Fig.12. Silver *siliqua* of Valentinian I (364-75), struck at Thessalonica, AD 364-7. RIC IX, 12a. Found in North Lincolnshire, NLM-B77AE2. © Portable Antiquities Scheme (19mm)

Fig.13. Silver *siliqua* of Valens (AD 364-78), struck at Constantinople, AD 375-8. This is the only *siliqua* from Constantinople for this period on the PAS Database. RIC IX, 42. Found in Kent, KENT-9076E2. © Portable Antiquities Scheme (19mm)

The standard silver coin was still the *siliqua*. The largest proportion of these coins come from Trier, Lyons and Arles (Figs.4, 8 & 9.), although a small number did travel from Italy, the Balkans and the East. The Rome coin is of one of only two known of its issue from the fourth workshop (Fig.10.). The *siliqua* of Valentinian I from Sirmium is rare (Fig.11.), while Thessalonica was to become an increasingly important mint in the late Roman period (Fig.12.).There is only one *siliqua* from Constantinople on the PAS Database (Fig.13.). *Siliquae* from Antioch are the most common of the Eastern mints which are found in Britain (Fig.14.). Some 300 *siliquae* of this period have been recorded with the PAS.

Revolt of Procopius (AD 365-66)

Procopius was a general who was also related to the emperor Julian who died in AD 363 (see previous chapter). While Valens was in the East, Procopius rebelled at Constantinople and gained control of the region around the Sea of Marmara. He struck coins at Heraclea, Constantinople, Cyzicus and Nicomedia. Coins of his are found in this region in significant numbers, but they are very rare in the West. The one coin of his on the PAS Database was found on the Isle of

Wight and it might have arrived by sea from the Mediterranean. It is quite possibly the only coin of Procopius ever found in Britain (Fig.15.).

Accessions of Gratian (AD 367-83) & Valentinian II (AD 375-392)

Gratian, the son of Valentinian, was only seven when he was made emperor in the West. Bronze *nummi* from Arles proclaimed GLORIA NOVI SAECVLI ("To the glorious new era") (Fig.16.). His coins were struck in copious numbers alongside those of Valentinian I and Valens (Fig.17.). Gratian was to take over from Valentinian I in 375; his half-brother, Valentinian II, was made emperor in the same year, although he was only four years old. Valentinian II's bronze coinage is very rare for the years 375-8, but a number of *siliquae* from Trier have been found in Britain (Fig.18.).

The Bronze Coinage

It is in the Valentinianic period that the bronze coinage ceases to have any silver added. Therefore the coins have little intrinsic value. Furthermore, initial metallurgical tests of *nummi* suggests that mints in the West (notably Arles and Lyons) added a significant quantity of lead to their coins (Fig.19.). This might explain why

Fig.14. Silver *siliqua* of Valens (AD 364-78), struck at Antioch, AD 367-75. RIC IX, 34b. This is one of six silver coins from Antioch on the PAS Database. Found in Bedfordshire, BH-32DD41. © Portable Antiquities Scheme (17.5mm)

Fig.15. Copper-alloy *nummus* of Procopius (AD 365-6), possibly struck at Constantinople: REPARATIO REIP type. This is the only coin of Procopius on the PAS Database, and possibly the only coin of his ever found in Britain. RIC IX cf. Constantinople 18-19 and Cyzicus 9. Found on the Isle of Wight, IOW-E6E981. © Portable Antiquities Scheme (15mm)

Fig.16. Copper-alloy *nummus* of Gratian (AD 367-83), struck at Arles, AD 367-75. This type was only struck for Gratian at Arles – GLORIA NOVI SAECVLI means "To the glorious new era". LRBC 529. Found in North Yorkshire, SWYOR-45E0A5. © Portable Antiquities Scheme (18mm)

Fig.17. Silver *siliqua* of Gratian (AD 367-83), struck at Trier, AD 367-78. RIC IX, 27f/46b. Found in Wiltshire, WILT-1096C3. © Portable Antiquities Scheme (18.5mm)

Fig.18. Silver *siliqua* of Valentinian II (AD 375-92), struck at Trier, AD 375-8. Silver coins of Valentinian II in the period AD 375-8 are relatively more common than bronze coins. RIC IX, 43/57a. Found in Hampshire, HAMP-D862E2. © Portable Antiquities Scheme (16.5mm)

Fig.19. Late Roman "grots" from Wiltshire. The larger red pieces are House of Valentinian *nummi*, nearly all from the mint of Arles. © Sam Moorhead

Fig.21. Copper-alloy *nummus* of Valens (AD 364-78), struck in Siscia, AD 367-75. LRBC 1477. Found in Buckinghamshire, BUC-B45BD5. © Portable Antiquities Scheme (17mm)

Fig.20. Copper-alloy *nummus* of Valentinian I (AD 364-75), struck in Siscia, AD 367-75. LRBC 1365-6. Found in Buckinghamshire, BUC-574243. © Portable Antiquities Scheme (16mm)

Fig.22. Copper-alloy *nummus* (AE1) of Valentinian I (AD 364-75), struck at Sirmium, AD 364. These large *nummi* are very rare and there are none on the PAS Database. RIC IX, 3. © British Museum (28mm)

Fig.23. Copper-alloy *nummus* (AE 2) of Gratian (AD 367-83), struck at Trier, AD 367-75. This is a very rare coin and none are recorded on the PAS Database. RIC IX, 29d. © British Museum (23mm)

these coins are now often heavily corroded or eaten away completely. They were made from an unstable alloy, unlike coins from Siscia which appear to have a better quality alloy (Figs.20 & 21.). In a recent hoard of Valentinianic coins from Devon found in very waterlogged conditions, the only coins which were clearly legible were those from Siscia.

There are a few very rare large *nummi* (AE1 and AE2) found across the Empire, but there are none on the PAS Database (Figs.22 & 23.). There are three very common types of smaller *nummi* (AE3):

GLORIA ROMANORVM
Emperor advancing right, dragging captive and holding standard
3,664 on PAS Dbase (Figs.21 & 24-7.)

SECVRITAS REI PVBLICAE
Victory advancing left, holding wreath and palm
5,026 on PAS Dbase (Figs.20 & 28-33.)

GLORIA NOVI SAECVLI (only struck for Gratian)
Emperor standing, holding shield and standard (Arles)
709 on PAS Dbase (Fig.16.)

There are a number of other rare types, but the only one which really figures on the PAS Database is a scarce issue from Trier:

GLORIA ROMANORVM
Victory advancing left, holding wreath and palm (Trier)
11 on PAS Dbase (Fig.34.)

Valentinianic *nummi* are incredibly common with 10,287 recorded with the PAS. Although Map 1 shows that Valentinianic coins are found across Britain, the density of their distribution is not uniform. I showed many years ago that there was a concentration of Valentinianic *nummi* in the West Country (Wiltshire and surrounding counties) and on parts of the East Coast. The PAS Data and Philippa Walton's research define the region more clearly, especially in the East where it is found around the Fenlands, into Lincolnshire and Nottinghamshire, and up to East Yorkshire. The two regions appear to be connected by a few sites in Northamptonshire. Those of you who have heard my lectures know that I think this is the region that the Roman army and tax collectors were exploiting to gain food to export to the Rhine to feed the Roman army. In contrast, there are very few Valentinianic pieces in the West Midlands up to Lancashire and Cumbria; furthermore, they are rare in parts of Sussex, Kent and Essex.

Fig.25. Copper-alloy *nummus* of Valentinian I (AD 364-75), struck at Lyons, AD 367-75. This particular issue can be identified by the crescent and dot on the reverse. LRBC 338. Found on the Isle of Wight, IOW-779230. © Portable Antiquities Scheme (16.5mm)

Fig.24. Copper-alloy *nummus* of Valentinian I (AD 364-75), struck at Trier, AD 365-7: GLORIA ROMANORVM type. LRBC 79. This is an unusually well preserved coin for the period. Found in Hertfordshire, BH-408355. © Portable Antiquities Scheme (18mm)

Fig.27. Copper-alloy *nummus* of Valens (AD 364-78), struck at Aquileia, AD 367-75. LRBC 1018. Found in Lincolnshire, LIN-4B8397. © Portable Antiquities Scheme (17mm)

Fig.26. Copper-alloy *nummus* of the House of Valentinian, struck at Arles, AD 367-75. Although there are around 230 of this type from Arles on the PAS Database, most are very heavily corroded, probably due to the effect of fertiliser on a poor alloy. LRBC 487-9. Found in Dorset, SOM-0FA377. © Portable Antiquities Scheme (15.5mm)

Fig.28. Copper-alloy *nummus* of Valens (AD 364-78), struck at Lyons, AD 367-75: SECVRITAS REI PVBLICAE. LRBC 340. Found in Surrey, SUR-229917. © Portable Antiquities Scheme (16.5mm)

Fig.29. Copper-alloy *nummus* of Valentinian I (AD 364-75), struck at Arles, AD 367-75. This coin was struck in the second workshop (OF II). LRBC 521. Found in Somerset, SOM-468460. © Portable Antiquities Scheme (18mm)

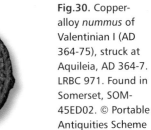

Fig.30. Copper-alloy *nummus* of Valentinian I (AD 364-75), struck at Aquileia, AD 364-7. LRBC 971. Found in Somerset, SOM-45ED02. © Portable Antiquities Scheme (18mm)

Fig.31. Copper-alloy *nummus* of Gratian (AD 367-83), struck at Rome, AD 367-75. This coin is from the fourth workshop (RQVARTA). LRBC 714. Found in Somerset, SOM-5A3203. © Portable Antiquities Scheme (18mm)

Fig.32. Copper-alloy *nummus* of Valens (AD 364-78), struck at Rome, AD 367-75. This has a distinctive mintmark with a leaf between the letters SM and RB. LRBC 725. Found in Lincolnshire, NARC-95BB10. © Portable Antiquities Scheme (18mm)

Fig.33. Copper-alloy *nummus* of Valens (AD 364-78), struck at Thessalonica, AD 364-7. This is one of eight coins from Thessalonica for this period. LRBC 1707. Found in Hampshire, HAMP-601EC4. © Portable Antiquities Scheme (17.5mm)

Fig.34. Copper-alloy *nummus* of Gratian (AD 367-83), struck at Trier, AD 367-75. The GLORIA ROMANORVM Victory type was only struck at Trier. LRBC cf. 108. Found in Kent, KENT-DE1FD5. © Portable Antiquities Scheme (18mm)

Fig.35. Clipped silver *siliqua* of Gratian (AD 367-83), struck at Trier, AD 367-75. This coin comes from a hoard that was buried in the late 4th or early 5th century. Coins that survived in circulation this long tend to be clipped. RIC IX, 27f/45c. Found in Essex, ESS-1FFA77. © Portable Antiquities Scheme (13mm)

Clipping of Coins

I will deal with the clipping of coins in my next chapter, but I should note here that I believe most of the silver *siliquae* were lost quite soon after they entered circulation because they are unclipped. There does appear to be light clipping in the second half of the 4th century (Fig.11.), but it is not until the early 5th century that heavy clipping occurs. The clipped *siliqua* of Gratian (Fig.35.) was found in a hoard with coins dating to the very end of the century. Hence, we know that this coin stayed in circulation a long time, long enough for it to be heavily clipped, probably after AD 400.

Mints

Table 1 shows how the vast majority of coins used in Britain at this time come from Arles and Lyons in Gaul. It is also clear that Trier was declining in importance as a mint, having been dominant earlier in the century. There are significant numbers from Aquileia and Rome, but noteworthy are the 300+ coins from Siscia in Croatia. These coins tend to come from a select number of issues of the mint, but as yet there is no satisfactory explanation for their presence in Britain. Mints to the east of Siscia are very poorly represented in British finds.

Disaster at Hadrianople AD 378

In 376, pressure from advancing Huns resulted in the Roman authorities on the Danube allowing the Visigoths to cross the river into the Empire. However, the Romans seriously mistreated the Visigoths who were forced to take up arms. For two years armies clashed across the Balkans. In the end, it was planned for the Eastern Roman Field Army (under Valens) to combine with the Western Roman Field Army (under Gratian) in order to eradicate the Visigoths. However, at Hadrianople, Valens decided to go it alone against the Goths – he did not want his nephew Gratian to share in the glory. The result was a disaster for Rome with Valens and most of his army being killed. In the next chapter I will explain how Theodosius I saved the day.

Mint	Count
Trier	258
Lyons	1,000
Arles	2,461
Aquileia	352
Rome	130
Siscia	386
Sirmium	1
Thessalonica	11
Heraclea	5
Constantinople	1
Nicomedia	2
Cyzicus	0
Antioch	15
Alexandria	2

Table 1. Number of coins found in Britain from various mints.

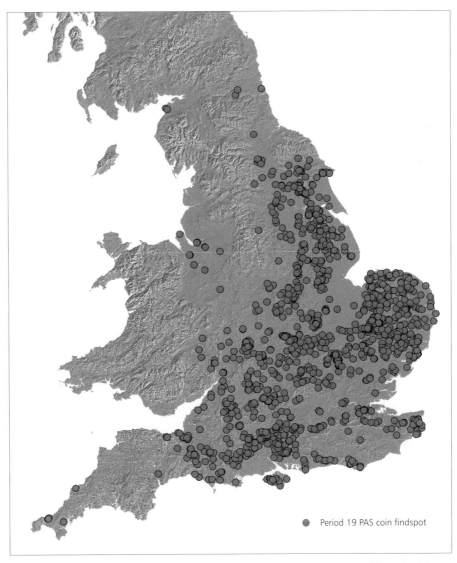

Map 1. Coins of the House of Valentinian (AD 364-78) recorded on the Portable Antiquities Scheme Database. © Philippa Walton (BM/UCL)

Chapter XXVIII

Coinage of The House of Theodosius to Post-Roman Britain

(AD 378-c.430)

Fig.2. Silver *siliqua* of Theodosius I (AD 379-95), struck at Trier, AD 379-83. RIC IX, 58b/84a. Found in Monmouthshire, NMGW-7D44F6. *Siliquae* are rarely found this far west in Britain. © Portable Antiquities Scheme (17mm)

Fig.1. Gold *solidus* of Gratian (AD 367-83), struck at Constantinople, AD 378-83. AVGGG on the reverse refers to the three emperors ruling at the time: Gratian, Theodosius I and Valentinian II. RIC IX, 45a. Found in Buckinghamshire, BUC-F59BB6. © Portable Antiquities Scheme (19.5mm)

Fig.3. Gold *solidus* of Valentinian II (AD 379-95), struck at Trier, 388-92. RIC IX, 90a. Found in Essex, ESS-2ED1F5. © Portable Antiquities Scheme (21.5mm)

Fig.4. Gold *solidus* of Aelia Flacilla (wife of Theodosius I), struck at Constantinople, AD 379-83. Flacilla's coins were mostly struck in the East and are extremely rare in Britain. RIC IX, 12. © British Museum (20mm)

Accession of Theodosius I (AD 379-95)

After the disaster at the Battle of Hadrianople in AD 378 (see previous chapter), the emperor Gratian (Fig.1.) turned to a seasoned general, Theodosius, who became emperor of the Eastern Empire (379-95). Theodosius I (Fig.2.) was the son of Count Theodosius who had led the Roman army in the suppression of the so-called "Great Barbarian Conspiracy" in AD 367. While Gratian and the young Valentinian II (Fig.3.) ruled in the West, Theodosius dealt with the Goths in the East. Theodosius was also to strike coins for his wife, Aelia Flacilla (Fig.4.), who died in 386 – these coins are extremely rare in Britain.

Coinage Reform of AD 379

In 379, yet another coinage reform was initiated. The gold *solidus* (Fig.1.), silver *miliarensis* (Fig.5.), and *siliquae* (Fig.2.) continued to be struck, but the copper coinage was overhauled. *Solidi* were now more common than in early periods of the 4th century with around 18 specimens on the PAS database (see Figs.1, 3, 12 & 32-3). Silver *siliquae* continued to be struck in large numbers (Figs.3, 14, 16, 19, 20, 25, 27-8 & 29). At times, a half-*siliqua* was struck as well (Fig.6.).

A new larger bronze *nummus* (AE2) was issued; this coin was to be common in the Mediterranean region, but such coins are rarely found

Fig.6. Clipped silver half-*siliqua*, anonymous issue, struck at Aquileia, probably c.AD 388-93. Half-*siliquae* are very rare. The date range for this issue has been suggested recently by Roger Bland. Found in Suffolk, SF-C35A06. © Portable Antiquities Scheme (13mm)

Fig.7. Copper-alloy *nummus* of Gratian (AD 367-83), mint unclear, AD 379-83. These large *nummi* are rarely found in Britain. Found in Leicestershire, LEIC-2A6DB2. © Portable Antiquities Scheme (21mm)

Fig.5. Silver *miliarensis* of Magnus Maximus (AD 383-8), struck at Trier. This is the only *miliarensis* of Magnus Maximus on the PAS database. RIC IX, 82. Found in Surrey, SUR-0BAFD0. © Portable Antiquities Scheme (24mm)

Fig.8. Copper-alloy *nummus* of Thedosius I (AD 379-95), struck at Aquileia, AD 379-83. This type is rarely found in Britain. LRBC 1071. Found in Somerset, SOM-E6C117. © Portable Antiquities Scheme (18mm)

Fig.9. Copper-alloy *nummus* of Gratian (AD 367-83), struck at Lyons, c.AD 379-83. This VOT XV MVLT XX type of Lyons is extremely common. Found in Yorkshire, SWYOR-D693C1. © Portable Antiquities Scheme (14.5mm)

Fig.10. Copper-alloy *nummus* of Gratian (AD 367-83), struck at Lyons, c.AD 379-83. This variety has an S on the top of the wreath. LRBC 378. Found in Lincolnshire, DENO-BE30F0. © Portable Antiquities Scheme (14mm)

Fig.11. Gold *solidus* of Magnus Maximus (383-8), struck at London. The AVG on the reverse stands for Augusta, the name of London at the time. RIC 2b. © British Museum (20mm)

in Britain (Fig.7.). The more regular size *nummus* (AE3) continued to be struck, but again this was more common in the Mediterranean region (Fig.8.).

Finally, the smallest *nummus* (AE4) was introduced. These coins had "Vota" reverses, celebrating jubilees of the various rulers. They were struck in large numbers in the West and are often found in Britain – the VOT X MVLT XV issue of Lyons for Gratian is the especially common (Figs.8-10.). These three bronze denominations were apparently valued at a ratio of 4:2:1.

Magnus Maximus & Flavius Victor (AD 383-88)

In Gaul, Gratian became increasingly unpopular with his court and army until in 383 a senior officer in Britain, Magnus Maximus, rebelled. Maximus (originally from Spain) declared himself

emperor and even struck coins at London where the mint had been closed since AD 325. He issued gold *solidi* and silver *siliquae* with the mintmark AVG(usta) which was the title of London – these coins are very rare (Fig.11.). He quickly took a large part of the British army to the Continent and defeated and killed Gratian; Valentinian II fled to Italy. Maximus now ruled over Britain, Gaul, Spain and Africa.

Maximus was to rule from Gaul for five years, striking coins in great numbers at Trier, Arles and Lyons (Figs.12 & 13.). In 387, he made a move on Italy; he made he son, Flavius Victor joint

Fig.13. Copper-alloy *nummus* of Magnus Maximus (AD 383-8), Lyons. These large *nummi* of Magnus Maximus are rarely found in Britain. RIC IX, 32. Found in Warwickshire, WAW-F25BA7. © Portable Antiquities Scheme (23mm)

Fig.14. Silver *siliqua* of Flavius Victor (AD 387-8), struck at Milan. RIC IX, 19b. Found in Dorset, SOM-8BDAD4. © Portable Antiquities Scheme (14mm)

Fig.12. Gold *solidus* of Magnus Maximus (AD 383-88), struck at Trier. This is the only *solidus* of Magnus Maximus on the PAS database. RIC IX, 77b. Found in North Lincolnshire, NLM-598885. © Portable Antiquities Scheme (21mm)

Fig.15. Copper-alloy *nummus* of Flavius Victor (AD 387-8), struck at Aquileia. This is a superb example of this issue. RIC IX, 55b. Found in Leicestershire, LEIC-BB65E2. © Portable Antiquities Scheme (13mm)

Fig.16. Silver *siliqua* of Magnus Maximus (383-88), struck at Milan, AD 387-8. Maximus only controlled the mint at Milan for a short time so these coins are scarce. RIC IX 19a. Found in Somerset, SOMDOR-477457. © Portable Antiquities Scheme (16mm)

Augustus to rule in Gaul (Figs.14 & 15.). Valentinian II fled east to Theodosius I; Maximus occupied Italy and struck coins at Milan, Aquileia and Rome in 387-8 (Figs.14-17.). However, Theodosius I would not accept the usurper and marched west. Maximus was defeated at the battle of Poetovio and executed at Aquileia; the Frankish general Arbogastes executed Flavius Victor in Gaul. Although Magnus Maximus was not in Britain long, his legacy was to live on in Welsh folklore where he is called Prince Macsen and is the ancestor of Welsh dynasties. It is possible that he withdrew the Roman army from Wales, possibly introducing mercenaries from Ireland to guard the region.

Magnus Maximus & the Tremissis

It is thought that it was Magnus Maximus who introduced a new coin, the *tremissis*, which was the third of a gold *solidus* (Fig.18.). This denomination was to become increasingly popular, especially among the Barbarian Kingdoms who succeeded the Roman Empire in the West in the 5th and 6th centuries. Late Roman *tremissi* are rarely found in Britain.

The Usurper Eugenius (AD 392-4)

Between 388 and 392, Theodosius and his son Arcadius (383-408) ruled in the East (Fig.19.),

while Valentinian II had control of the West. The most common coins of this period found in Britain are silver *siliquae* (Figs.19 & 20.) and *nummi* of the SALVS REI PVBLICAE and VICTORIA AVGGG types (Figs.21-4.). These *nummi* are often very poorly preserved and most of the ones that I see are retrieved from detectorists' "grotpots". It is crucial that these coins are recorded because they are often the latest coins from sites in Britain.

However, the Frankish general, Arbogastes, had other ideas about who should rule in the west, and in 392 rebelled, putting an aged pagan, Eugenius, on the throne. Eugenius was to last two years, striking coins at Trier, Lyons, Arles, Aquileia, Milan and Rome. His gold is rare, but a significant number of *siliquae* and *nummi* are found in Britain (Figs.25 & 26.). As with Maximus, Theodosius did not take kindly to the new ruler and Eugenius died at the Battle of the River Frigidus, also near Aquileia – it was here that Alaric and his Goths took heavy casualties while fighting for Theodosius.

AD 395 – The Empire Splits

Theodosius I died in 395. His son Honorius (393-423) (Fig.27.) became emperor of the Western Empire (ruled from Milan and then Ravenna); his other son Arcadius (383-409) took

Fig.17. Copper-alloy *nummus* of Magnus Maximus (AD 383-88), mint unclear, AD 387-8. These camp-gate types are normally poorly preserved. Found in Hampshire, SUR-34C027. © Portable Antiquities Scheme (14mm)

Fig.18. Gold *tremissis* of Magnus Maximus (AD 383-88), struck at Trier. This denomination was apparently first issued by Maximus. RIC IX, 79b. © British Museum (14mm)

Fig.19. Silver *siliqua* of Arcadius (AD 383-408), struck at Milan, AD 388-93. RIC IX, 27a Found in Yorkshire, NCL-9A6D66. © Portable Antiquities Scheme (18mm)

Fig.20. Clipped silver *siliqua* of Theodosius I (AD 379-95), probably struck at Trier, AD 388-95. This coin has been heavily clipped, but SIVS is still legible. RIC IX cf. 94b/106a. Found in Hampshire, HAMP2855. © Portable Antiquities Scheme (13.5mm)

Fig.21. Copper-alloy *nummus* of Theodosius I (AD 379-95), struck at Heraclea, AD 388-95. SALVS REI PVBLICAE coins are very common, but Eastern mint examples are scarce in Britain. RIC IX 26b. Found in Bedfordshire, BH-D86984. © Portable Antiquities Scheme (13mm)

Fig.23. Copper-alloy *nummus* of Valentinian II (AD 375-92), struck at Arles, 388-92. This VICTORIA AVGGG type was the major type struck at the Western mints. LRBC 562ff. Found in Hampshire, HAMP-849EE4. © Portable Antiquities Scheme (13mm)

Fig.24. Copper-alloy *nummus* of Arcadius (AD 383-408), struck at Lyons, AD 388-92: VICTORIA AVGGG. LRBC 392. Found in Greater London, SUR-A7D9F2. © Portable Antiquities Scheme (13mm)

Fig.22. Copper-alloy *nummus* of Valentinian II (AD 375-92), struck at Siscia, AD 388-92. This VICTORIA AVGGG type of Siscia is rare in Britain. LRBC 1575. Found in Buckinghamshire, BUC-FA8C48. © Portable Antiquities Scheme (13.5mm)

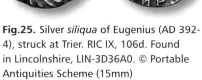

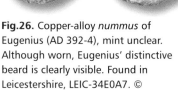

Fig.25. Silver *siliqua* of Eugenius (AD 392-4), struck at Trier. RIC IX, 106d. Found in Lincolnshire, LIN-3D36A0. © Portable Antiquities Scheme (15mm)

Fig.26. Copper-alloy *nummus* of Eugenius (AD 392-4), mint unclear. Although worn, Eugenius' distinctive beard is clearly visible. Found in Leicestershire, LEIC-34E0A7. © Portable Antiquities Scheme (16mm)

Fig.28. Clipped silver *siliqua* of Honorius (AD 393-423), struck at Milan, c.AD 397-402. This is the last major issue of *siliquae* to arrive in Britain. Most of these coins are found clipped. RIC X, 1228. Found in Hampshire, SUR-8DB041. © Portable Antiquities Scheme (13.5mm)

Fig.29. Clipped silver *siliqua* of the House of Theodosius, probably struck at Milan, c.AD 397-95. This heavily clipped piece is typical of coins of this period. RIC X, 1227-8. Found in Yorkshire, DUR-B12F35. © Portable Antiquities Scheme (11mm)

Fig.27. Clipped silver *siliqua* of Honorius (AD 393-423), struck at Milan, AD 393. This rare coin was struck between January and September 393 at the start of Honorius' reign. RIC IX, 26. Found in Oxfordshire, BUC-3E3CF2. © Portable Antiquities Scheme (14.5mm)

Fig.30. Copper-alloy *nummus* of Honorius (AD 393-423), struck at Aquileia, AD 393-402. SALVS REI PVBLICAE *nummi* were only struck at Rome and Aquileia in the period 395-402. LRBC 1111/1113. Found in Leicestershire, LEIC-F11800. © Portable Antiquities Scheme (14mm)

Fig.31. Copper-alloy *nummus* of Arcadius (AD 383-408), struck at Cyzicus (AD 395-401). A coin of this VIRTVS EXERCITI type on the PAS database was found on the Isle of Wight but is in too poor condition to illustrate (IOW-85AAB2). RIC X, 66. © British Museum (18mm)

the Eastern Empire (ruled from Constantinople) (Fig.19.).

In the West, Honorius was largely under the control of the half-Roman/half-Vandal general, Stilicho. However, the Western Empire was already on the decline and the mints of Trier, Arles and Lyons were largely to cease operating in 395. Between 395 and 402 only coins from a few issues arrive in Britain. The last large batches of silver *siliquae* are the VIRTVS ROMANORVM issue of Milan (Figs.28 & 29.).

The last bronze coins to arrive in any significant number are SALVS REI PVBLICAE *nummi* from Aquileia and Rome (Fig.30.). The odd exotic coin is occasionally found in Britain. For example, a VIRTVS EXERCITI *nummus* from an Eastern mint, struck between 395 and 401, has been found on the Isle of Wight (Fig.31.). Gold coins did continue to arrive, the Hoxne hoard suggesting that they did come in significant numbers (Fig.37.).

Constantine III (407-11) & End of Roman Administration in Britain

In 402-3, the Goths invaded Italy, but were driven back by Stilicho. However, Honorius moved from Milan to Ravenna (Figs.32 & 33.). More barbarian raids culminated in a massed

crossing of the frozen Rhine by Vandals, Alans, Suevi and Burgundians on New Year's Eve, 406.

Britain was increasingly cut off and in 406-7 three usurpers arose in the Province. The first two (Marcus and Gratian) did not last long, but the third, Constantine III, was able to establish himself and then take the British "field army" to support his claim on the Continent. He was to rule Gaul and Spain, striking gold and silver coins at Trier, Lyons, Arles and Milan (Figs.34-6.); he struck coins for his son Constans at Arles. Constantine III was briefly acknowledged as a joint emperor by Honorius at Ravenna, but he was eventually captured by a general of Honorius, Constantius, and executed in 411.

It was in the reign of Constantine III that Britain appears to slip out of the control of the Roman Empire. Traditionally, people cite Honorius' letter telling the British towns to defend themselves; this letter, however, almost certainly referred to some Italian cities. Instead, the sources suggest that the aristocracy of Britain rebelled against Rome in 409, probably because they were still being taxed but received no benefits such as protection; the Roman administration was thrown out and the Romano-Britons began to rule themselves.

Fig.33. Gold *solidus* of Honorius (AD 393-423), struck at Ravenna, AD 402-6. Ravenna became the capital of the Western Empire in AD 402. Found in Hampshire, HAMP-F6F384. © Portable Antiquities Scheme (21.5mm)

Fig.34. Gold *solidus* of Constantine III (AD 407-11), struck at Lyon, AD 407-8. There are no *solidi* of Constantine III on the PAS Database. RIC X, 1508. © British Museum (22mm)

Fig.32. Gold *solidus* of Honorius (AD 393-423), struck at Milan, AD 395-402. Milan was the capital of the Western Empire until 402 when Alaric's Goths invaded Italy resulting in the imperial court moving to Ravenna. RIC X, 1206. Found in Yorkshire, YORYM-6F08B4. © Portable Antiquities Scheme (21mm)

Fig.35. Silver *siliqua* of Constantine III (AD 407-11), struck at Lyons, AD 407-8. There are no *siliquae* of Constantine III on the PAS Database. RIC X, 1526. © British Museum (17mm)

Fig.36. Clipped silver *siliqua* of Constantine III (AD 407-11), struck at Lyon, AD 407-8. This coin is from the Coleraine Hoard (see Fig.40.). RIC X, 1529-30. © British Museum (13mm)

Fig.37. A selection of coins from the Hoxne Hoard (Suffolk) which contained 580 *solidi*, 60 silver *milirenses*, 14,565 *siliquae* and 24 bronze *nummi*. It was buried sometime after AD 407-8 and was discovered by Eric Lawes with a metal detector in 1992. The discovery also included hundreds of silver and gold items, ranging from spoons to bracelets. A selection is on display at the British Museum. © British Museum

Fig.38. The Stanchester Hoard (Wiltshire) of three gold *solidi*, 1168 silver *siliquae* and one bronze *nummus*. The latest coins are AD 402-6. This hoard is typical of late silver hoards in Britain and is on display in the Wiltshire Museum in Devizes.
© British Museum

Fig.39. A view across the late-Roman Saxon Shore Fort at Richborough. © Sam Moorhead

Late Roman Coin Hoards

A large number of coin hoards were buried in the late 4th and early 5th centuries in Britain. There are a few very large hoards, such as the celebrated Hoxne Hoard of over 15,000 gold and silver coins (Fig.37.). There are a few other smaller gold hoards, normally with only a handful of coins. However, there are over 100 silver hoards containing *miliarenses* and *siliquae* – some of these hoards do contain the odd gold coin, as at Stanchester (Fig.38.).

These hoards represent around two-thirds of all such hoards recorded for the entire Roman Empire! In addition, a number of Theodosian bronze hoards have been found, notably at Richborough in Kent (Fig.39.) and Caerwent in South Wales. Much work needs to be done to determine why these hoards were buried. It might well have been insecurity, but some hoards might have been votive deposits and others might even be people burying money which was no longer of any practical use.

Clipped Siliquae

Many of the silver *siliquae* found in coin hoards and as single finds have been clipped. Some are lightly clipped around the edges (Figs.14, 27 & 28.), but others are heavily clipped so that only the ruler's head is visible (Figs.20 & 29.). There has been much debate about when this clipping happened. It is quite likely that some light clipping occurred, probably to make illegal gains, from the time that the coins were issued in large numbers by Constantius II and Julian (AD 357-63). However, recent research suggests that clipping really started after 402 and it is quite likely that it continued beyond 407-11.

Why clipping occurred is not known, but we can surmise that it was an attempt to make dwindling silver supplies last longer – some of the clippings appear to have been used to make contemporary copies of *siliquae*. Also, it has been argued that the clippings might have been used to make ingots, like those found in the Coleraine

Fig.40. The Coleraine Hoard (Co. Antrim, Northern Ireland) of silver *siliquae*, ingots and hack-silver in a silver vessel. The latest coin is a clipped *siliqua* of Constantine III (see Fig.36.) dating to 407-8. This hoard was traditionally interpreted as loot; now, we think it might have been payment by Romans to an Irish mercenary. The hoard is on display in the British Museum. © British Museum

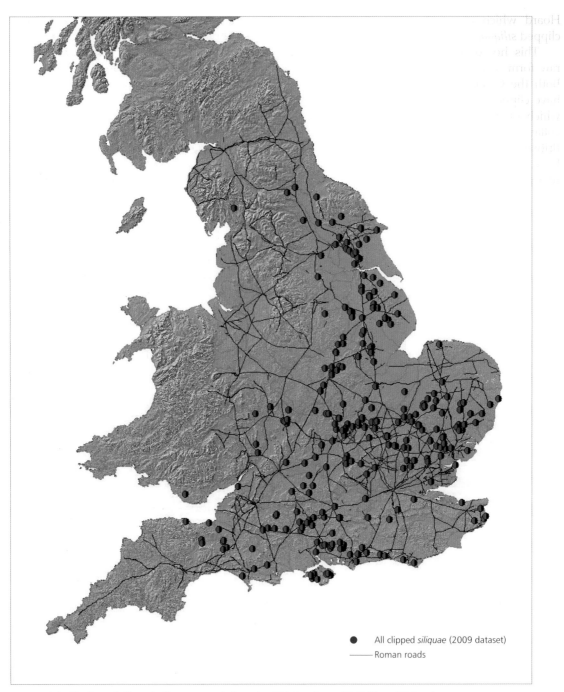

Map.1. Distribution of clipped *siliquae* recorded on the PAS Database. (© Philippa Walton)

Hoard which also contained hack silver and clipped *siliquae*.

This hoard does suggest that silver, in its raw form, was taking over from coins (Fig.40.). Both the Coleraine and Hoxne hoards (Fig.37.) have clipped *siliquae* of Constantine III (407-11) which suggests that clipping continued after the collapse of the Province (Fig.36.). Clipping is a British phenomenon – the recent discovery of a hoard of clipped coins in the Pyrenees probably represents the money of a British soldier who went to fight with Constantine III on the Continent in 407.

End of the Monetary Economy in Britain

Gold coins continued to arrive in Britain in small numbers after 411, a *solidus* of Jovinus (411-3) being recorded on the PAS database (Fig.41.). However, new silver coins do not arrive and it is possible to argue that clipped *siliquae* continue to be used for some years after 407-11, possibly down to 430. The PAS data shows us that clipped coins were not just hoarded, but also circulated freely (Map.1.). Furthermore, some bronze coins are found in hoards with clipped *siliquae*. This might suggest that some bronze coins were also still being used. A coin from the GLORIA ROMANORVM issue with three emperors on the reverse, struck in 406-8 for Arcadius, Honorius and Theodosius II, has been recorded from just north of Hadrian's Wall (Fig.42.).

It is also very interesting that five *nummi* of Valentinian III, struck c.425-35, have been recorded in Britain, although there is no specimen on the PAS database (Fig.43.). One of these coins came from Richborough where over 20,000 late *nummi* were found in excavations – was this fort an outpost of the Roman army after 407/11? (Fig.39.).

It is therefore possible that down to around 430 some people in Britain were using gold, silver or bronze coins; it was in 429 that St Germanus met the town elders of Verulamium (St Albans), suggesting that there were still people attempting to lead a Roman way of life (Fig.43.). The PAS data has made an important contribution to this debate about the end of coin use in Roman Britain.

Fig.41. Gold *solidus* of Jovinus (AD 411-13), struck at Trier. RIC X, 1704. This is the only coin of Jovinus on the PAS database. Found in Kent, KENT-DEF360. © Portable Antiquities Scheme (20.5mm)

Fig.42. Copper-alloy *nummus* of the House of Theodosius, struck at an Eastern Mint, AD 406-8. The reverse is GLORIA ROMANORVM with three emperors standing. Found in Northumberland, NCL-EE2655. © Portable Antiquities Scheme (13.5mm)

Fig.43. Copper-alloy *nummus* of Valentinian III (AD 325-50), struck at Rome, c.425-35. Five *nummi* of Valentinian III have been found in Britain. LRBC 845. © British Museum (13mm)

Emperor Rarity

In this period, Arcadius, Theodosius I and Honorius are the most common rulers represented on the PAS Database. Flavius Victor and Eugenius are rare. The one coin of Jovinus is exceptional. We still await our first coin of Constantine III which is not from a hoard (see Table 1.).

Distribution of Coin Finds

Map.2 shows that coins of the period 378 to 402 are found across England, but it is interesting that they are rare in the far South West, in the West Midlands and the North West. This does suggest that the monetary economy was shrinking.

Gratian (378-83 only)	171
Valentinian II (375-92 only)	158
Theodosius I (379-95)	223
Magnus Maximus (383-8)	108
Flavius Victor (387-8)	32
Eugenius (392-4)	41
Arcadius (383-408)	350
Honorius (393-423)	160
Constantine III (407-11)	0
Jovinus (411-13)	1
House of Theodosius (uncertain ruler)	1,030

Table 1. Rarity of coins by emperor (excluding Welsh data).

Fig.44. A view of St Albans Abbey through the walls of Roman Verulamium. © Sam Moorhead

212

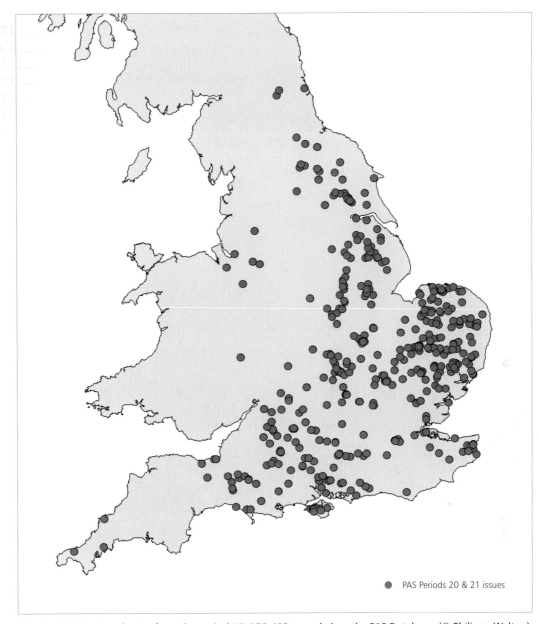

Map.2. Distribution of coins from the period AD 378-402 recorded on the PAS Database. (© Philippa Walton)

Appendix I
Glossary of Terms

Caduceus	Wand of Concord with entwined snakes, held by Mercury and some personifications
Cornucopiae	Horn of plenty – oversize ram's horn with fruits
Die	The engraved block of metal used to strike coins
Exergue	The area under the reverse type, often defined by a line above (ground line), in which the mintmark often appears on late Roman coins
Field	The area on the coin between the head or reverse type and the legend
Flan	The circular piece of metal which is struck to make a coin
Legend	Numismatic term for the inscription
Mappa	Cloth used by emperors to start chariot races, sometimes held by late Roman emperors
Modius	Corn measure
Officina	Workshop in a mint
Parazonium	Sword sometimes held by the emperor
Patera	Dish used for sacrifice
Petasus	Winged hat of Mercury
Pileus	Cap of Liberty, often held by Libertas
Obverse (Obv)	Head side of the coin
Reverse (Rev)	Tails side of the coin
Thyrsus	Staff entwined with ivy and topped by a pine cone held by Bacchus
Trabea	A special decorated toga worn by consuls

Appendix II
Further Reading

Roman Empire
For information about the Roman Emperors, there are two major Roman sources that are available in English translation:
Suetonius *The Twelve Caesars* (Penguin Classic)
The Lives of the Later Caesars (Penguin Classic)
The most accessible guide to the Roman emperors is:
Chris Scarre *Chronicle of the Roman Emperors* (Thames and Hudson, 1995)

Roman Britain
For general introductions to Roman Britain, there are three recent books which provide an overview of the history and archaeology of the province:
Sam Moorhead and David Stuttard *The Romans Who Shaped Britain* (Thames and Hudson, 2012) – this book includes much about Roman coins
R. Hobbs and R. Jackson *Roman Britain* (British Museum Press, 2010)
G. de la Bedoyere *Roman Britain* (Thames and Hudson, 2010)

Introductions To Roman Coinage
Many books have been written on Roman coinage. The most accessible introductions and dictionary are:
D.R. Sear *Roman Coins and Their Values* (4th Revised Edition, Spink, 1988)
D.R. Sear *Roman Coins and Their Values* (4 vols., Spink, 2000-2011)
A. Burnett *Coinage in the Roman World* (Seaby, 1987)
J. Melville Jones *A Dictionary of Ancient Roman Coins* (Seaby, 1990)
Other books that you might be able to find are:
R.A.G. Carson *Coins of the Roman Empire* (Routledge, 1990)
R. Reece *Roman Coins* (Ernest Benn, 1970)
C. Foss *Roman Historical Coins* (Seaby, 1990)
The most comprehensive coverage of Greek and Roman coinages to be published recently is:
W.E. Metcalf (ed.) *The Oxford Handbook of Greek and Roman Coinage* (Oxford University Press, 2012)
If you want to find out more about Roman Provincial coins:
K. Butcher *Roman Provincial Coins: An Introduction to the Greek Imperials* (Seaby, 1998)
D.R. Sear *Greek Imperial Coins and Their Values* (Seaby, 1982)

General Books On Coinage In Roman Britain
R. Reece *The Coinage of Roman Britain* (Tempus, 2002)
P.J. Casey *Roman Coinage in Britain* (Shire, 1980)
R. Abdy *Romano-British Coin Hoards* (Shire, 2002)
R. Reece *Coinage in Roman Britain* (Seaby, 1987)
P. Guest and N. Wells *Iron Age and Roman Coins from Wales* (Moneta 66, 2007)
R. Bland and X. Loriot *Roman and Early Byzantine Gold Coins Found in Britain and Ireland* (Royal Numismatic Society, No. 46, 2010)
A.S. Robertson *An Inventory of Romano-British Coin Hoards* (Royal Numismatic Society, No. 20, 2000)

A major new re-appraisal of Roman coinage in Britain, including much information from the Portable Antiquities Scheme data, has been written by the Deputy National Finds Adviser for Iron Age and Roman Coins, Dr. Philippa Walton:

P. Walton *Rethinking Roman Britain – Coinage and Archaeology* (Moneta 137, 2012)

Initial Identification Of Roman Coins

R. Reece and Simon James *Identifying Roman Coins* (Seaby, 1986)

Also do look at the Roman coin guides on the Portable Antiquities Website: http://www.finds.org.uk/romancoins/ – these will be completely rewritten in the next few years

Major Reference Catalogues

In this book you will see that I have made frequent reference to the following catalogues. They are often quite expensive, but can occasionally be found second hand:

RRC	M. Crawford *Roman Republican Coinage* (Cambridge, 1973/1995)	
RIC	Mattingly et al *Roman Imperial Coinage* (10 vols., Spink, 1923-2007)	
BMC	Mattingly et al *Coins of the Roman Empire in the British Museum* (6 vols., 1923-62)	
LRBC	P.V. Hill, J.P.C. Kent & R.A.G. Carson *Late Roman Bronze Coinage*, AD 324-498 (Spink, 1965)	
CHRB	*Coin Hoards from Roman Britain* (Since 1979, 13 volumes have been published by the British Museum, Royal Numismatic Society and Moneta)	

For 3rd century "radiates", two hoard publications are essential:

Cunetio	E. Besly and R. Bland *The Cunetio Treasure* (British Museum, 1983)
Normanby	R. Bland and A. Burnett *The Normanby Hoard and other Roman coin hoards* (British Museum, CHRB VIII, 1988)

(Spink is preparing a new joint edition of these volumes, introduced by Sam Moorhead)

A number of online resources are available. A couple that might be of interest are:

British Museum Collections Online: http://www.britishmuseum.org/research/publications/onlineresearchcatalogues.aspx

Wildwinds: http://www.wildwinds.com/coins/

Various Other Works On Roman Coins

If you are interested in votive assemblages and especially in 2nd century AD "Coins of British Association", see:

D. Walker, "Roman Coins from the Sacred Spring at Bath" (Part 6 of Barry Cunliffe (ed.), *The Temple of Sulis Minerva II: Finds from the Sacred Spring* (Oxford, 1988)

For ancient forgeries/contemporary copies, the best overview is still:

G.C. Boon, "Counterfeit coins in Roman Britain" in Casey, P. J. and Reece, R. (eds.), *Coins and the Archaeologist*, 102-189 (Seaby, 1988)

A brief introduction to the recently discovered Frome Hoard (Sam Moorhead is working on the final publication):

S. Moorhead, A. Booth and R. Bland *The Frome Hoard* (British Museum Press, 2010)

An account of the discovery of this hoard is written by Dave Crisp in *Metal Detecting* (Greenlight Publishing, 2012)

Iron Age Coinages

P. de Jersey *Celtic Coinage in Britain* (Shire, 1996)

C. Rudd *Ancient British Coinage* (Chris Rudd, 2010) – this supersedes all other catalogues

R. Hobbs *British Iron Age Coins in the British Museum* (British Museum Press, 1996)

R.D. Van Arsdell *Celtic Coinage of Britain* (Spink, 1989)

Byzantine Coinage

D.R. Sear *Byzantine Coins and Their Values* (Seaby, 1987)

Appendix III

Archaeological and Numismatic Societies

If you are interested in the archaeology of Roman Britain, I urge you to join the Association for Roman Archaeology – membership means you can join tours of sites, gain free access to major Roman sites in Britain and receive publications keeping you up to date with news about Roman Britain: http://www. associationromanarchaeology.org/.

Membership of The Society for the Promotion of Roman Studies means that you can receive the annual journal *Britannia*: http://www.romansociety.org/

There are two national numismatic societies in Britain, the Royal Numismatic Society (RNS) http://royalnumismaticsociety.org/ and the British Numismatic Society (BNS) http://www.britnumsoc.org/ Both publish annual journals.

The RNS concentrates on coins across the world, but often publishes articles about Roman coins; the BNS concentrates on coins of the British Isles, but includes articles about coins from Roman Britain and lists recent coin hoards and important single finds in the *Coin Register*. There are numerous other numismatic/coin societies/clubs across the country and these can be found by looking at the British Association of Numismatic Societies (BANS) website which lists them – http://www. coinclubs.freeserve.co.uk/